A GARDEN OF PAPER FLOWERS

I wish I could say I was immune to the Oxford myth, but like my compatriots, I ate up stories of Oxford, the more anachronistic and improbable the better. I waded through Dorothy Sayers' *Gaudy Night*, Lady Antonia Frazer's *Oxford Blood*, the adventures of Colin Dexter's Inspector Morse, Max Beerbohm's *Zuleika Dobson* and of course Evelyn Waugh's *Brideshead Revisited*. I paged through tour guides promising a glimpse of the "real" Oxford, and on a trip to England when I was eighteen I joined the throngs of tourist clogging the muddy paths of Christ Church Meadows, elbowing each other into the Cherwell in their frantic efforts to get a glimpse of some authentic Oxford students, actually punting. As I watched the punts go by, filled with undergraduates resolutely ignoring us tourists, it was easy to believe that they knew some secret of life not available in the USA.

Rosa Ehrenreich was born in New York City in 1970. She was educated at Harvard University and at Christ Church, Oxford, where she spent two years on a Marshall Scholarship. She has been published in several American magazines, including *Harper's* and *Glamour*. She is currently attending Yale Law School, and trying to earn enough through freelance writing to pay her tuition bills.

ROSA EHRENREICH

A GARDEN OF
PAPER FLOWERS

An American at Oxford

PICADOR ORIGINAL

A Picador Original
First published 1994 by Picador

a division of Pan Macmillan Publishers Limited
Cavaye Place London SW10 9PG
and Basingstoke

Associated companies throughout the world

ISBN 0 330 32794 1

The author and publishers gratefully acknowledge permission to reproduce
copyrighted material in this book. All attempts have been made to identify
copyright holders. If any have been inadvertently omitted, the publishers
will be happy to make proper acknowledgement at the earliest opportunity.

David Segal: from "Bill and Friends' Excellent Adventure," in the *Washington Monthly*,
December, 1992. Reprinted by permission of David Segal and the *Washington Monthly*.
Louis MacNeice: from "Autumn Journal," in *The Collected Poems of Louis MacNeice*, edited
by E. R. Dobbs. Reprinted by permission of Faber and Faber Limited.
Martin Jacques: from an article entitled "The Establishment: It's Back," in the *Sunday
Times*, London, 17th January, 1993 © Martin Jacques/Times Newspapers Limited 1993.
Reprinted by permission of Times Newspapers Limited.
Hugh Trevor-Roper: from *Christ Church*. Reprinted by permission of the Governing Body
of Christ Church, Oxford.
John le Carré: from *Tinker, Tailor, Soldier, Spy*. Reprinted by permission of Alfred A. Knopf.
Richard Levin: from his speech to incoming Yale College freshmen, September, 1993.
Reprinted by permission of President Levin and Yale University.
Richard Brodhead: from his speech to incoming Yale College freshmen, September, 1993.
Reprinted by permission of Dean Brodhead and Yale University.

1 3 5 7 9 8 6 4 2

A CIP catalogue record for this book is available from
the British Library

Typeset by CentraCet Limited, Cambridge
Printed by Cox & Wyman Ltd, Reading, Berkshire

ACKNOWLEDGEMENTS

The author also wishes to thank a number of people for their help and moral support. The following small army of people read and commented upon early drafts: Michael Callahan, Janet MacIntosh, Tim Snyder, Milada Vachudova, Bart Moore, Ruth Davis, Dr. A. Christodoulou, Wayne Plasha, Alexandra Robert, Trevor Darrell, Sharon McQuaide, John Ehrenreich, Barbara Ehrenreich, Gary Stevenson, Georgie Boge, Andrew Myers, Frank Taylor and Jerome Wilson. Jane Moody, Maria Sherwood-Smith, Kenji Yoshino, and Jeff Dolven provided insight and anecdotes.

The undergraduates and graduates of Christ Church provided material, frequently unbeknownst to themselves; I thank them all for making my two years at Oxford interesting, thought-provoking, and frequently a lot of fun. I cannot possibly express my gratitude to the British Marshall Commission, which provided me with funding for my time at Oxford. Finally, Jerome Wilson's presence in my life lent meaning to what might otherwise have been two pleasant but aimless years.

. . . Certainly it was fun while it lasted . . .
But in case you should think my education was wasted
     I hasten to explain
That having once been to the University of Oxford
     You can never really again
Believe anything that anyone says and that of course is an asset
     In a world like ours;
Why bother to water a garden
     That is planted with paper flowers?

—Louis MacNeice

CONTENTS

IDEALIZATION

Oxford Myths 3
About this book 7
How to get to Oxford 12
Correspondence from the Censor 26
Briefings 30

BEWILDERMENT

Carts and Christians 45
Touring, Eating, and another Christian 54
I Remember I'm American 77
Pretending to be an Oxford Student 91

DISILLUSIONMENT

Content-Free Learning 115
The Sulks 131
I Join the Élite, Briefly 151
A Hiatus 176

CONTENTS

INSIGHT

CLASS, HIERARCHY, AND APATHY   185
REGRESSION   201
RUGBY   218
THE SWITCH   230

EPILOGUE

SOME SORT OF LEARNING PROCESS   257
QUOTH THE ANCIENT MARINER   264
CLOSE ENCOUNTERS: THE QUEEN   272
DEATH THROES?   280

PART ONE

IDEALIZATION

Oxford Myths

At a New Year's Eve party in Key West, I decided to write this book. After graduating from college in the United States, I had gone to Oxford on a two-year fellowship.

I was talking to a man who had recently written a best-selling thriller. I told him shyly that I was in the middle of my first year at Oxford, and that I was thinking of writing something about my experiences there. He thought it was a great idea.

"Just think how it could sell!" he told me. "Write about the orgies! Write about your memories of Bill Clinton!"

"I don't *have* any memories of Clinton," I pointed out. "He was at Oxford twenty-five years ago. Before I was born."

"The orgies and the illegal drugs, then!"

"Uh—"

"The passionate affairs in the Bodleian Library!"

"Well, uh, I haven't really been invited to any orgies."

"So?"

"And unlike Clinton, I haven't even been offered the *option* of choosing not to inhale marijuana. *Some* people at Oxford definitely take drugs, but I don't seem to go to the right parties. I haven't been offered any drugs at all, not even the legal kind, like aspirin."

"So? Make it all up!"

I thought about this. "I don't think I could do that," I objected.

My friend gave me a pitying look. "All right. You can't, I see that. I make things up, but I suppose that's because I write fiction. But I'm sure there's something interesting, and true, to say about Oxford."

I thought about my first term at Oxford. "Yes, I suppose so. Maybe you're right."

"Do it," he said. "You have nothing to lose but your literary reputation, and I wouldn't let that bother you. I lost mine long ago. Here's to the book." He toasted me with his champagne glass. "I'll help you find an agent. You'll need one now."

When I was a seventeen-year-old freshman at Harvard, home for Christmas vacation, I watched the movie *Heaven's Gate* with my family. "This was filmed at Harvard," my stepfather told me as the opening credits rolled.

"Oh, really?" I said. Sure enough, the words "Harvard University, Cambridge, Massachusetts" appeared on the screen. A group of young men ran shouting into an ivy-covered quad. "I don't recognize those buildings."

I looked more closely. The quad didn't look anything like Harvard Yard. It looked older, more beautiful. It looked better.

"That's not Harvard," I said. "It looks like some other place. More like Oxford, maybe."

"Sshh!" said my brother.

A year or so later, I discovered that the reason "Harvard" had looked like Oxford was that it *was* Oxford. Some Hollywood mogul in charge of shooting *Heaven's Gate*

4

had decided that Harvard didn't look as grand as it ought to look. The reality—Harvard Yard's stern and unhandsome colonial red brick—wasn't classy or archaic enough. So the opening scenes of the movie were shot at Oxford instead, amidst the spires and crumbling gargoyles.

I don't know when I first heard of Oxford. It was just a place that most Americans seemed to know about, to have learned about through some strange form of cultural osmosis. To most Americans, Oxford has always represented all that America isn't. When I saw *Heaven's Gate*, I had only seen pictures of Oxford, but Oxford had been permanently engraved in my mind. A college as grand as the one in *Heaven's Gate* couldn't have been in America. To put it bluntly, in the eyes of the average, mildly Anglophilic American, Oxford is old, while America, even Harvard at the age of three hundred and fifty-five years, is new. Oxford is gracious, while America is rushed and ill-mannered. Oxford is sophisticated and aristocratic, while America is naïve, gauche, self-made.

During my second year at Oxford, the American presidential contest between George Bush and Bill Clinton testified to the durability of this image of Oxford. Although it is difficult to imagine a more privileged member of the American political and educational élite than George Bush (Andover, Yale, son of a senator), Bush managed to score a few political points by claiming that he could hardly be expected to have Clinton's polished debating skills: after all, Clinton was a sophisticated *Oxford* man, steeped in privilege, while poor George was just a regular guy! This despite the fact that Clinton came from a far more "regular" American family than Bush— which is to say, a poor one.

I wish I could say I was immune to the Oxford myth, but like my compatriots, I ate up stories about Oxford, the more anachronistic and improbable the better. I watched the movie *Oxford Blues,* in which brat-packer Rob Lowe learns about loyalty and the stiff upper lip from aristocratic young rowers at Oriel College. I read, and later watched, Evelyn Waugh's *Brideshead Revisited.* I waded through Dorothy Sayers' *Gaudy Night,* Lady Antonia Fraser's *Oxford Blood,* the adventures of Colin Dexter's Inspector Morse, and Max Beerbohm's *Zuleika Dobson.*

I paged through tour guides promising a glimpse of the "real" Oxford, and on a trip to England when I was eighteen I joined the throngs of tourists clogging the muddy paths of Christ Church Meadows, elbowing each other into the Cherwell in their frantic efforts to get a glimpse of some actual Oxford students, actually punting. As I watched the punts float by, filled with undergraduates resolutely ignoring us tourists, it was easy to believe that they knew some secret of life not available in the USA.

ABOUT THIS BOOK

THIS BOOK IS about my first year at Oxford. The emphasis in that sentence should be on the word "my" as well as on the word "Oxford;" I can only describe what I experienced myself. Some readers will complain that the Oxford I describe is nothing like the Oxford they knew. I'm sure that this is true—Oxford is large enough to be many things to many people, and I only knew my own corner of it.

I was a member of Christ Church, a college that is considered by many to be more traditional and élitist than the average Oxford college. As a foreign graduate student, I had little contact with undergraduates from colleges other than Christ Church; most of my friends at other colleges were graduate students, and many of them were foreign. I knew little about the undergraduate subcultures that centered around the Oxford Union, the student newspapers, or the world of drama and the arts. There were, undoubtedly, Oxford undergraduates whose worlds never intersected in any way with my own. My view of Oxford, as set forth in this book, is necessarily partial.

My Oxford was not a very charming place. It was filled with pretension and apathy. It was profoundly anti-intellectual. This was true especially among the under-graduates. Academic programs seemed poorly thought out and stagnant, with much teaching and advising char-acterized by muddle and negligence.

And yet there were wonderful people at Oxford, and

exciting courses. Among the undergraduates as well as the graduates and the dons, there were people who were broadminded and thoughtful, humorous and kind, politically and socially responsible and engaged. There were people who were motivated by a genuine love of learning.

I don't speak much about these people in this book. This isn't because they didn't exist. They were there—but they were very difficult to find, because the dominant culture pushed them off center stage and into hiding, into libraries and private rooms and cafés. Every university and every community contains a certain number of genuine intellectuals, but some communities encourage these people and make it possible for them to thrive, while other communities greet them with apathy and derision. In my experience, this was what Oxford was like for undergraduates. The overall ethos of the university was sufficiently anti-intellectual, laddish, and alcoholic that the best and most interesting undergraduates either voted with their feet by retreating to the privacy of their rooms or, in self-defence, censored their real thoughts and pretended to be as boorish as their peers.

Academically, I left Oxford feeling strongly that the value of an "Oxford education" is overrated. Little teaching appears to take place at Oxford, and less learning. I have two main criticisms of academic life at Oxford. First of all, the claim that on the graduate level there are "taught courses" at Oxford represents a false promise. Students are provided with little guidance, and are expected somehow to pull together the threads of poorly articulated and disparate approaches on their own. Oxford would be fine as a think-tank. But it claims instead to be a teaching institution, and ought therefore to be expected to *teach* something to its students. Many students, especially foreign students, end up feeling misled—the catalog promises them a taught course, and they arrive to discover that for £8,000 a year, they're on their own.

Second, I argue that getting a good education at Oxford is far too much of a hit or miss process. Success depends on picking the right subject, because it is very difficult to change courses once having begun them (unlike in the US, where a major is not chosen until after two years). Success also depends on getting good tutors or supervisors. An undergraduate may have only three or four tutors over three years; a graduate will usually have one supervisor for two or three years. As tutors are the only people monitoring the student's work and providing feedback, one or two mediocre or incompetent tutors can severely reduce a student's odds of having a profitable academic career. And for undergraduates, degree quality is determined solely by examination performance at the end of three years, leaving little room for error, for poor exam takers, or for those who had the misfortune to have bad tutoring. It's all rather arbitrary.

Critics of this book will charge that I came to Oxford with the wrong attitude and that I simply failed to understand the unique Oxford approach to teaching and learning, an approach which emphasizes self-motivation and individual intellectual curiosity.

This may be true, but to the extent that this "wrong attitude" is shared at least by several thousand foreign students, I don't think it's an adequate response. I think that coming to Oxford from a different culture gave me a perspective on the University that few natives could have. And I am certain that most foreign students will agree with at least the broad outline of my views on Oxford. As I was writing this book, I had dozens of conversations with Oxford students and dons, both foreign and English, and everything I heard served to reinforce my views.

In the end, it comes down to a philosophical question about the nature of the university. Should the university adopt a "take it or leave it" approach to education, allowing students to graduate with minimal knowledge if they aren't motivated enough to persevere through possibly mediocre tutoring? I.e., should the university be like a think-tank, providing students with a few resources and then more or less leaving them to their own devices? Or should the university take a more active approach to teaching, and take the steps necessary to ensure that virtually *all* undergraduates and graduates will have equal access to good teaching and continuous assessment? Does the university have a responsibility to make sure that, once accepted, students *learn* something? Does it have a responsibility to try to make sure that academic success is not arbitrary and to create a community that encourages love of learning and civilized behavior?

Throughout this book, I compare Oxford to the better American universities. I don't mean to idealize universities like Harvard and Yale: they have their flaws. But by and large, they adhere to the second conception of the university, and assume that it is their responsibility to make sure students learn to think and to foster an environment that encourages mutual respect amongst students. Oxford adheres to the first conception of the university: the assumption is that if students fail to understand their subjects, that's the student's problem, not the university's. If students choose to opt for alcoholic escapades instead of responsible, mutually respectful behavior, that's their affair.

And by making this assumption, Oxford fails its students. To me, the proof of this is in the undergraduate culture, apathetic and unintellectual. Bright students resent it when they aren't being taught anything; at

Oxford, they respond by behaving like sulky adolescents, instead of mature university students.

This book was written during my second year at Oxford, when I was still very close to the experiences I describe. Undoubtedly my views will mellow and change with time. But I think that the emotions I had during my first year were shared by at least the vast majority of foreign graduate students, and for that reason it seems worth while to record those emotions before they fade into nostalgia. Many readers of this book, especially foreign readers, will be taken aback by how critical I am of Oxford. Most Oxford graduates take care to perpetuate, not puncture, the myth of Oxford's superiority. This should hardly surprise us. Élites are rarely willing to jeopardize their status by criticizing the institutions that gave them that status.

This book is not a work of fiction. Everything described here actually occurred. However, my experiences are *fictionalized:* in some cases I have altered the order of events, and in many cases I have conflated several people into one person for narrative purposes. There is thus *no necessary one-to-one correspondence* between any given character in this book and any particular real-life person. Student names and background details have been changed. I have taken less trouble to disguise dons and administrators, as they are, to some extent, public figures.

HOW TO GET TO OXFORD

AT THE BEGINNING of my last year at college, I realized that I needed to think of something to do after graduation.

I presented myself at the Office of Career Services and requested an interview with a counselor. "Well, what do you *want* to do next year?" she asked kindly. She was a tired-looking middle-aged woman, and I was probably the tenth confused senior she had seen that day.

For some reason, this question surprised me. It was so obvious that I hadn't thought about it. "Uh . . . well, nothing really. I mean, nothing in particular," I answered, realizing as I spoke that this was, in fact, true. The thought of moving into the real world of jobs, bills, and health insurance terrified me. It wasn't that I had no ambitions. It was the opposite. I had too many ambitions, but no idea how to turn my vague goals into realities, and no appetite for climbing arduous career ladders. But I could hardly say, in answer to the counselor's question, "Actually I'd kind of like to be a senator next year," or, "Well to be honest I was thinking of being a movie star after I graduate." I wanted to be famous, powerful, and rich, in that order, without doing any work. I was aware that this was unrealistic.

The counselor was still gazing at me, so finally I blurted this out. "I don't know *what* to do. I can't really think of any *jobs* that I would enjoy. I want to do something fun, but I want to get paid while I do it."

She looked at me glumly. Clearly she thought I was a Bad American, completely lacking in the work ethic.

"Well, you could try robbing a bank," she finally said, with mild sarcasm. "Or winning the lottery, or maybe embezzlement."

I laughed sheepishly. "Yes, but of those three options, one is unlikely and the other two are illegal."

"I have an idea," said the counselor. "Apply for a fellowship to Oxford."

"Oxford?" It was another world. Only Very Special People went to Oxford.

"Sure, Oxford, why not?" The counselor was warming to her theme. "You've done well academically, you're head of a student organization. I'm sure you could win some sort of fellowship. Apply for the Rhodes, the Marshall, the Fulbright, the Rotary. Think of something to study at Oxford. It's good preparation for pretty much anything. Governor Bill Clinton was at Oxford. So was the actor Kris Kristofferson." The star of *Heaven's Gate*. I remembered him. "Besides, the terms at Oxford are only eight weeks long, and you get six-week vacations in between. You can travel a lot. Oxford will look wonderful on your CV, and maybe after two years there you'll have figured out what you want to do."

This sounded good to me. I still would have preferred to become a senator, but the more I thought about it, Oxford came a close second. Two years at Oxford would give me the time I needed to come up with some sort of game plan for my life. I thought of all the books I had read about Oxford, and tried to imagine myself graciously pouring a glass of wine for my companions as we glided smoothly down the Cherwell in our punt, discussing Milton. Or staring dreamily out of my seventeenth-century room at fog-obscured spires, contemplating life. I was hooked.

★

Fellowships are a fantastic deal: in exchange for showing "potential", a group of people you have never met before gives you a large amount of money with which to do something fun. The only problem with getting a fellowship is that there are a lot of hoops to jump through before the first grant instalment is safely deposited in your bank account. Getting a fellowship isn't easy.

This is not because you need to be fabulously intelligent: many fellowship winners aren't that sharp, to say the least. The Rhodes Trust in particular is thought to look with forbearance upon the "Gentleman's C". Nor must you be an all-around achiever, or a brilliant athlete, in order to win a fellowship. Plenty of Rhodes, Marshall, Fulbright, and other fellowship winners seem to have no particular talent or sport.

For instance, the year I was a junior in college, a good friend of mine won a Rhodes, a scholarship which historically has emphasized athletic talent. Jamie was a brilliant mathematician and social scientist, but was not noted for what the Rhodes Trust refers to as "physical vigour". The selection committee wanted to give him the scholarship, but found this slightly embarrassing, and questioned him closely.

"Jamie, do you ever go for walks?"

"Er, well, sometimes, I guess," replied the bewildered Jamie.

"Have you ever . . . gone for a walk . . . in a *forest*? Or up a hill?"

"Uh . . . I think so. Probably."

"Jamie"—the chairman of the committee leaned closer to impress upon him the importance of what he was about to say—"Jamie, from now on, if anyone ever asks you, you *hike*."

What you do need, in order to win a fellowship, is patience. Essays ("Tell us, in less than five hundred words,

14

something important about yourself") must be written, forms must be filled out, six identical passport-sized photographs are demanded for applications. I spent hours in a local store, trying to straighten out crumpled dollar bills: the store had an instant photo booth with exacting standards of dollar-bill crispness. I laboriously (I had lost my calculator) converted my grade-point average from Harvard's unintelligible fifteen-point weighted scale to the more usual four-point scale, and even had the thrill of discovering that, mysteriously, my grades were higher in the four-point scale. I humiliated myself by racing around begging every former teacher, employer, and advisor for letters of reference. I scoured every clothing store in Cambridge for something to wear to interviews.

To win a fellowship you also need the ability to reduce your life to a series of snappy yet sincere sound bites. Those candidates lucky enough to be offered interviews need the ability to remain cool, respectful, and good humored while a selection committee composed of tax lawyers, real-estate developers, and other such unsympathetic characters picks apart their records and their aspirations.

At interviews, anything goes, as far as the questions are concerned. The lawyers use the interviews as an opportunity to ask the kind of questions that would be objected to and struck off the record by any fair-minded judge, questions of the "Have you stopped beating your wife yet?" variety. I tried to come up with feisty yet charming answers to questions like, "Don't you think your record shows that you're just an academic dilettante?" and "You've done all this community service work. Wouldn't you say that you're just a naïve and radical dreamer to think that you can actually bring about social change?" The questions got worse, ranging from the merely rude to the outrageously irrelevant. "Wouldn't you say that your politics are totally out of line with what people in this country think?" "So who cares about your senior thesis topic?" "If you could be any kind of vegetable, which would it be?" "What would your mother think about that?" "Do you have any pets?"

Another talent the would-be fellowship winner must cultivate is the ability to shine at cocktail parties. The Rhodes is notorious for having pre-interview cocktail parties, at which the lucky dozen chosen for interviews in each region vie with each other to impress the selection committee in an "informal" setting. Of course, the setting is anything but informal. In Boston, this cocktail party is held in the stodgy and all-male St Botolph's Club on Commonwealth Avenue. (Does it not occur to the committee that holding interviews at an all-male club might make female candidates uncomfortable? Actually, perhaps it's no accident: the year I applied for a Rhodes, only five of the thirty-two American Rhodes Scholarships went to women.)

Before the cocktail party begins candidates lurk anxiously outside the massive doors, unwilling to be the first inside, trading whispered rumors about just what the (presumed to be sadistic) interviewers might be watching for.

"Be really careful not to drink too much," said a smooth-looking fellow in an Australian trenchcoat, from Groton via Princeton. "They have these things to weed out the alcoholics. They watch you to see how much you drink."

"But you have to drink *something* alcoholic," added a Yale student, an artist who eventually won the scholarship. "If you don't drink at all they'll think you're a prude with no social graces."

Perhaps he was right—I stuck to club soda all night, and as it turned out the Rhodes selection committee

16

neglected to select me. But I'm not sure that any committee members actually noticed, half of them appearing far too inebriated themselves to pay much attention to the candidates. At one point I found myself wedged into a corner of the room by the headmistress of a prominent but now defunct girls' boarding school. She was about five feet tall, rather stout, and looked to be well over seventy. She was drinking scotch, straight. Her breath nearly knocked me over as she boozily urged me to tell her about my most interesting summer job. When I finished my carefully phrased answer, she gushed, "That sounds *wonderful!*" and suggested we go and refresh our drinks.

It was a horrendous affair. The candidates all chittered non-stop and poured drinks down their shirts through anxiety. The members of the committee alternated between smiling benignly through a haze of liquor and outdoing each other in an apparent effort to make arrogant and belittling comments about the candidates' qualifications. One committee member, a "real-estate developer," responded to a young black woman's statement that she hoped to be a high-school teacher by sneering, "Well, how *interesting*." He looked pityingly at her as though she had just revealed an ambition to metamorphose into a cockroach. "I think however that you'll find, if you look through a list of past Rhodes Scholars, that most of them do things that are more . . . prestigious. In fact," he said smugly, "I really don't think most Rhodes Scholars would wish to . . . be teachers." His thoughts were written openly on his well-fed face as he looked at her: *not* Rhodes material.

The poor woman looked like she might cry. I was furious. I began to burble irately. "Don't you think that teaching, a profession our country desperately needs, would *have* more prestige if talented people like Rhodes

17

Scholars would condescend to *be* teachers, instead of going into jobs that make them a lot of money and contribute nothing to society?" I tried to make it evident from my expression exactly what I thought of real-estate developers. Sub-cockroach level. He merely chuckled. "I see we have a radical here!" he said gleefully.

I walked away, and, in my righteous indignation, rounded out a perfect evening by attempting to stroll gracefully through a large mirror which had cunningly disguised itself as a door. I had been too vain to wear my glasses.

Somehow, when it was all over, when the interview dress ("Conservative, but not too businesslike. Feminine. Nothing Ethnic!" said the Harvard fellowships advisor) had been carefully hung in the closet and the tasteful pearl earrings, borrowed from my roommate, had been returned ("Don't wear dangling earrings!" added the fellowships advisor. "It distracts people. You want the interviewers to stare at your ears the whole time? Go for small. Go for pearls."), somehow, after all this, I found that I had won a Marshall Scholarship to spend two years at Oxford.

The Marshall Scholarships are provided by the British Government. Begun in the early fifties, they are meant to express British gratitude to America for the Marshall Plan, George Marshall's post-war European reconstruction scheme. Originally only about a dozen scholars were chosen each year, but by now there are about forty. Marshalls can go to any British university, but since the scholarship's inception about half have chosen Oxford, with most of the rest divided between Cambridge, London, and Edinburgh. The Marshall Commission encourages scholars to go to the newer, less traditional universities, but few scholars pay much attention: after all, many American scholarship winners have never heard of any British university other than Oxford.

After the Rhodes Scholars, Marshalls make up the largest group of Americans at Oxford. Historically, the Marshall has been a more "academic" scholarship than the Rhodes, placing a good deal of emphasis on grades and scholastic achievement, while the Rhodes, in keeping with its Imperial provenance, placed more emphasis on athletics and "leadership." In recent years, however, these stereotypes have been changing; both scholarship committees seem to have become uneasy about their images. The Rhodes has tried to pick more "scholarly" scholars, and the Marshall has increasingly been emphasizing extracurricular leadership and community involvement.

Looking back, it seems rather odd that the Marshall and Rhodes fellowships interviewers all took it for granted that wanting to spend two years at Oxford was a natural thing to do. What else would a graduating Harvard senior do, their silence suggested, but go on to Oxford? What else is there? So I was never asked why I wanted to go to Oxford, or even what exactly I would do there. Which was just as well, because I wouldn't have known what to answer. My image of Oxford was formed by books, most of them written decades ago, if not centuries ago. My longing for Oxford was a longing for an imagined peace and graciousness, for a quiet oasis of the mind. But I couldn't have articulated this longing, perhaps because voicing it would have forced me to acknowledge how unrealistic it was.

Only later, when the question of why I was in Oxford came back to haunt me, did I realize that this should have told me that going to Oxford was a somewhat foolish idea.

*

By the time spring came, I had gotten over the initial euphoria that gripped me when the congratulatory letter arrived from the scholarship committee. And I panicked. Until that point I had had no time to worry—worry? I was far too busy straightening out dollar bills and choosing which earrings to wear. That was when I wasn't praying for a fellowship, my ticket to a happy two years. But suddenly it hit me that two years was a long time, and that I was really going to have to go through with it, going to have to go live in Oxford, to read for a degree of some sort, to leave behind my boyfriend and my family and my friends. I would have to leave behind most of my books, my posters, my bicycle, my pots and pans, my platform bed, my plants. To calm myself down, I tried to reassure myself that I knew what I was getting into. I thought of all the movies about Oxford I had seen, all the books I had read.

What did I know about Oxford? I knew that undergraduates at Oxford were an unstable lot, liable to dash about in dinner jackets with teddy bears tucked under their arms, and to plunge suicidally into rivers at a moment's notice. That was when they weren't busy rowing, playing cricket, or hosting elegant cocktail parties. The dons were a different story: they seemed to divide their time between murdering people, if Antonia Fraser was to be trusted, and merely penning nasty anonymous notes to one another, as in *Gaudy Night*. The townspeople were just as bad. In the fourteenth century they had slaughtered quite a few Oxford scholars, and according to Colin Dexter, author of the Inspector Morse series, they still had a tendency towards violence, with rotting corpses popping up every week or so.

This was not soothing. I decided that it was time to find some more up-to-date, hard-headed, and realistic information about Oxford. Harvard's Office of Career

Services asks all graduates who win fellowships to send back letters describing their experiences, for the use of future fellowship applicants and winners. I knew that the Career Services Library kept a fat file of these reports from graduates who had gone on to Oxford, and I resolved to go read these reports, and take notes.

I settled myself in at a table in the Career Services Library, surrounded by other seniors. The woman next to me was reading something called "Careers in International Finance" and biting her nails. The man sitting across from me was chewing on a pencil while he scrutinized the Harvard Business School Catalogue. Across the room a woman sucked her thumb while she scanned the shelves of the legal careers section.

But when I opened the fat binder labelled "Oxford and Cambridge: Alumni Reports," there was almost nothing there about Oxford. There were reams of paper about Cambridge, dozens of letters written by alternately homesick and euphoric recent graduates. But in the Oxford section, the most recent report was dated January 1972. For that matter, when I looked on the shelf where the Oxford graduate prospectus was supposed to be, I couldn't find it.

I went to the librarian. "Where," I asked, "do you keep the up-to-date alumni reports on Oxford?"

"Ah," she said. "Oxford."

"Yes, Oxford, in England."

"Ah. We don't have them." She looked at the ceiling.

"Could you tell me, please, where I could find them?"

The librarian jolted upright in her chair and then leaned towards me. "You can't!" she nearly shouted in my ear. "They've been stolen!"

"Stolen?" I was bewildered. "Who would steal them?"

The librarian slumped back in her seat, and said, in a

21

normal voice, "One of last year's Rhodes applicants, we think. He even cut the article on Oxford out of the *Encyclopaedia Britannica* in Widener Library. We never found out who it was, or if he got the fellowship."

"That's really sick," I said.

She shrugged, and gestured at the reading room. "Look around you."

I left the library, thankful at least that my own fascination with Oxford had stayed within the realm of normal behavior, if only just. And aware more than ever before of just how powerful a grip Oxford holds on the American imagination. Powerful enough to make a graduating Harvard student, someone with a lot going for him regardless of whether he won a Rhodes, stoop to cutting articles from the encyclopaedia, in order to prevent other students from learning something about Oxford that might give them the tiniest edge in the competition for fellowships.

In a further effort to learn about Oxford, I called my old friend Justin, an English major at the University of Chicago. We had gone to the same junior high school and had been friends, but Justin's family had moved away when he was fourteen. We had kept in touch only sporadically, and I knew from friends that Justin had spent his junior year at Exeter College, Oxford. He had also won a Rhodes Scholarship, so I would be seeing him at Oxford in October. I wasn't sure what to expect when I called Justin—after all, I hadn't seen him in eight years. For all I knew, he had changed a lot.

He sounded as confident and cheerful as ever, but there was an angry edge to his voice when I asked him about Oxford.

"Did you like it?"

"I hated it," he replied.

This surprised me. "Why?"

His answer was bitter. "Oxford is rigid and hierarchical and filled with snobs who hate Americans, especially Americans there just for a short time, who aren't matriculated. When I went to Oxford junior year I didn't have anyone, and all the English students shut me out completely. It was like not existing for a year."

"Why do you want to go back, then?"

Justin snorted. "You remember when I was little, how much I hated being bullied by Tommy Winch? But I kept right on provoking him? It's a bit like that, I suppose," said Justin. "Oxford intimidated me and bullied me. Well, now I'm going back, I'm older, I'll be doing a D.Phil. and I'll be on a prestigious scholarship. This time I'll have friends and I'll have some social entrée. This time I'm going to show them." He stopped, embarrassed by his vehemence. "Terrific, laudable revenge mission, huh? But it makes me angry. Oxford is disgusting, but I'm going to show them I can be just as disgusting if I have to."

"Well," I said somewhat uncomfortably, "I'm sure Oxford can't be all that bad."

"Wanna bet?"

This wasn't terribly reassuring. I sighed. "Well, Justin, I hope you don't get a bloody nose for your trouble this time."

In the months that followed, I tried as hard as I could to forget Oxford. Realistically, I knew that it was a university like any other, filled with the usual mixed bunch of students. Whatever Justin said, it couldn't be *all* bad. There would be some snobs, some athletes, some artists, some students interested only in their work, some hateful people and some kind ones.

I would survive it, whatever it was like. I decided to choose Christ Church as my college, and to study for a second bachelor's degree in PPE: Politics, Philosophy, and Economics. This seemed like a reasonable choice—I had done some coursework in all three areas, so it wouldn't be completely unfamiliar, but I still had a lot to learn. And doing a second BA would bring me into more contact with British undergraduates than I might otherwise have.

After making this decision, I threw myself into life at Harvard. I only had one more term, and I wanted to enjoy it. I finished up my term as head of Harvard's public service organization. I took a poetry-writing seminar. When the Gulf War began I got involved in student protests against the Bush administration's military policy. I finished my senior thesis on images of women doctors. I studied haphazardly for my general exams, belatedly realizing that, despite a major in the History and Literature of England and America, I knew nothing whatsoever about several centuries' worth of English history. I rowed for Lowell House, getting up at five and seeing the sun rise over the Charles River.

In May and June I sat with classmates on the grass in the outer courtyard of Lowell House, drinking endless cups of weak iced coffee, getting a suntan, and waiting for graduation. Madonna was always on the radio, the grass was soft and green, the trees swayed in the wind, and it was always sunny. Not true, of course, but that's how it seemed in the long month between the end of classes and the beginning of Commencement Week. At least, that's how it seemed to a senior eager to avoid thinking about the future.

And then it was Commencement Day, and Harvard Square was filled with over-dressed, anxious parents escorting seniors who tripped awkwardly in unfamiliar gowns. A lot of nervous giggling, beach balls, champagne, everyone trying hard to remember the words to "Fair Harvard," and then it was over. Rented gowns were returned to the store, dorm rooms were swept clean, overflowing boxes filled with the detritus of four years were jammed into station-wagons, and college was over, in the same flurry of irritability, heat, and anxiety with which it had begun, four years before.

CORRESPONDENCE FROM
THE CENSOR

THE SUMMER PASSED quickly. After graduating I worked until mid-August, earning spending money to augment my grant, then took it easy. I went to the beach and went hiking in the mountains of Washington State. I tried not to think about Oxford.

This was not entirely possible, however, as the summer was punctuated by a series of odd communiqués from someone at Christ Church who called himself the Senior Censor. He advised me that while a duvet would be provided I would be wise to bring my own tea crockery. He further informed me that Cathedral time was five minutes after Tom and I would be expected to budget my time accordingly. As a commoner my gown would cost me about £14, he added helpfully. Overnight guests were not permitted. Scouts were to be given a minimum gratuity of £3 per term, and as an overseas student, I would be permitted to remain in my rooms during the vac between Michaelmas and Hilary.

This was so much gibberish to me. It might as well have been in Latin, a language I had never studied but had an uneasy suspicion might be necessary at Oxford, given the comment that I should obtain *sub fusc* clothing promptly upon my arrival. Would the dons think I was stupid? (An image of Marlon Brando in *The Godfather* flew to my mind. I cowered in the corner as he sat slouched in his gown. "Whatsa matta wit you," he grated in his low, dangerous voice. "Doncha know you gotta wear *sub fusc* when ya see the Don?")

Dozens of questions and worries darted through my mind. What was a duvet? What was a scout? What was a vac, and what was Michaelmas? Who was Hilary? Why was I a commoner? Was this the insidious British class system at work already? It hardly seemed fair: I hadn't even arrived at Oxford and already I'd been relegated to the lower classes. How did they know? Had it been something I'd let slip in my application?

What was Tom, and why was it five minutes before Cathedral time? (Tom, I later discovered, was the large bell in Christ Church's "Tom Tower". Early on at Oxford I found myself seated next to an archdeacon at dinner. Trying to think of something to say—I didn't think I had much in common with an archdeacon—I asked him why Tom rang five minutes before the Cathedral bells. He replied, in a tone that suggested that only a moron would ask, that certain pedantic former Christ Church scholars had determined that Tom Tower was five longitudinal minutes away from Greenwich. I nodded sagely, only afterwards realizing that this made no sense at all, as there is not a one-to-one correspondence between longitudinal minutes and minutes in time.)

Most of all, who was the Senior Censor, and what business was it of his if I wanted to have overnight guests in my room? As a card-carrying member of the American Civil Liberties Union, I was damned if I was going to let some middle-aged Brit tell me who I could have in my room overnight.

I would have liked to call the Marshall Commission in London and have some of these things cleared up, but I was far too frightened of the secretary to do so. Her name was Ruth Davis and she sent out innumerable thick letters full of extremely detailed schedules and precise rules governing the administration of Marshall Scholarships. Her letters generally started off with stern phrases like, "Scholars shall *not*," after which would follow a lengthy list of forbidden activities. The letters from the Marshall Commission were my first exposure to a very British form of bureaucracy. Mrs. Davis even sent out large stickers saying "MARSHALL" on them in red letters. "Scholars are advised to affix these to their belongings and preferably to their person while *en route* to Britain."

I later found that Ruth Davis was extremely kind-hearted, wise, tolerant, and good humored, and, like the rest of my class of Marshall Scholars, I came to rely on her to bail me out of trouble when necessary. I even began to suspect that some of her letters to us, such as the one advising us to wear "MARSHALL" stickers, were distinctly tongue-in-cheek. But that summer she scared the wits out of me. In the spring, I had decided that I didn't want to do a BA in Politics, Philosophy, and Economics after all. Instead, I wanted to do a graduate degree in Politics. I decided to call Ruth Davis to ask whether or not this would be possible.

Sitting in my dorm room, I heard the sharp "Brrring!" of an English phone. When it was answered it was by a sound that was, to my American ears, sharper still. "Ruth Davis!" barked the voice on the other end of the phone.

I was startled. In America, people answered the phone by saying "Hello?" One then says, "Hello, is this so and so?" I was befuddled by the unusual response. "Oh!" I said foolishly. "Is this Ruth *Davis?*" as though there might perhaps be two of them.

A stony silence. Then, "Yes."

Completely unnerved by now, I made a fatal *faux pas*. "Oh! Mrs. Davis, this is Rosa Ehrenreich. Uh, how are you?"

There was an *extremely* long silence. Finally: "I'm fine, thank you." And then more silence.

I realized, agonizingly too late, that I had yet again said the wrong thing. In America, "How are you?" is a standard and meaningless pleasantry, exchanged with anyone one has met or corresponded with, often on the telephone as well as face to face. It was obvious from the chilly silence on the other end of the line that in England one does *not* say "How are you?" when speaking to strangers on the phone.

I plunged resolutely into my question about switching courses.

"We discourage scholars from attempting to make changes," Mrs. Davis responded crushingly, clearly thinking to herself, another frivolous American.

I finally promised to rethink my situation and managed to bring the conversation to an awkward close. And from then on I was too scared to have any further dealings with the Marshall Commission, at least by telephone. Well over a year later, when I told Ruth Davis of my initial fear of her, she told me with amusement that her long silences over the telephone had been due not to disapproval but to the delays in timing caused by a poor long-distance satellite-linked conversation.

BRIEFINGS

FORTUNATELY, IT LOOKED like I was not going to be left at sea with my dozens of questions. The British government was funding thirty-nine Marshall Scholars in addition to me, of whom twenty were headed for Oxford. And Her Majesty's Government, represented by the British Embassy in Washington, was not going to unleash forty raw young Americans on the unsuspecting English academic world without giving us four days of "briefings." I relaxed as soon as I heard this: something about the word "briefings" is so very reassuring, suggesting by its similarities to the words "brief" and "briefcase" something full of concise, efficient, businesslike chunks of information.

It was not to be. The briefings took place first at the Embassy in Washington, and continued after two days in the seminar room of a dingy hotel near London's Tavistock Square. The Washington briefings were conducted by a pair of harassed and rumpled young embassy officials, who clearly regarded the job of babysitting for us as the equivalent of a posting to Siberia. They were polite but exceedingly glum.

The forty of us sat uncomfortably on folding chairs. We had lots of questions. Was Oxford friendly? Anti-American? Could we change courses on arrival? What was the weather like, really? What was the food like? (Ah, so naïve . . .) Would we be able to take classes in faculties other than our own? What were the differences in reputation between the various Oxford colleges?

Unfortunately, the lecturers didn't know. They would respond to each question by gazing quizzically around. "Well, right. I'm not really sure about that. I haven't really been to Oxford in some time. Hmm. Right. But I feel sure that you'll enjoy being there. Ah. Any other questions then, or shall we take a break?" This was how I learned that the English use "right" as Americans use the word "OK": it's an all-purpose word, insertable anywhere.

"Er, right, a duvet, right. Well, it's a—one uses it rather as a blanket. Or rather like a cover, perhaps. It's hard to describe but you'll understand when you see one, no doubt. Right. Next question?"

But we were not about to give in. We hadn't gotten to the exalted state we were now in, as fellowship winners, by giving up easily in the face of non-answers. The questions continued.

A black woman raised her hand. "What would you say race relations in England are like?"

Our briefers looked at each other anxiously. "Oh, well, right. Rather good, I should say. Difficult, though. Highly complex situations, you see. Nothing to worry about."

"Oh, good. Because as you probably know, in some parts of the US race relations are really bad. I went to a very racist college in Alabama. That's why I carry a gun with me everywhere."

We all eyed her nervously, searching our minds to expunge any thoughts that might conceivably ever be misconstrued as racist.

The lecturers looked at each other again. In unison, they said, "Umm, right. Let's break for tea now, shall we?"

Lectures were supplemented by a videotape of a television show called *Britain Today*. The lights went out dramatically. "I haven't viewed this yet," warned the more junior of the embassy officials (the more senior having taken the opportunity, under cover of darkness, to depart for greener embassy pastures). "But I'm told it's quite good."

The first scene was of men with face-masks and snorkels slithering about the bottom of a pool, hitting a hockey puck around. Ten minutes were then spent on an adulatory interview with a champion of this strange new sport, which was said to be taking Britain by storm. The second vignette involved a Welsh lorry driver who drove throughout Europe delivering machine parts. His life was made difficult because he had to be able to converse at least a little with people who spoke all sorts of foreign languages. He sometimes drove through countries where they drank coffee instead of tea. Still, it was a decent job and he felt that modern man would get nowhere unless he learned to adapt to foreign ways even if they seemed strange at first. Midway through a scene in which the lorry driver explained, to a rapt interviewer, how he memorized the rules of the road in each country, our babysitter turned off the television.

"Ah. Well. Enough of that. Perhaps this wasn't exactly . . . I think at this point we'd best move on for our visit to the White House."

Yes, the White House was part of our "briefing". We had been promised a meeting with the then-President George Bush, but at the last minute he had gone to DisneyWorld instead. (It was just as well: several of us had been agonizing over the question of what we would say to Bush if we had two seconds to make any point or ask any questions. "George: shape up?" or perhaps just "George: it's the economy, stupid!" a line later made famous by the

Clinton campaign.) As a substitute we were offered a White House official called Roger Porter, together with all the White House former Oxonians that Porter had been able to round up.

It took a while for us to warm to Roger Porter, though, because in the enthusiasm of his opening remarks, he neglected to introduce himself. We therefore had no idea who he was. He had been at Oxford himself. He instructed us to make full use of our tremendous opportunity, and urged us to go into public policy. He gave an adoring portrait of President Bush: "He wanted to meet you himself but was unfortunately called away on a trip to Orlando, Florida, to deal with some . . . things . . . there. Which illustrates the fact that despite what the liberal media have been saying, the President spends exactly fifty percent of his working hours on domestic issues." He then urged us to ask him any questions we might have.

There was a long silence. Finally, I raised my hand.

"Ah, yes! The young lady at the end there," he said encouragingly.

"Uh . . . I'm afraid that some of us missed your, ah, introduction of yourself," I said as politely as I could, "and I was wondering if you could perhaps say a bit about yourself and your job."

"Oh," he said, and rather grudgingly explained that his name was Roger Porter and he was Bush's Advisor on Domestic Policy, the domestic equivalent of Brent Scowcroft. (This, I thought to myself, was obviously why no one had ever heard of him, the Bush administration never having had any domestic policy to speak of.)

After that, everyone had a question. Most of them were politically hostile. As question after question on poverty, the economy, the recession, education, was thrown at him, Porter grew more and more brusque. He was obviously beginning to regret having agreed to see us in the President's stead. Finally the last straw came.

The question came from Warren, a good-natured young man who was a former national bridge champion, and it started off reassuringly enough, for Porter. "I guess what I'm about to ask is not as pressing as poverty or anything," said Warren apologetically. "It's about the plight of baby veal calves, Mr Porter." The question became exceedingly detailed and pointed, and Warren, probably through nerves, inadvertently referred to the calves from the second sentence on as "the baby veals". He ended by asking what George Bush planned to do to protect the abused baby veals.

The question was fair, thoughtful, and intelligent, although Warren's phrasing was a bit odd. Porter didn't seem to appreciate Warren's obvious concern.

"I don't know anything about that," said Porter. "And I don't think George does either." He rose. "That'll be all for now. It was a pleasure. Goodbye." And he stood up, signalling the abrupt end of our little chat.

Besides the briefings and the White House visit, the Marshall Commission and the British Embassy had arranged several parties on our behalf, at which former scholars and prominent political and business leaders were assembled to wish us well. Unfortunately, they managed to schedule every party during what would normally be considered a major mealtime. Yet at these events there was rarely much food, forcing all of us new scholars to crouch desperately by the door to the kitchens, waiting for the next tiny tray of *hors-d'œuvres*. Fights broke out over watercress sandwiches, and a minuscule slice of roast beef was yanked into shreds by three of Stanford's brightest graduates.

The situation was exacerbated by the fact that although there was little food, there was lots to drink. (I soon learned that in order to survive in Oxford, one needs to get used to this sort of situation.) Each reception soon degenerated into a drunken frenzy, with crowds of staggering Marshall Scholars vying with one another to recite their accomplishments to any important people within earshot and simultaneously make a grab for the *crudités*. No one was sufficiently satiated or sober to mingle successfully with the well-known people thoughtfully assembled for our benefit, and those who tried reported that it was unrewarding.

My friend Janet discovered that an English author she had always admired was at one of the receptions. Approaching him, she expressed her delight at having the opportunity to meet him, and asked politely whether he was connected officially to the Marshall Commission in some way. He leaned over to whisper salaciously in her ear, "No! I'm here because tucked into my breast pocket, I have compromising photographs of the British Ambassador engaging in sexual congress with a baboon!"

Let me just mention one major disappointment connected to our four days of briefings. It was rumored that when we got to London, we were going to get to meet Prince Charles. Yes, that's right, Charles, the Thinking Man's Prince. But in the end he didn't show up. Imagine the sense of let-down. (This was in those heady, innocent days before the Monarchy began so spectacularly to self-destruct.) And then, to add insult to injury, the following year's batch of Marshalls got to meet Princess Diana. Rumor has it that they forever disgraced the Marshalls by allowing one of their number to make an unimaginable gaffe. Someone asked the Princess whether she found it difficult to live under constant media scrutiny. She answered politely, saying that yes, it was in fact difficult, because one was always being quoted out of context, and approached by people who undoubtedly liked you for your fame, not yourself. At this point a new Marshall from a small university in Illinois interrupted: "Oh, I know *just* what you mean," she warbled blithely. "I mean, when I got a *Marshall Scholarship*, all the campus papers kept *quoting* me wrongly! And all these people I barely knew were so nice to me, and I'm sure it was just because I had a *Marshall Scholarship*!" And on she went, oblivious to the agonized cringing of the people around her.

I have never been a fan of Princess Di, but for the record, I am told that she responded graciously.

My year's group of Marshalls was not so self-assured as the group who met Princess Di. We stifled our gloom over not meeting the Prince of Wales, and muddled our way through the events planned for us. We were thrilled and grateful at getting to meet so many important people; for most of us, a party at the British Embassy, a visit to the West Wing of the White House, and a tour of the Houses of Parliament were undreamt-of privileges. In Washington and in London, we kept looking uneasily at one another: we felt that we were just kids, really, and yet here we were, being flattered and fêted. Were we the future power élite? It was a heady thought, but also a frightening thought. Most of us wanted, with at least half of our minds, to shrivel up shyly and head back to our monastic dorm rooms. Our nervousness meant that we got little sleep, and the combination of excitement, sleeplessness, hunger, and alcohol lent a surreal quality to the four days of briefings. It was a shame, because had we been more alert and less petrified, we would undoubtedly have gotten more out of the activities planned for our benefit.

By means of compensation, perhaps, by this time we were getting to know one another quite well. Take forty bright young people between the ages of twenty-one and twenty-five, cram them two to a hotel room, put them through a series of activities that are cunningly scheduled so as to deprive them of sleep and of regular meals. In the middle of this stick them on a night flight to London, a time zone five hours later than Washington. When they arrive at Heathrow, nearly immobilized by exhaustion and vast quantities of baggage, take them immediately on whirlwind tour of the Houses of Parliament. Give them little British currency and no opportunity to change money, thus making the purchase of food and other essentials entirely out of the question. By the end of four days they will have *bonded*.

There was Warren, the amiable bridge champion committed to the plight of the baby veals. There was Lizzie, the gun-toting Alabaman. There was Janet, a fellow Harvard graduate, who planned to study PPP, Psychology, Philosophy, and Physiology. There was Carter from Williams College, who was rather quiet but smiled broadly at everyone. There was James, who was very serious and responsible. There was Richard, a philosophy major from Berkeley. There was Jack from West Point, who helped everyone with their bags in a kindly if military manner. There was Jorge, from Michigan State, who was Puerto Rican and took a liking to me because my first name was a common Spanish name; he was going to live with his fiancée, a Rhodes Scholar. There was Miranda from Stanford, who was the daughter of Czech dissidents.

There was Jonah, a precise and obviously brilliant linguist who looked like a youthful Albert Einstein (same wild hair) and was also going to Christ Church. There was Natalie from Columbia, who wanted to write novels. She was a wonderful mimic and kept us amused with imitations of Marshall officials. There was Celia, who planned to do a degree in Middle Eastern Studies. There was Ron the Princeton mathematician, Joanna the Russian Studies major, Alfred who had worked for IBM for two years.

Also in our group were a number of shadowy people who were going off to universities the rest of us had never heard of, like Reading and East Anglia (which sounded to me like a wild outpost deep in the central nervous system), whose names I never quite caught and whom I never saw again after those first four days. I'm sure they were all very nice and interesting but you know how it is: you tune out when you discover a fact that makes it clear that there is absolutely no possibility of future contact with someone, i.e. they're leaving the next day for a six-year government posting to Peoria, or they're about to begin their second year in a chartered accountancy training program. Unlike the rest of us, these brave souls had taken the trouble to look beyond Oxbridge. I regret to say that those of us who were Oxbridge-bound treated them as though they were mentally ill. But in the end, perhaps they made the wiser choice.

During those four days we traveled everywhere *en masse,* never in groups of fewer than fifteen. This was partly because we liked each other—looking back even now, I feel a surge of gratitude at my luck in finding my fellow Marshalls to be so wise, tolerant, and good-humored. Several of them became close friends during the course of the year, and especially in those first days, the Marshalls were like a big, quirky group of siblings, sometimes cantankerous, gossippy, and disorderly, but always kind and supportive.

We went around together, then, partly because we liked each other, but also because we were terrified. Terrified of what? Of getting lost. Of being attacked by hooligans. Of running out of money, or, worse yet, of simply finding, when confronted with an irritable storekeeper, that there was absolutely no way of figuring out which coin was worth what amount of money. The possibilities for misfortune and humiliation seemed truly endless. Our normally robust egos were fragile after four sleepless nights, our nerves frayed by our diet of cucumber sandwiches and white wine. I'm not sure exactly what it was that *I* feared about going out alone: perhaps that some supercilious person would come up to me on the street, look me over, and sniff, "Ha! *You* think *you'll* make it at *Oxford!* How naïve!" At which I would undoubtedly have run sobbing back to the hotel.

Being in a foreign country, about to start a new life of sorts, is scary. This is true even when the same language is spoken. perhaps that makes it all the more frightening: in a foreign country where people speak a different language, you *expect* things to be difficult. You expect to be baffled by what would otherwise be simple transactions: buying a newspaper, going to the grocery store, making a telephone call from a pay phone. But when the language is the same, you're caught off guard. You expect things to be easy; only accents, surely, will be different. This makes the ensuing culture shock all the worse.

For me, nothing was worse than the discovery that I did not know how to make a telephone call. My parents traveled frequently when I was growing up, and most major life crises—illnesses, temper tantrums, fights with friends—were resolved over the telephone. A child of the modern age, I was practically brought up over the telephone. So naturally, the first thing I tried to do, on arriving at our hotel, was call home.

Unfortunately the pay phone in the lobby did not take coins. There was a little slot for a card. I tried feeding it my credit card, which it summarily rejected. I tried to call the operator to get information, but naturally I did not know the number for the operator. I tried at random several combinations of numbers, but none worked. Finally I summoned up the courage to ask the adolescent desk clerk. "You need a phonecard," he said obnoxiously.

"Where do I get one?" I asked.

"Newsagents," he replied curtly, and went back to looking at a tabloid picture of a semi-nude woman.

What was a newsagent? Where was a newsagent? If I found one, would I be brave enough to go in and, in the face of a probably incomprehensible regional accent, ask for a phonecard, then purchase it with the correct coins? I had ten minutes before we had to leave for a cocktail party. (The very one to which Charles didn't show up.) Stymied, I gave up.

The next day we were summoned by Ruth Davis to the hotel's conference room. Those of us going to Oxford were each handed a small envelope containing the exact amount of money (down to the penny) necessary to take a train from Paddington. We were also given a small cash "arrival allowance" and a check for the remainder of the term's stipend. Natalie leaned over and whispered to me: "Do you think this will be enough money to last us until we can cash these checks?"

"I don't know," I replied anxiously. I had been wondering the same thing. "Should we ask Mrs. Davis if there's a way to get some more cash now?"

"I'd like to but I don't dare," replied Natalie. "I'm afraid she'll look at me like in *Oliver Twist*: 'More? You want more?'"

In a way, this was an apt metaphor for our common state. We felt like a group of orphans. We had no sense of entitlement (that came later). We couldn't contact our loved ones because we didn't know how to make phone calls. We were dressed in wrinkled rags because our clothes had been crammed into bursting suitcases for four days. Our remaining possessions had, in theory, been shipped ahead of us. We were dependent entirely upon government charity and the kindness of strangers.

In this sorry state we staggered off to Paddington, where we stood in a forlorn huddle until our train arrived. When the train pulled in Jack from West Point formed us into an efficient assembly line to get our luggage inside— no one person was capable of carrying all his or her own luggage. As soon as the last bag had been carefully stowed, a conductor arrived to announce that our luggage was in the wrong place and had to be moved to the other end of the train. He oversaw the process with obvious relish. Finally we all climbed in next to our luggage. My God, I thought with mixed elation and terror, in an hour I'll be at Oxford. Then I promptly fell asleep.

PART TWO

BEWILDERMENT

CARTS AND CHRISTIANS

I woke to a gray landscape of low, treeless hills and the occasional sheep. Then we passed vast industrial complexes. And then we were at Oxford Station.

Somehow we got our luggage off the train before it pulled away. Richard, the philosophy student from Berkeley, had spent his junior year in college as a visiting student at Oxford, and the rest of us gratefully let him take charge. At his suggestion, we decided to meet that night for dinner at an Indian restaurant on the High Street. We separated then for the first time in days, boarding taxis to our respective colleges.

Jonah and I were both going to Christ Church, so we got into a taxi together. "Christ Church, please," we told the taxi driver, a glum-looking fellow who spoke no known variant of English. He nodded, and sped off.

"I don't see any spires," said Jonah after a minute or two had passed. "Maybe we're going the wrong way."

I didn't see any spires either. Nothing but laundromats, fish and chip shops, warehouses, and liquor stores. We went under a dark, echoing underpass and passed what looked like a bus station. I wondered idly if the taxi driver was deliberately taking us somewhere other than Oxford, kidnapping us to sell us into white slavery in Kathmandu. "Maybe he misheard us," I told Jonah.

But soon enough we began to see spires. And more spires. Spires *ad nauseam*. We screeched towards an enormous phallic tower. (I mean that. Everyone these days says

that buildings are phallic. Tom Tower really is.) I recognized it from the pictures. The taxi, to my alarm, actually
sped up, cut into the oncoming traffic, and swerved right
through the gate, coming to a sudden halt directly beneath
Tom Tower.

"Christ Church," said the driver.

Christ Church looked like a fortress. Behind Tom
Tower's bulk, Tom Quad stretched out, vast, grandiose,
and empty, all forbidding yellowed stone, hard lines,
harsh light reflected off the high windows. It didn't look
like a place that had ever accommodated anyone under
eighty years old.

We staggered out of the taxi, dragging our bags along
with us into the porters' lodge. Two porters stared at us
sceptically.

"Oh, look," said Jonah. "The boxes I shipped over are
here."

In the center of the lodge was an enormous heap of
boxes. There were at least a dozen of them, all neatly
identified by their laser-printed labels: *Jonah Kramer*.

The porters told us both to sign a piece of paper
mysteriously labeled "Coming Up List", and we received
two keys, one to our rooms and one to the gate of Tom
Quad and St. Aldate's Quad, the mostly graduate quad in
which our rooms were located. Then we stood helplessly
staring at our bags and at Jonah's pile of boxes, which
looked bigger and heavier by the second.

"Do you happen to have a cart we could use to move
our luggage to our rooms?" I addressed the friendlier
looking porter, a small, emaciated man whose white head
was almost swallowed by his bowler hat (black suits and
archaic bowler hats are, for some reason, *de rigueur* for
Christ Church porters).

He gave an asthmatic wheeze, and launched into a
cheerful stream of words, gesturing us towards the door.

I could only understand every third word. Like most Americans, I was familiar only with more upper-class "BBC English" accents, and found regional accents nearly impossible to understand for at least the first month of my stay. The porter also wheezed constantly, further obscuring his meaning. I nodded encouragingly, and eventually managed to piece together the fact that we needed to sign for the cart, an enormous piece of rusting metal which was cleverly hidden behind the gate, wedged tightly into a little stone nook.

Jonah and I managed to drag the cart out, to the accompaniment of numerous piercing creaks and clanks. The porters had decided that we were a very amusing pair, and came out of the lodge to watch as we loaded our bags into the cart. They were joined by several camera-toting tourists who snapped our photograph.

"Ah, it's easy to get the cart out," said the taller, younger looking porter.

"But very hard to get it back in!" cackled the wheezing older porter hilariously.

"And first you've got to get across the street," reflected the tall porter.

"That's not an easy one," agreed the wheezer. "Now you just turn left, go up to the second gate in the wall, then cross St. Aldate's and go in through the keyhole-shaped gate. All right then?"

"There's a lot of traffic," warned the tall porter.

Jonah and I gave them a sickly smile. "Well, wish us luck," I said. "We'll be back soon."

"If you make it across that street," the wheezer said sourly. "God bless you in the attempt."

We started creakily off, blinking as we left the shadow of Tom Tower. The cart, like many American supermarket shopping carts, had a will of its own, and wanted only to go to the right. I tried not to regard this as an ominous sign about Christ Church's fabled conservative bias. The cart was also so heavily loaded that whenever we went downhill it accelerated rapidly, dragging us along with it.

In this way we crossed the street, relying largely on the cart's momentum to carry us safely through the traffic and through the keyhole-shaped gate.

St. Aldate's Quad looked, from the outside, rather like a Holiday Inn in some south-western American town. From the inside, it also looked like a Holiday Inn, or, more charitably, like a ski-lodge in the Sierras. There was a metal plaque outside of staircase two, where my room was. It had a date on it, in roman numerals, and I laboriously—I could never remember what "L" meant—interpreted it to mean 1986. The rest of the plaque was unfortunately in Latin, and the only words I could make out were "*novum quad.*"

My room was reasonably large, and had a closet containing a built-in sink and a well-lit mirror. It was on the second floor, and had two large windows. Unlike a Holiday Inn, alas, my room also had what looked like the world's narrowest bed.

We looked around quickly. My room was off a hallway with two other bedrooms, and there was a small kitchen next door. There was also a bathroom with a very large bathtub. It had two faucets, one for hot water and one for cold, and no shower head or shower curtain. I couldn't understand this. Surely shower technology had reached Britain by 1986? And there didn't seem to be a phone jack anywhere, or even a pay phone.

Jonah's room was in the next staircase, and was similar in size and layout to mine. His windows looked over the small quad. His hallway, though, had a shower as well as a bath, and a pay phone. I could see that I would be spending a lot of time visiting Jonah. At least, after I figured out where to buy a phonecard, I would.

After our brief inspection of the rooms, we dragged the cart back up the street to the porters' lodge. The two porters were waiting for us. Fortunately, the clump of tourists seemed to have dissipated.

"Ha. Never thought we'd see you two again," wheezed the old one. We grunted noncommittally. He stood back to let us by.

"You don't have to help me with my boxes," said Jonah. "Really, I can get them myself." He stared hopelessly at the pile in the lodge.

"Of course I'll help," I said. "I would never have been able to get my bags up without your help. It won't take long if we both carry boxes."

"If you're sure . . ."

"Absolutely."

We each picked up a box and walked out to the cart.

"Whoa!" said the old porter. He glared at Jonah. "You're not going to let the young lady carry your boxes for you, are you?"

Jonah looked aghast. The problem of my being a young lady had crossed neither of our minds.

"Don't worry!" I chirped. "We American girls are tough! We tame broncos every day back home!"

Shaking his head disapprovingly, the porter retreated into the lodge.

Half an hour later, the last of the boxes safely stored in Jonah's room, we returned the cart. As the porters had warned, it proved very difficult to wedge the cart back into its space. The elderly porter stood by shouting orders at Jonah, who tried to steer the cart back in. The porter refused to allow me to help. "Oh no," he said, giving Jonah a dirty look. He had apparently decided that Jonah had too little sense of male chivalry. "*He'll* do it."

The cart was finally stowed back behind the great gate. Jonah and I went into the porters' lodge and discovered that we each had a mailbox, which the porters referred to as a "pigeon-hole," stuffed full of little envelopes. My envelopes contained a stern letter demanding that I report as soon as possible to the office of the Senior Censor, and innumerable letters urging me to join the Christian Union and discuss Jesus over tea. There was also a lengthy letter from the Chaplain (whose name, improbably, was Michael Jackson). The Chaplain wanted me to feel that I could come to him at any time to discuss all manner of personal concerns. He also invited me to tea.

Finally, I had two small embossed cards, one from the "Dean, Canons, and Students of Christ Church", inviting me to a "Newcomers' Drinks Party", and another from the same group of people inviting me to dinner in Hall the following week. *Dark suit,* said the card. *No gown.* I decided to assume that "dark suit" did not apply to me. (Correctly: women are still such a relative novelty at Christ Church that no one dares tell them how to dress.)

The mention of "Canons" unnerved me. I grew up in an entirely pagan household, blessed, among my parents and step-parents, with one lapsed Protestant, one lapsed Jew, and two lapsed Catholics. Furthermore, it was a family of socialists, all of whom, while differing from Marx in many instances, fully agreed that religion was the opiate of the masses. Why were there Canons at Christ Church? Why was it a cathedral? And most of all, why did I have so many kind letters from Christian Unionists and the Chaplain, when Jonah reported that he had none at all? Was I viewed as easily convertible? Was Jonah beyond salvation?

Pondering these questions, we repaired to the nearest restaurant, the St. Aldate's Coffee Shop, only to discover the sinister fact that the coffee shop was run by St. Aldate's church. Religious books and posters of Jesus were for sale along with teas and pastries. The menus offered an unap-

50

petizing selection of curries and potatoes, and urged us in a few discreet lines to feel free to join the staff in their morning prayers. We were too hungry to keep going at this point, so we gave in and ordered. The waiters and waitresses were all ominously friendly and welcoming. In my exhausted state I was beginning to understand what it was that made people join cults.

"Enjoy your time here!" said the waitress as we left. "If you're ever feeling lonely, do come by for tea! Or prayers!" The entire staff joined her at the door to wave goodbye to us.

We trudged back down the street to St. Aldate's Quad, past a large sign that declared chirpily, "Christian Life is in the Fast Lane!" I was clearly unsuited for Christian life. Jonah and I parted back at the quad and I went to my room to unpack.

When I started to unpack I noticed for the first time that there were no drawers in the room. There were a few shelves in the closet, but that was it. For the time being I resorted to just stuffing everything into little heaps in the closet. I would have to figure something out later, or at least acquire a lot more coat-hangers. But all in all my room seemed acceptable. I removed the stained and horrible thing lying on the bed (the duvet?) and replaced it with my own sheets and down comforter. I had been warned by many Americans that the British do not believe in central heating, so I was relieved to discover that the radiator by the window was already pumping out large quantities of extremely hot air. I became somewhat less relieved when I discovered that there was no visible way to turn the heat *off*.

It was, in fact, rather hot and stuffy in my room. I opened my window to get some air and discovered two things. The first was that I had a wonderful view of the front of Christ Church. The sun had come out and was low in the west, and the decorative ramparts on top of the great hall glowed in the long light. To the right, the War Memorial Garden was filled with flowers and the meadows stretched out towards the river. It was like looking out on a grand palace. I decided right then that that view would make up for a lot of things.

It had to. My second discovery was that I was not the only person to like that view. St. Aldate's, the street directly under my window, was thronged with double-decker tourist buses, all of which were pausing to allow the tourists to gawp. Several competing loudspeakers crackled on in a number of different languages:

"When Cardinal Wolsey fell from power in 15–"

"Et quand le roi Henri huit—"

The worst thing was that sitting on the upper level of the double-deckers, tourists were uniquely placed at exactly the level of my windows. As I admired the view, several tourists turned enthusiastically to admire me and my room. "Ooh, a student!" I found myself staring into their curious faces, less than three feet away, and hastily closed my curtains.

I decided to run a bath. The hot water, I discovered, was very hot. The cold water was very cold. There was no way to mix the hot water with the cold except by letting both taps run together into the tub, which was of dubious cleanliness. I stifled my concerns about hygiene and lowered myself into the water, wondering apprehensively how on earth I was going to be able to rinse the shampoo out of my hair. The answer, I soon discovered, was that I was *not* going to fully rinse my hair. There were still suds in it as I towelled myself off. Clearly something was going to have to be done, and soon.

That evening, soapy but refreshed, I went out to join

the other Marshalls for dinner. We met at a High Street Indian restaurant. We had the restaurant pretty much to ourselves, because most students would not arrive for a few days more. Oxford marks time in weeks: terms last eight weeks, and one speaks of the date as "Thursday of Sixth Week," or "Sunday of Third Week." We were not even in 0th Week (pronounced, by the English, "Noughth Week"); that would start the next day. "0th Week" had an apocalyptic ring to it, sort of like "Zero Hour."

Our impresario for the evening was Richard. He seemed to know the ropes. "Learn to drink port," he told us. We laughed nervously. "I'm not kidding," said Richard. "That's what they drink here." And then, in an astonishing gesture, he bought us all a round of port. For most of us it was our first glass of port, ever. "To us," said Richard. "And to taking Oxford by storm." Again, we all laughed nervously.

TOURING, EATING, AND
ANOTHER CHRISTIAN

THE FOLLOWING DAY was devoted to exploring, shopping, and to doing some research on Christ Church. I met
up with Janet, Natalie, and Miranda and we wandered
around Oxford, seeing the sights. We admired the old city
wall at New College, the Tower and deer parks at
Magdalen, the Bridge of Sighs at Hertford. We also visited
the University buildings proper: the Radcliffe Camera, the
Bodleian, the Sheldonian.

There is a joke about some American tourists at
Oxford, who stop a student on the High Street and ask to
be directed to "the University." This is supposed to
provoke gales of mirthful laughter from those in the
know, because—ho ho—there is no "campus" in the
American sense. Oxford is made up of lots of autonomous
colleges, each of which admits its own students, owns its
own buildings, has its own large or small endowment,
and provides its own teaching. This is actually a stupid
joke, and serves merely as an example of the worst sort of
Oxford smugness. Because regardless of the technical
autonomy of the colleges, they are all part of the University, and share University libraries and lecture halls like
the Examination Schools, the Bodleian, and the Sheldonian. Any friendly passer-by could easily explain to a tourist
that standing on the High, one is smack in the middle of
the University, surrounded by the High Street colleges
and mere yards from the main University buildings.

After looking around, we went to buy gowns. Gowns

were required for the matriculation ceremony the following week, and Christ Church required that gowns be worn at "Formal Hall," the later dinner seating attended by most postgraduate students. We bought our gowns in a dimly lit men's store on the High, surrounded by dignified older men who called us "madam." At American universities, gowns are only worn at graduation and are rented for the occasion; the idea that we might have to wear them frequently seemed silly but was not unappealing. Every day would be like Hallowe'en!

I discovered to my relief that "commoner" simply meant that I was doing an undergraduate degree and was not on a college scholarship. This meant that I was supposed to purchase a short, ugly gown that looked like a genetically engineered mutant vest. ("Waistcoat," to the English.) Natalie and Miranda, doing M.Phils, got slightly more respectable looking garments.

After buying our gowns, we set off in search of white blouses, another part of the "*sub fusc*" outfit required for matriculation. *Sub fusc,* I learned, simply means dark clothes, although the Oxford authorities are mighty specific about just what sorts of dark clothes qualify. "For men, dark jacket, dark trousers, dark shoes, white shirt, white tie, and gown. For women, dark skirt, dark stockings and shoes, white shirt, black tie, black jacket if desired, and gown." These clothes must also be worn, absurdly enough, at all official University examinations.

Finding a white blouse was harder than one might expect, and I ended up paying a wopping fifty pounds for a plain-collared shirt. However, as a special bonus I persuaded the salesgirl at Lewis's department store to give me two dozen left-over coat hangers. I also bought some plates, mugs, and basic food provisions, and, blessedly, I stumbled upon a small rubber gizmo designed to funnel the water from separate hot and cold taps into one unified stream. I bought it instantly, and bidding goodbye to my friends I raced home to rinse the remaining shampoo out of my hair.

Bathing was still not exactly easy—as there was no shower curtain one had to crouch in the tub, shivering in the icy air (unlike the bedrooms, the bathroom was not overheated), trying not to spray water all over the room. It took forever to get clean, because at any given time one had to have one hand on the sprayer and therefore had only one hand free to soap and rinse. But it was a big improvement.

After my bath I settled down with a fat guidebook on Oxford and an elegant little volume on the history of Christ Church, compiled by Hugh Trevor-Roper, the historian of Hitler Diaries infamy. I had settled on Christ Church as my college for several rather arbitrary reasons. For one thing, it was said to be very beautiful. (While the view from my window was certainly lovely, I had promptly decided, upon arrival, that as far as I was concerned the inside of the college was phenomenally unpleasant. Huge, empty, stone—it was symmetrical and entirely devoid of any softening influence, like trees or flowers. It occurred to me that standing in Tom Quad, one would have absolutely no clues as to what season it was in the rest of the world.)

Christ Church also had the Meadows. I had seen enough of Oxford on my brief visit several years before to know that it was nothing if not a busy city, filled with blaring horns and exhaust fumes that discolored the ancient stone of the colleges. I wanted to go to a college that had some nice green places attached to it. And the Christ Church Meadows were beautiful, just beginning to turn amber and red with the coming of autumn. They stretched down to the Thames (called the "Isis" by Oxonians) and to the row of college boathouses, past grazing cows and one lone horse. (Why just one? The horse's solitary state was an unending source of puzzlement to me.)

Christ Church was also old, rich, and famous. As an American, I wanted my money's worth of Oxford (or rather, the Marshall Commission's money's worth). There seemed hardly any point in going to Oxford only to be swallowed up by some modern, international college like Nuffield or Wolfson or St. Antony's, surrounded mostly by other foreign graduate students, and far from the center of town. Christ Church somehow seemed to be the "real" Oxford.

Finally, Christ Church was one of the few well-known colleges to lack an enormous American ghetto. Most of the Americans I knew were at places like Balliol, New College, and Magdalen, where Americans make up about half of all graduate students. Christ Church, in contrast, had only three Americans other than me out of the fifty graduate students who entered that year. There was Jonah. There was a forlorn boy on a junior year abroad. He was called Bob, and he came from Purdue University (or, as he put it in his thick New York accent, "I'm Baaahb, from Purdooo." The English students found his accent as incomprehensible as I found the accents of the porters). And there was a smiley young man named Bill who was said to be a mathematics wunderkind.

(After a few months Bill started going out with Christ Church's one pseudo-American, a flaxen-haired English undergraduate called Tina who spoke with a perfect American accent. She was outgoing and voluble; when I first met Tina she told me that she was American but had been to school in England; later, some other undergraduates told me that Tina was as English as the Queen and had only been to America for two weeks in her life. She had a strange obsession with America which caused her to pretend to be American. Tina's other oddity was that she claimed to have a health condition which prevented her from eating anything other than raw vegetables. Since the Christ Church kitchen remains unconvinced that raw vegetables are edible, she had a tough time. In Hall, she was continually racing to and fro between her seat and the kitchen, begging the servers for extra platters of raw carrots, cucumbers, and celery. When salad was served she would eat everyone else's salad as well as her own, saying piteously, if they objected, "You *know* it's all I can eat. I'm just hungry all the time. [*sniff*] I really think they're trying to starve me here." People called her "the Veg Girl.")

When I was choosing a college, I had considered this shortage of Americans at Christ Church to be good. I figured that I would see my American friends no matter what, and that if I lived with them too I would never meet anyone else. Only when I arrived did the lack of my compatriots seem frightening. Sitting in my room, curtains closed against the tourist buses, I recollected the reason that Christ Church had so few Americans: grand and imposing, it was said to be a bastion of upper-class snobbery and élitism, and to be pretentious and cold to outsiders, be they outsiders for reasons of class or nationality. It was not said to be a very friendly sort of place. More male students came from Eton than from any other school, with Westminster close behind. Women had only been admitted in the early eighties, and the male–female ratio was still five to two.

Back in my dorm room at Harvard, the previous March, it had been easy to dismiss this side of Christ Church's reputation. Surely they didn't really care about all that class stuff anymore, did they? A high-school friend who had herself done a junior year abroad at Oxford assured me that Christ Church was very friendly. But now I was doubting that. Here I was in a college of more than five hundred students, most of them strangers to me, most of them foreigners! And on my desk lay an unfriendly letter from the Senior Censor.

I opened my guidebook, and then read the booklet by Hugh Trevor-Roper ("also Lord Dacre," proclaimed the book somberly. So which is it, Hugh?). Neither book was able to tell me whether or not I would ever make any friends at Christ Church. I did, however, learn more than I ever wanted to know about the history and architecture of Christ Church.

Christ Church is not one of the oldest colleges. It was founded in the 1520s by Cardinal Wolsey, then at the height of his career. Built on the ruins of the medieval priory of St. Frideswide, the patron saint of Oxford, Christ Church is visually the grandest, if not the most accessible, of Oxford's colleges.

Christ Church has two oddities. One is its dual nature as a college and a religious institution. (Thus the canons.) Most colleges at Oxford have chapels, but Christ Church has a cathedral. A small one, to be sure, but a cathedral none the less, serving all of the diocese of Oxford. The Dean of Christ Church (at other colleges called the master, the provost, or the president) must be an Anglican clergyman, and Christ Church has many clergymen affiliated with it.

Christ Church's other oddity stems from its nature as a royal establishment. The Queen is the official Visitor of Christ Church; when she comes to Oxford, Christ Church is her home away from home. Because of this, Christ Church has historically attracted an aristocratic student body; although this is much less true today, it is still thought to be the most élitist and conservative of the Oxford colleges. In Hall, there are frequent toasts to the Queen, and royal portraits abound. Reading Trevor-

Roper's book, it was hard not to conclude that Christ Church is a smug sort of college. After a long list of famous Christ Church graduates, the book ends with the following comment:

> To end on a proper note of humility, we should perhaps add that, in one respect, we are admittedly defective. We have produced no saints. But this, of course, is a mere accident of chronology: saints were not made in England after the foundation of Christ Church.

That night, I decided that it was time to try eating dinner at Christ Church. I wanted to get the hang of things before all the undergraduates arrived.

In most American universities, the place where meals were obtained and consumed is known simply as "the cafeteria". Harvard, trying to be classier, pompously calls its cafeterias "dining halls". At Oxford, the word "dining" is dropped, and one simply eats in "Hall," with a capital "H".

This alone was enough to intimidate me. "Hall" struck me as having masculine and militaristic associations: Hall was where the warriors in *Beowulf* hung out drinking mead late into the night after a tough battle, fighting and flinging bones over their shoulders to the mangy dogs who snarled for scraps. Fearful of being struck in the head by a flying bone and knocked unconscious, I went out to look for Jonah. I wanted to persuade him to accompany me to dinner. He would be able to ferry me discreetly to the hospital if necessary.

Jonah's staircase had the outer door locked. (My staircase door wouldn't lock; this puzzled me, I am embarrassed to say, for months, which was the time it took me to discover that this was because somebody had put a pebble at the bottom of the doorjamb.) I shouted up at his window and he tossed down the key. When I got to his room, I discovered that he was talking to a dark-haired young man wearing a white V-necked sweater with navy blue bands around the collar and waist, the kind that Americans call a "tennis sweater." His sweater, in fact, said "O.U.L.T.C.," and under that was a pair of crossed tennis racquets. He introduced himself as Jerome. He had what sounded to me like an English accent.

"Jerome is a second-year graduate. He lives across the hall," explained Jonah. "He says he'll go across to dinner with us."

"Oh, great. Where are you from, Jerome?" I asked politely.

"South Africa," he replied.

South Africa! I backed up a bit. Everyone knows that white South Africans are evil.

"What does your sweater say?" I asked suspiciously.

"Oxford University Lawn Tennis Club."

Lawn tennis? Sounded like a sissy sport to me. "What's lawn tennis?"

"Just regular tennis. It's the Blues team. The English just call it by an old-fashioned name."

Our conversation proceeded awkwardly. I learned that Jerome was in Oxford on a South African Rhodes Scholarship, studying for a second bachelor's degree in law. I couldn't decide what to think of him. He seemed intelligent and friendly, but he also seemed, superficially at least, to be alarmingly at home at Christ Church. In an effort to seem natural, I asked a number of foolish questions about the "scouts," women who come in each morning to clean. Would they report me if I had an overnight guest?

Jerome raised his eyebrows. "Are you planning on having a lot of overnight guests?"

I blushed, and suggested that we all go change for dinner.

"Don't forget your gown," Jerome warned, "or you won't get in." He looked severely at Jonah. "Tie and collar, too. They're quite strict."

"Do I need to wear a skirt?" I asked anxiously.

Jerome surveyed me. He looked unnervingly like a representative of an ancient hierarchical tradition. "No. You're female. There's no dress code for women."

At 7.20, sharp, we marched into Hall.

Superficially, it looked grander than I imagined Beowulf's hall to be. High-ceilinged, cavernous, and dark, the walls were lined with busts and portraits of famous Christ Church graduates: John Locke, Lewis Carroll, W. H. Auden, more than a dozen prime ministers. The High Table, where the tutors and fellows sit, was on a raised platform at the far end of the room. Above the high table was a looming life-sized portrait of Henry VIII, in all his portly glory, looking about to leap down on to the table below and belt out an aria. All the tables in the room were long enough to seat at least a dozen on a side, and they were wedged in tightly enough to make it impossible, once seated, for anyone in the middle of the room to leave before the people at the end tables. The tables held small lamps that seemed to have sprouted from the wood, and were laid with plates and silverware. There were only about forty people scattered around the room.

I had put on a skirt, just in case. Jerome led the way.

"Ah," he said, heading for a long table at the far right corner of the hall. "There are some other graduates. We'll sit there."

Jonah and I obediently followed along and clambered over the high narrow bench in front of the table. I immediately saw the true argument for not wearing a skirt: tight skirts make it extremely difficult to step over high benches. I sat down as gracefully as I could and stared at my plate. The plate was decorated with a small picture of what I took to be a cowboy hat with a lasso (it later turned out to be a rendering of Cardinal Wolsey's ecclesiastical hat and tassels).

I waited for Jerome to introduce us to the two men sitting opposite us, but he just smiled vaguely in the direction of a bust of Queen Elizabeth and began to tap on his dinner roll. The roll sounded hollow. The two young men across the table didn't look at us, although they had earlier given Jerome a friendly greeting. They seemed to be talking about sports: "We have more Blues than Univ," said one.

I picked up my roll. It was rock hard. "Are they always this stale?" I asked Jerome.

"They re-use the uneaten ones day after day," he explained. "Last year someone carved a hole in his roll and put a slip of paper inside with his name and the date. It turned up again on an undergraduate's plate a month later."

The hall had filled up and voices echoed loudly off the walls. Suddenly two sharp cracks of a mallet brought the noise to a stop. Everyone instantly rose. I shot up, banging my knee against the table.

Ten feet away a young man gazed soulfully at the ceiling as he bellowed out a Latin grace, of which I understood next to nothing. Finally, with the words "*Dominum nostrum*", everyone mumbled "*Amen*" and sat down. Dinner had officially begun.

The food was at odds with the elegant atmosphere. Which is to say that it was awful. I mean *really* awful. Worse than awful. Limp noodles with a sauce made out of what smelled like rotting lamb, served with both baked and fried potatoes. Did they think that one derived different sorts of nutrients from different sorts of potatoes?

Wasn't *one* kind of potato enough? At Lowell House, the food had been mediocre, but at least there were hamburgers, sandwiches, and a salad bar with yogurt. At Christ Church there were no such options. You didn't have any choice about what to eat. White-coated servants brought around plates and dropped them in front of the diners. You ate what was there, or else went hungry. As an American, I found it embarrassing to be waited on; I kept wanting to apologize to the servers for putting them to so much trouble. It was with an effort that I prevented myself from leaving a tip when we left.

No drinks other than pitchers of water were provided, but the men across the table from us were drinking beer. I wanted to ask them where they had gotten it, but didn't dare; although they each smiled vaguely if I happened to meet their eye, they made no attempt to talk to any of us, despite the fact that they were sitting directly across the table. Had I been in the US I would have simply introduced myself, but here, I suspected, that would only give me a reputation for being a brash American.

Jerome, digging industriously at his food with the stoic expression of one who has been eating institutional fare for most of his life, explained that if you wanted anything other than water, it had to be purchased separately, before dinner, in the "Buttery" in the antechamber. As the buttery sold nothing but drinks, I can't imagine why it was called a buttery. The food was so bad that, with only water to wash it down, I could hardly eat anything, and there was apparently no chance of getting coffee.

(My mother visited later in the year and I took her to a Special Guest Dinner in Hall. This was shortly after a controversial book came out, claiming that Princess Di was bulimic. The dinner was black tie, but the food was as disgusting as ever: sweet and sour veal kidneys with apple purée. My mother's only comment, as she stared dolefully at her kidneys, was to suggest that perhaps Di's bulimia was merely a tactful response to the food consumed by the English élite.)

Luckily, I didn't have long to think sad thoughts about the food, or to be intimidated by the men sitting opposite, because after about twenty minutes the plates were removed and the lights were dimmed. Christ Church apparently frowned upon leisurely after-dinner conversation. Dinner was over. As we filed out, I asked Jerome if he knew the men who had sat across from us. "Sure," he said. "Neal and Bill." I explained that I had found it odd that they had not spoken to us at all. He laughed. "Don't take it personally. The tables are so wide that people almost never talk to people sitting across from them. Besides, they're English."

"So you think I was right to decide not to introduce myself? Would it have been seen as too American?"

"Hmm. Probably."

The next morning I couldn't put it off any longer. It was Monday. I had to obey my summons to go see the Senior Censor. I wasn't sure, but I suspected that he wanted to see me because Ruth Davis had told him of my desire to switch courses, dropping my plan to do a second bachelor's degree in Politics, Philosophy, and Economics (PPE) in favor of doing an M.Phil. in Politics.

Switching degrees or subjects, I knew from my previous chat with Ruth Davis, is not encouraged by the powers that be at Oxford. Unlike in the US, where students are in college for four years and choose a major subject only after a year or two of general studies, British undergraduates are in college for only three years. They apply to study a particular subject, and once admitted to a college it is very difficult to change courses. For graduates, especially American graduates, things are a bit more flexible: the British seem to take it for granted that Americans will be academically undisciplined and flighty. At any rate, such high fees (about four times the amount paid by British students) are extracted from Americans that it makes fiscal sense for colleges to humor them rather than risk having them leave, money and all.

Before going to see the Censor, I decided to go see the Tutor for Student Welfare. His title was less ominous than the Censor's, and I thought he might be able to answer some preliminary questions about course switches. According to Jerome, who was becoming an essential source of information, the Senior Censor essentially fulfilled the functions of a dean. Christ Church, alone among the colleges, used the odd title of "Censor." Still, it seemed safer to arm myself with information from the Welfare office first. I brought my friend Janet along for moral support.

Unfortunately, the Tutor for Student Welfare was guarded by a fire-breathing assistant. She was a deceptively pleasant-looking middle-aged woman, and her nameplate identified her as Mrs Edgerton, Assistant for Welfare and Special Events.

"Good morning," I said to Mrs. Edgerton. She glared at me. "I'm trying to switch courses and I—"

"That's not possible," she said instantly.

"Yes, well, I thought perhaps the Tutor for—"

"Only the Censor handles those issues," she snapped.

"Oh, I'm terribly sorry then." I looked at my watch. It was 4:30. A note in the Christ Church rule book had said that the Censor was only to be approached between 9 and 9:30 a.m. I wasn't sure if these hours applied only to walk-ins or to appointments as well. I thought that I had better check with Mrs. Edgerton, for fear of meeting with another rebuff if I walked into the Censor's office at the wrong hour.

"If I want to see the Censor, should I walk in or make a special appointment to see him?"

"If," Mrs Edgerton returned venomously, "*if* you had taken the *trouble* to read the rule book, you would *know* when to come see the Censor." Then she shot a vicious look at Janet, who had been hanging back politely, idly thumbing through a copy of the aforementioned rule book that she had picked up from the window-ledge. "Would you kindly *put* that *down!*" she spat. Janet dropped the booklet in horror, and together we backed out the door, goggling at each other.

"Was it something I said?" I asked Janet finally.

"I don't think so. She was—she was—well, I hate to say this about any woman, but the way she acted made me think she was just a *bitch*."

(I later learned that quite a few students considered Mrs. Edgerton to be unpredictably rude. Some days she was friendly and helpful, other days—beware. She seemed to particularly dislike Americans. Mark, an American friend of mine, finally got fed up when he went in one day to inquire about the deadline for filing a particular form. She refused to give him the date, telling him snidely that she couldn't understand why, when all the *English* students had figured that out for themselves, he couldn't figure it out. Mark had had a bad day and he hit the roof, telling her that her rudeness was inexcusable and that he was writing a letter of complaint to the Tutor for Welfare, the Dean, and the Queen of England if necessary. She blanched and apologized profusely, making Mark something of a folk-hero with us from then on.)

Needless to say, before going to see the Censor the next morning I practically memorized the Christ Church rule book. I discovered, among other things, that in order to see the Censor, one needed to put on a silly costume. Said the rule book: "Gowns are worn when consulting the Censor on official business."

I thought that was great. Not "Gowns should be worn," or "Gowns are required." Just that bland phrase stating an unarguable proposition: "Gowns are worn." This is the way we do things here.

Especially after my run-in with the Tutor for Welfare's assistant, I wasn't feeling particularly tolerant. Wearing gowns to see the Censor did not strike me as a quaint Oxford tradition. It struck me as an affirmation of hierarchy. As in, "I have power and you don't, and I'm going to rub it in by insisting that you wear something absurd in order to speak with me."

The Senior Censor didn't know what to do with me when I finally arrived, begowned, in his office. He was a mild and soft-spoken fellow. He didn't seem at all annoyed at me, but he didn't look thrilled to meet me, either. A tall, soft-looking man with a pink, lined face and a rushed, reedy voice, he was obviously dismayed by my last-minute request to switch courses. "I really don't know if that's possible," he said, mouth sagging.

I begged and reasoned, and finally he sent me off to see Hugh Ford, a politics tutor.

Ford seemed overjoyed to see me. He was a large man, and compared to the Censor he was positively jolly. He zestfully rubbed his hands together.

"Certainly you can switch!" he exclaimed when I had explained my situation. "Switch by all means! Why waste your time doing undergraduate work? Put undergraduate days behind you!"

"Oh! Really! That's wonderful. I was given to understand that switching would be quite difficult."

"Nonsense, nonsense." He leaned forward conspiratorially. "I'm quite in favor of people studying what they want to study, you know. The Censor—he's a fine man. But like so many people here you may find him rather *limited* in his views. No imagination. Fine people all. But—" he lowered his voice—"they've never left Oxford, you see."

"Oh. I see."

"Quite, quite. Rather parochial. I myself spent a year at New York University." He leapt up and began to pace to and fro. "There's just one thing. One problem. At this late date it may be difficult to find someone to supervise you if you switch to the Politics M.Phil."

My spirits dropped. "But then—"

"However, I have a possible solution for you. An offer." He chuckled. "I am the director of a brand-new program, the M.Phil. in European Politics. It's not dissimilar to the Politics M.Phil. If you were to switch to that, I would supervise you myself. With your academic credentials I would be very happy to let you into the program."

"But I don't know anything at all about European Politics."

He stopped pacing and gaped at me. "Surely you wouldn't want to study something you already knew?"

There was logic in this. "Well . . ."

"Think it over, think it over. Do you speak anything other than English?"

"Uh . . . a bit of French."

"That's all right then. You'll do fine. I'll send the paperwork over to you this afternoon."

I stood up. It was obvious that our meeting was over. "Well . . ."

"Oh yes. One more thing." Ford's round face took on a kindly, sympathetic look. "You may find the examinations here quite difficult to get used to."

"The examinations? Why?"

"Well, at the end of two years you will have to take

four three-hour examinations. You're probably used to composing at a computer and you may, er, not know how to write an essay for three hours, under time pressure. It's rather a long time, three hours, you'll find . . . and there are four exams."

"Dr Ford," I said, as delicately as I could. "Um. Actually . . . at most American universities students take four three-hour exams every few months, for four years."

Ford looked at me, astounded. "*Really!*" he said, in the tone adults usually reserve for five-year-olds who demonstrate unexpected maturity. "Really. Ahem. Well, then, you should be fine." And, beaming again, he ushered me out the door.

By now other students were beginning to arrive. A steady stream of people came and went with the cart from the porters' lodge. I was pleased one day to come upon two porters harassing some young men as they struggled with the cart. At least it hadn't just been Jonah and me. The young men were red in the face and sweat dripped from their foreheads. A small serious crowd of Japanese businessmen recorded their movements with hand-held video cameras as they attempted to wedge the cart back into its corner. I gave them a pitying smile and walked on.

The two other rooms with which my room shared a kitchen and bathroom were both now occupied. My new flatmates were both men, which surprised me somewhat: technically I was allowed no overnight guests, yet here they were making me share a bathroom with men I had never met before. (This was later explained by one of my scouts, who told me that the "no guests" rule was not so much designed to prevent pre-marital sex, but to ensure that the college could earn money by renting out guest rooms to students with visiting friends.)

Peter was tall and thin and very friendly. He had curly hair and a perennially surprised look. He was from Australia and was doing an M.Phil. in economics. Like many Australians, he loved sports and all outdoor activities; he spent his vacations mountain-climbing in the Himalayas. He hovered amiably by the kitchen door as I unloaded various groceries, examining each item with undimmed curiosity.

"Oh, look, what's this? A lettuce!"

"Come on, Peter," I'd say. "Surely you have lettuce in Australia."

"Oh yes. I've never bought one myself though. I can't cook."

"I guess it's Hall for you, then. But Peter," I added kindly, "you don't *have* to cook lettuce. You eat it raw."

"Oh, I know. It's just that I'm surprised that they have them here in England. I didn't know they *ate* vegetables here."

Obviously, Peter had liked his meal in Hall almost as much as I had liked mine. This became a recurring theme in my conversations with Peter: the inadequacies of English food. Peter soon decided that virtually nothing in England was satisfactory, and took advantage of having a sympathetic non-English flatmate to whom he could air his complaints. He stopped me in Tom Quad the day after I met him to inform me irately that there were no mountains in England. As the year wore on and the weather worsened, Peter took to compiling obsessive little lists of what was wrong with England. The lists, which were revised weekly, usually included a number of permanent entries: "Pasty-faced people. Drizzle. Exhaust fumes. No showers. No vegetables. Decadent. Corrupt. Anaemic," and a number of up-to-the-minute complaints: "People too lazy to go skiing with me in Germany. Censor ruddy and fat. Kidney for dinner Tues followed by monkfish Wed."

My other flatmate was Ian. Ian was English, which alone caused Peter to try to keep a safe distance from him. Ian was a physicist from the University of Warwick. He was short and had tufty blond hair which stood on end.

Ian was either extremely shy or he just hated me. He fiddled and twitched uncontrollably whenever I spoke to him, and spoke only in rushed, desperate monosyllables. He darted furtively back and forth between his room and the kitchen, continually checking his watch like the White Rabbit. All in all there was definitely something starved and rabbity about him: he had little pink eyes and a twitching nose. In the kitchen he filled several cupboards with exotic spices and ingredients, and he cooked himself large and enormously complex meals, which he then ate alone in his room.

That afternoon I went off to the "Newcomers' Drinks Party." It was in the Junior Common Room. The phrase "Junior Common Room" (JCR) denotes both an actual set of rooms, containing newspapers, vending machines, et cetera, and all people who are "members" of the JCR: in this case, all undergraduates. Thus one might say, "I'll meet you in the JCR," but one might also use the phrase to mean the group of members, as in, "The JCR is against the new rules governing library hours." Graduate students had their own set of rooms, the GCR, upstairs from the JCR. While graduates were entitled to use the JCR as well, few did, and undergraduates were not allowed to use GCR facilities. The dons and "senior members" of Christ Church had their own Senior Common Room, off limits to students.

The JCR was packed when I arrived, the air thick with the intermingled odors of beer, sherry, and cigarette smoke. I noticed for the first time that English students smoke a lot more than their American counterparts; at most college gatherings in the United States, smoking is not permitted indoors. Someone thrust a can of not very cold beer into my hand. (I had been warned about this when I set off for England, and I am happy to report that for the most part, it is Not True that the English drink warm beer. Only at student events do you frequently get warm beer; the idea of filling a bucket with ice and putting the cans in the ice doesn't seem to have occurred to anyone at Oxford. Give them a few years.)

I allowed myself to be carried gently into the room on a tide of bodies. I looked around. I knew not a soul. There seemed to be about three men for every woman in the room, and after a few minutes a very polite boy came and stood beside me. He looked very sweet, and he also looked like he was about sixteen. Way too young. But I was glad of someone to talk to, so we went through a ritualistic exchange of information: Where are you from? What subject? Where are your rooms? Will was from Yorkshire and he planned to read History. His rooms were in the Meadow Buildings. He had visited America once. He was actually eighteen. (Still way too young, I thought.) He urged me to come by for tea some time. I told him that I would like to but that I wasn't sure if it would be legal.

After a while I noticed that some of the older-looking people in the room wore name tags and carried clipboards. They seemed to be representatives of various college clubs, so I detached myself from Will and went to scout out what clubs to join. I signed up for rowing. I also signed up to sing in the college choir, a non-auditioning group that sounded just about my speed; I had sung in choirs all through school but by now was badly out of practice.

I had broken up with my boyfriend of two years when I left for England. The relationship hadn't seemed fated to survive a 3,000-mile separation. By the time I arrived in Oxford, I missed my boyfriend terribly, but I was also glad to be on my own. For two years, I had been one half of a couple; now I was suddenly free to flirt if I wanted to, to go out dancing and to parties with whomever I wanted. It was a little frightening, but it was also liberating. Here I was, in a new country. Who could say that England might not hold the man of my dreams? Perhaps a minor lord with, say, a teeny tiny castle on the Cornish coast?

The prospects didn't seem all that bright at the Newcomers' Drinks Party, though. Looking around, I decided that there was only one decent possibility within striking distance. He wore a nametag, which I took to be a good sign—it meant he was at least not a fresher. His tag said *John Christian, Union*. I was pleased, because this gave me a good reason to go talk to him. I had been trying to make up my mind about whether or not to join the Oxford Union, the famed debating society. It seemed to be part of the Oxford of myth, but on the other hand it cost £80 to join, and a lot of people had told me it wasn't worth it.

My luck was good. John Christian caught my eye and smiled. "Hello," he said.

"Hi," I beamed. "I'm Rosa. I see you're from the Union."

He beamed back. "Yes, I'm John from the Christian Union. Are you interested in Jesus?"

I recoiled in embarrassment. Looking closely at his

name tag I saw that it did, in fact, say *John, Christian Union*, not *John Christian, Union*.

"Uh, no thank you, John," I said quickly. "I mean, not that I have anything against Jesus or anything. It's just that—well, actually I was just leaving." I turned and dove into the crowd, making for the door.

On my way back to my room I noticed a new sign up outside of St Aldate's church: "Jesus takes us by Surprise," it warned.

It was just as well. He was probably nineteen anyway. Too young.

This was, in fact, a sad realization. Like many Americans, before my arrival at Oxford I had enthused about Getting to Know the English Undergraduates. I wanted to share in a different cultural tradition by spending all my time with the natives. When I applied for a Marshall, I was an undergraduate myself, and this seemed like a perfectly realistic goal. Like most young people who have never been attracted by a career in academia, I considered graduate students to be a separate breed. Undergraduates were normal people. Grad students were a hunted, pale, sickly lot, with lots of books but no friends. I found it very difficult to keep in my mind the fact that at Oxford, I would *be* a graduate student myself. And almost all the English students would be undergraduates, between the ages of eighteen and twenty-one. In other words, they would all be younger than I was.

This was true particularly because of the fact that English undergraduates only do three years at university, while Americans almost always do four years of undergraduate work. This makes most first-year American post-graduates at Oxford at least two years older than third-year undergraduates. This was a disappointment. I had come to Oxford ready to be awed by the people around me, but many institutions soon lost some of their glamor. For instance, attending a debate at the Oxford Union for the first time, I was disillusioned to discover that it was run by pretentious and acned nineteen-year-olds.

Needless to say, this was unfair of me. When I was nineteen, and involved with undergraduate societies, my peers and I took ourselves extremely seriously, and would have been quite put out if older people had failed to take us at our own estimate. But even knowing this didn't make me any less disappointed by the extreme youth and apparent callowness of most of the people around me.

I REMEMBER I'M AMERICAN

MY OLD SCHOOLFRIEND Justin came over for dinner that night. I had met him for tea the previous day, and had been slightly taken aback—he had, naturally, grown a lot taller since I had last seen him, and he now towered over me. He had also surprised me by the formality of his dress and by his slightly reserved manner. I had asked what the occasion was for his suit and tie, and he had shrugged. "I always try to look good."

Sure enough, when he arrived for dinner he was again wearing a jacket and tie. He had brought a bottle of wine and we cooked a simple meal in the kitchen, under Ian's watchful eye. Ian seemed convinced that if he didn't watch me closely I might steal a pinch of his spices (which indeed I would have done, out of pique). He shuddered visibly when I asked if I could use one of his pots, but agreed—he could hardly refuse, as I had caught him in the act of using my garlic press that very afternoon. I had seized the opportunity to generously invite him to make use of everything I owned, knowing that he would then be obligated to let me occasionally borrow from him.

I told Justin about my first few days. He shrugged. "All the undergraduates here are useless people," he told me.

"They all seem perfectly nice and friendly, though," I protested.

"They're not," he insisted. "They're awful people. Believe me—I spent a year here at Exeter College, remember? I was an undergraduate myself. I had a rotten time.

The British undergraduates are incredibly anti-intellectual. And class matters here. It doesn't in the US, or, at least, upward mobility is seen as a good thing. People let you in. My mother's a secretary and my father's a builder, but that never mattered at home. But here they never will let you in unless they think you're one of them."

"Who's 'them?'" I asked.

"Upper-class snots. They're all over this college." Justin looked mistrustfully at the closed curtains, as though the upper-class snots might at that very moment be observing us through the window.

"Come on, surely they're at St John's too."

"Of course." He shrugged. "They're everywhere. You can't escape them."

"Don't be paranoid," I responded. "It seems to me that not being 'one of them' should be a good thing. We can't be one of them, because we're foreigners. We don't belong. We're on the edge, just observing. We don't get judged by the same standards."

"Sure, but do you want to be on the edge the whole time? Wouldn't you rather be inside?"

I thought about this. "I'm not sure. In some ways, yes, I suppose so. But in other ways, no. My life isn't here. I'm just a visitor here. My life is in America. That's my reference group, that's the culture that matters to me. I don't *want* to get enmeshed in this culture."

"Well, you're lucky, then. My problem is that I do want to be accepted here, in the same way I always wanted the bullies to acknowledge me in junior high. I don't know why but I do. And I know I never will be accepted or acknowledged here."

"Well, then you're screwed," I said cheerfully, trying to inject a little levity into the conversation.

"Yes," he agreed. "I am. The world is a hostile place but I want to be in it."

This struck me as an unnecessarily pessimistic view of life. "So what should we do?"

"Get to know the little snots anyway. Beat them at their own game."

The next day was a busy one, because it was the day of the University matriculation ceremony, at which all new students would be ritualistically initiated into Oxford. I got up early and raced to the lodge to check my pigeon-hole. The previous day I had written a note to Winston, the President of the GCR, asking if I could come talk to him sometime. Jerome had suggested that I visit Winston. He was Australian and was doing a second bachelor's in PPE. Before I irrevocably switched out of PPE I wanted to talk to a student who knew something about it.

Sure enough, my pigeon-hole contained the expected note of response: "Sure, four o'clock tomorrow would be fine. Come to my room."

I dashed off a grateful note, promising to be there at four the next day.

My pigeon-hole contained four other things as well. One was a memo from the Senior Censor advising me that Dr Watson would be my Moral Tutor and would be in touch with me soon. Moral Tutor? This was worrying. I would have to ask someone what it meant. There was a letter from a Dr Trunk, politics and philosophy tutor, saying that he wished to speak to me about my desire to switch out of PPE.

There was a letter from the captain of the women's lacrosse team, congratulating me on my Marshall Scholarship and encouraging me to join women's lacrosse. This was odd, because Marshall Scholars, unlike Rhodes, are not exactly known through the world for their stunning athletic prowess. And finally there was a letter from the student billing office at Harvard, informing me that I owed them $7, past due. I tore that up. Harvard had already gotten $80,000 out of my family, and as far as I was concerned they could whistle for the last seven bucks.

I left the lodge and wandered up to the graduate common room. The GCR consisted of a large, dingy room with musty chairs and sofas, all arranged in a semicircle around a television set. Off to one side was a small kitchen stocked with candy bars, fruit, and drinks, all of which could be signed for. To the other side was a door through to the GCR dining-room, where lunches were served each week day by Les, the steward. Down the hall was a computer room, a study room, a photo-copying room, and a pay phone. I sat down with the *International Herald Tribune,* and then flipped through the unfamiliar London papers.

After a while I left to change into *sub fusc* clothes for the matriculation ceremony. Glancing once more at my mail, I realized to my horror that what I had previously taken to be a reply from Winston was in fact a reply from Jeff, a college friend now at Magdalen. I had written him a note suggesting tea. I had been so sure that there would be a note from Winston that I hadn't even glanced at the signature.

I raced back to the lodge, hoping I could still remove my note from Winston's box. But I was too late. It was gone. In my own box was a puzzled note from Winston saying that he was a bit confused by my note as he had not written to suggest four o'clock, but that if I really was desperate to see him, four the next day would be fine.

Unfortunately even damage control was no longer possible. I could hardly cut my losses and go see him the next day at four, because Jeff was expecting me for tea at four. So I had to write an awkward apology to Winston, explaining that it was all a big mistake and could we pick another time? I went back to my room feeling like an idiot. Only a few days into the term and already the President of the GCR thought I was batty.

The matriculation ceremony was an anticlimax. It takes place in Christopher Wren's Sheldonian Theatre, which was not designed with audience comfort in mind. One sits on hard wooden benches, and the theatre is too small to fit all new students at once. Colleges take it by turns to go in. This takes a lot of the glamor out of the ritual, because by the time we got in, it was overwhelmingly obvious that the university Vice-Chancellor was already sick to death of welcoming people to Oxford. Still, it was fun. In my *sub fusc* clothes I felt like an extra in a movie about Oxford. I sat with other new graduates from Christ Church directly above and behind the Chancellor, and we all jostled and laughed in the glare from the bright overhead lights.

After the ceremony I met up with all of the other Marshalls. We had decided to have a short photo session: everyone's Mom and Dad would want pictures of us in our *sub fusc*. When we all felt we had enough pictures, we went *en masse* to register at the Bodleian Library, a ceremony that involved promising not to kindle flame in the building. (Why not just say "no smoking"?) I was excited to get my Bodleian card, though. The Bodleian is world famous, and as a copyright library it has every book printed in England. (At least, in theory it does; I soon learned that this was rarely the case in practice.) The thought of all those millions of books just waiting for me practically made my mouth water.

There was just one other ritual to be completed that day. In addition to registering at the Bodleian, our British entrance visas required us to register with the police. The police, for some reason, wanted to keep tabs on us, as we were "resident aliens," an insulting term that sounded like

81

it had been picked from a sci-fi movie. As Americans, we prefer to view other people as the aliens. We made little alien bleeping noises at each other as we straggled back from the police station, registration cards in hand.

It was a very busy week, filled with introductory dinners, meetings, and rituals. I went to see Winston, who informed me stiffly that he quite forgave me for all my contradictory notes. He advised me to switch out of PPE. I went to see Dr Trunk, who advised me not to switch out and reproached me for trying. He was peevish. He seemed to think that I had intended to do an M.Phil. all along, but had slyly applied to do PPE because I thought it would be easier to get into Christ Church that way, as M.Phil. programs are more rigorous and selective. The previous two Harvard students at Christ Church had apparently also applied to read PPE and then switched up, causing Dr Trunk to suspect a conspiracy. He accused Harvard of advising students to use this clever ploy to be admitted to M.Phil. programs.

I blinked in astonishment and assured him that this was not the case. Most American students are in awe of Oxford socially, but also have the impression that Oxford is a lot more interested in getting their money than in getting their minds, and I must say that at most colleges this seems to be true. It wouldn't occur to most Americans from good universities to adopt such a devious ploy in order to gain admission. But Dr Trunk was obviously feeling slighted enough as it was, so I decided to keep this to myself, and told him at great length of my enormous respect and esteem for PPE.

I visited Dr Ford to ask him whether I should be doing any academic work. He said yes, and told me to go write an essay on the topic, "France: superficially multipartite but essentially bi-polar." This meant absolutely nothing to me, but I promised to write something and give it to him in ten days. Ford also gave me a list of seminars to attend. The list was long. If I were to go to all the seminars and lectures, I would be busy forty hours a week.

"Do I have to go to all of these?" I asked dolefully.

"Why, yes, I think it would be best, since you have no background in European Politics."

I nearly fainted. He took pity on me then, and explained that only two of the seminars were completely essential, and designed for the M.Phil. program. These were on Comparative European Political Institutions and on European Integration. The other seminars were ones that might provide useful background or related material. In addition to these, I would have tutorials with him every two weeks or so, and could arrange additional tutorials with other people in the Politics faculty if I so desired.

Like all courses at Oxford, there would be no formal assessment until the end of the two-year program, at which point there would be four exams, one in Comparative Institutions, one in European Integration, and two in other subjects that I would choose from an approved list. A short thesis of thirty thousand words would also be necessary. In the mean time I was expected, although not technically required, to attend my seminars and write about five ten-page essays a term. These would not be graded, but Dr Ford would discuss them with me. In April I would have to pass a "qualifying exam" in order to remain in the program, but no grades would be recorded for that exam.

"Oh," he added, "I prefer that you type your essays."

I had never not typed an essay. I could barely remember how to write longhand. "What else would I do to my essays?" I asked.

"Well, undergraduates write them out longhand and

then read them out loud at tutorials. But I prefer to get them in advance, typed."

This was one of many things that astonished me about undergraduate education at Oxford. Undergraduates have one or two tutorials a week, with an essay due at each. (Tutorials are meetings with one's "tutor," the faculty member who is teaching a particular subject. They usually last about an hour.) Essays can be fairly short, usually five to eight sides of notebook paper, and are on set topics each week. Undergraduates are encouraged to attend relevant lectures, but are not required to do so, and are neither required nor, generally, offered the opportunity to go to seminars.

Oxford is rightly proud of its tutorial system. Meeting individually with faculty members can be an ideal way to learn. In America, students are often just part of a large crowd in a lecture theater, and may never really interact with anyone above the level of a graduate student section leader. At Harvard, most departments offered weekly one-on-one tutorials (in conscious imitation of the Oxbridge system), and my own tutorials were definitely very rewarding: they provided me with a chance to pursue my own intellectual interests with the support of a more experienced scholar.

But weekly tutorials at Harvard were in *addition* to lectures, sections, and seminars. I think Oxford students are lucky to have tutorials, but it seems a shame that they don't have seminars as well. Learning from one faculty member can't really replace the sort of discussions that occur in a well-run seminar. Arguing with other students is an equally essential form of learning. Also, arts students at Oxford rarely do their own research. Essays are short and are on assigned reading, which means that most students, unless they go on to do advanced degrees, never learn the pleasures and frustrations of following up on lead after lead until finally something interesting and worthwhile emerges.

I later discovered that often Oxford graduate students aren't encouraged to do creative research, either. But I am getting ahead of my story, because at that point all of these discoveries were still ahead of me.

I had one further question for Dr Ford before taking my leave.

"Dr Ford, can you tell me what a 'moral tutor' is, and why I have one?"

"Ho ho," he said, looking at me humorously. "Do your morals need taking care of?"

"I'm not sure if it's any business of Christ Church's," I replied.

He laughed. "'Moral Tutor' is just an archaic phrase for your College advisor."

"I thought that you were my advisor," I said.

"I'm your University supervisor. It's just coincidence that I'm also affiliated with Christ Church. You have a moral tutor so there's someone you can go to about non-academic issues. For instance, if I were sexually harassing you you could go and tell your moral tutor."

I shrugged uncomfortably.

"Should I go and introduce myself to my moral tutor?"

"Well, who is it? Dr Watson? I shouldn't bother, he'll probably get in touch. He'll invite you to dine at High Table once a term."

(In the event, I never heard a word from Dr Watson, and never met him. It turned out anyway that he had been assigned to me on the assumption that I was doing PPE, and some months later, when the College authorities finally processed the fact that I was doing an M.Phil. instead, he was removed as my moral tutor, and replaced with Hugh Ford. That meant Ford was both my Univer-

85

sity supervisor and College advisor. This didn't bother me, but Ford was quite put out. "I can't understand this," he said. "This will have to change. This must never happen. It's a conflict of interest. You need an objective advisor." But nothing was ever done, and Ford remained my moral tutor.)

I went to the Freshers' Fair. It took place in the Examination Schools buildings on the High Street. The large, high-ceilinged rooms were filled with little tables put out by every student group. I stopped to look at the tables put out by *Isis* and *Cherwell*, the student newspapers, and the Union, but managed to avoid Women's Lacrosse and the Medieval Society (never trust people who dress in thirteenth-century garb). I waved to Jerome, who was manning the OULTC table. He told me sadly that too many people wanted to play tennis, and that most of them were no good.

I finally left, toting a bushel of paper. I am unable to resist picking up flyers for activities I know perfectly well I will never do, like the Hang-Gliding Club and the Spelunking Society. It makes me feel that life is full of possibilities. For a few short days I am not a physical coward. No, not at all: I am a brave woman who is seriously considering hang-gliding! After I skip the first meeting I return to my usual state of cowardice. Still, it's a pleasant, though transitory, illusion.

The Freshers' Fair was reassuring. It was just like home. Every college in America has some similar event, at which student clubs vie for new recruits. I had spent a lot of time myself manning those tables, trying to get interested people to sign up. The hurly burly of the Freshers' Fair made Oxford seem a bit less frightening.

Any feelings of comfort slipped away that night. It

was the night of the welcome dinner for new students, and it coincided with the "installation" of the new Dean of Christ Church. The Dean started by giving a short speech. His speech was rather nice: he said that as he was new himself, he understood how intimidating Oxford, and Christ Church, could be. He told us to make it our own.

This is easier said than done. History weighs as heavily on Oxford as the age-encrusted stone of the buildings. It is on the plaques and the statues (Here Peter Boyle formulated the Gas Laws . . . Here John Locke lived . . . Here Archbishop Cranmer was burned at the stake for heresy . . .), in the buildings, and in the books in the library, so many of them written by brilliant past students. It is sometimes inspiring, but sometimes oppressive.

The university was founded sometime in the twelfth century. Within a hundred years, several of the colleges that still thrive today had been founded: University College in 1249, Balliol in 1263, Merton in 1264, Queen's in 1341, the anachronistically named New College in 1379. A list of Oxford's famous graduates reads like a list of England's most famous men—and, since the end of the nineteenth century, women. (Lady Margaret Hall was founded in 1878, Somerville in 1879.) Graham Greene, Matthew Arnold, Richard Burton, John Donne, Cardinal Wolsey, Cardinal Newman, Cecil Rhodes, Samuel Johnson, Christopher Wren, Percy Bysshe Shelley, Oscar Wilde, John le Carré, Gladstone, Peel, Harold Wilson, Stephen Hawking, Indira Ghandhi, Benazir Bhutto, Antonia Fraser, Shirley Williams, Margaret Thatcher: all went to Oxford.

As an American, would any of this ever be mine? I was comfortable claiming the English literary tradition as my own, but Oxford itself was different. Oxford was a completely different world in so many ways. It seemed not at all like America; at best, it was a bit like America in the 1950s. What did I know about gowns and servants, wine cellars and port, the Church of England and the playing fields of Eton? My ancestors were Scottish, English, Jewish, Hungarian, Irish, and Russian. They were farmers, innkeepers, frontiersmen, miners, and tailors. Only in the last few generations have they lifted themselves into the educated middle class. Many of my ancestors were communist and socialist political activists, eccentrics and rebels all. It's possible that if you go back far enough, you'd find some Oxford men in my family tree—my earliest ancestors were in America by 1720, and they had to have come from somewhere. But it's not too likely.

I was out as an American, and doubly out as a woman. Oxford, despite coeducation, remains an almost stiflingly male institution; its most coveted social rewards are for men only. I would never have the alcoholic chumminess of all-male clubs like Vincent's or the Bullingdon, or even the questionable camaraderie of singing obscene rugby songs in the college bar. That was for men. I was the only woman at my table, and next to me were an archdeacon and the Bishop of Oxford. Throughout the meal, I made labored conversation—the archdeacon got a bit tipsy and took a liking to me, happily rambling on about the pleasures of the SCR and a recent fox-hunting weekend. Did I *want* all this to be my own?

"Make it your own" was a nice thing to say, but it wasn't going to be easy, and I wasn't even sure if it would be good. From a distance, I was fascinated by Oxford and the élite world it represented. I was intimidated, awed, and even admiring. At the same time I didn't like it one bit. It represented something that Americans have been trying to escape for four centuries: a rigid, class-bound world in which ancestors and schools and accents and clothes matter tremendously, in which a tradition of deference often precludes the possibility of change. This world was very much in evidence at Christ Church; at other places, it's a little better hidden, but still present.

Looking back, I can see something that I tried to deny to myself at the time: I was scared. Really, genuinely, deep-down scared.

For the first time in years, I was completely at sea. I didn't know any of the rules. What mattered at Oxford? What was success, at Oxford? How should I act? It wasn't that I necessarily wanted to obey all the rules. I had always taken a not very secret pride in being a rule-breaker. But in order to break rules with panache, you first need to know what the rules are. And I didn't have a clue.

At the time, pride prevented me from admitting this even to myself. Sure, I was a bit nervous, I told myself as I lay wide-eyed and awake at night, but no more so than I might be if I were starting graduate school somewhere in the States. But I was kidding myself. In the US, I was confident that I knew all the rules. I would be nervous and excited at starting a new venture, but I knew that I could handle whatever America could throw at me.

I have heard English people complain that America is a terrifying country. They say it frightens them because it seems that there *are* no rules, and those that *can* be discerned are constantly in flux. It is true: this is not an original observation, but America's oddity is that it is a nation continually engaged in reinventing itself. The myth-making and the rewriting of history never end. The rules are made up as needed and abandoned when no longer useful. It is a culture of extreme openness: Americans will pump your hand and tell you their deepest sorrows, their cherished hopes, immediately upon meeting you. Yet it is a culture of cruelty and deceit as well, one in which contradictions are resolutely ignored, in which conscience is only sporadically heeded. Poverty and wealth, great greed and great generosity, worship of the rich and contempt for the rich, worship of learning and contempt for intellectuals. It see-saws giddily from the comic to the tragic. It fills me with longing and disgust. America has all the charm and the cruelty of a child, and a child's ability to break your heart.

What can I say? It's my country, and I love it, and leaving it showed me just how much. It's inside me, and I know the rules and the contradictions as well as I know myself. I can trace the pathways of the ever-changing rules, see the shadows left by rules that have fallen by the wayside, the pockets of quicksand freedom all around. I'm stuck with it in the same way I'm stuck with my own self. I don't always like that, but there it is. (You can take the boy out of the country, but you can't take the country out of the boy.) I came to Oxford because I was looking for something better, some dreamt-of graciousness, the elegant life of the mind, away from the hustle and the garishness of change. Did that world ever really exist? Fog and spires, Bertrand Russell reading in his Cambridge rooms. But life is unfair: there are some things you can't ever have unless you were born to them, and I think that understanding a culture is one of those things.

And England? A settled country. A country which has been inhabited and crowded for so long that not a square foot can confidently be said to be untouched by humans. I didn't know what the rules were but I could sense them all around me, a thick dusty web of rules. They attracted: come into my parlor. We love the things we lack. But we fear and resent them as well.

That's how I felt: like a fly exploring a spider's web.

PRETENDING TO BE AN
OXFORD STUDENT

PROBABLY I AM overdoing things. Even that first week, most of the time I was just being a happy, cheerful, excited new university student. I was shopping, eating, meeting new people, seeing old friends. The only thing that did alarm me, consciously, was the lack of routine. At risk of seeming boring, I like having a routine. And in those first weeks I did not have one. More than that: not only did I not have a routine, but I couldn't *imagine* having a routine. Ever. Each time I climbed the stairs to my room in St. Aldate's, I thought, "*I* live here? Do I?" I couldn't imagine not waking up every single morning for the next two years and thinking, "I'm at Oxford. *Oxford.*"

I still felt that I was only visiting, that each day would hold something unlike each other day: a new sight, a new museum, a new food. How very interesting, how amusing—if you get to go home at the end of a short time. Somehow I couldn't adjust to the fact that I wouldn't be going home in a few weeks, to tell entertaining Oxford stories and to get on with my *real* life.

This worried me, because I knew that in accepting the Marshall Scholarship I had agreed to let Oxford, not America, be my real life for the next two years. I couldn't absorb this emotionally, so I made myself do the next best thing: pretend.

Pretending that Oxford was my real life, I went and bought posters for my room. I bought dishes for the kitchen. I opened a bank account and agreed, when asked for my address, that I lived at Christ Church. I bought several books on European politics. I figured out where to buy phonecards. I tried not to sound lonely and lost when I spoke to my friends and my parents on the phone.

Some things were just like home. Hugh Ford told me that I should attend a class called "Statistical Methods for Social Scientists." I went, and it was inordinately tedious. What could be more familiar than sitting in a classroom, watching with dazed incomprehension as an awkward section leader mumbles inaudibly and scribbles formulae on a blackboard? Boredom, as every student knows, can be an actual physical sensation. The head becomes heavy and a certain stuporous but desperate blankness overtakes one. It said something about the state of my nerves that I was glad to be bored.

All of the other European Politics M.Phil. students had to take Statistical Methods too. I was relieved that Miranda, my fellow Marshall, had switched from International Relations to European Politics. Miranda was from Washington State. Her parents, Czech dissidents, had fled Czechoslovakia when Miranda was a small child, and had struggled to earn a living in the United States. With her experience of being an outsider, and of economic struggle, Miranda tended to look upon social pretension and "tradition" with a skeptical eye. Although we were different in many ways, we were brought together by being in a country full of strangers.

There were only about a dozen of us on the European Politics program, and people's personalities quickly became apparent. Henry, who was English, had been in the Navy for several years. He was something of a know-it-all, and always spoke as though giving orders. So did Austrian Rudolph, who immediately alienated Miranda and myself by telling us, with contemptuous pride, that his girlfriend made him lunch and dinner every day. Why? "Because," he said smugly, pointing to his crotch, "she just can't get enough of this. She *begs* for it. She does everything I say." Anne was fussy, blonde, pretty, and ever-so-slightly plump. She was from London and was something of a spoiled princess; her parents, fearful that she might find inferior housing at her college, simply bought her a small house for her personal use.

Vincent was a Belgian of Dutch extraction and he leered. His last name, which probably sounded fine in Dutch, sounded exactly like "Four-fart" in English. Far from being embarrassed by this, Vincent was proud, and enthusiastically pointed this out to anyone who would listen. ("You see," he'd say companionably, "it's Four-faaaart. Like fart. Like four farts." He would then laugh uproariously.) French François was rather unprepossessing but, like Rudolph, he was convinced that he was God's gift to womankind. (I was to meet many men at Oxford who were also convinced of this.) François took an enormous liking to Miranda and followed her down dark alleyways, flirting in a particularly horrible way. "Ah, Miranda," he would leer happily, "I see we go the same way! Tonight, perhaps I shall come over to see you!"

"I'm afraid that my boyfriend is coming over tonight," would be the firm reply.

"Ah, your boyfriend! You mean me," insisted François, insinuatingly batting his scaly eyelashes.

"No," said Miranda, "I mean Tom."

Within days of arriving at Oxford, Miranda had begun going out with Tom, another American at her college. "He comes over at night and reads stories out loud to me," she confided in a note to me during our first Statistical Methods class.

I rolled my eyes. "Spare me."

She laughed. "You're just jealous because you miss your old boyfriend!"

"True, true. That's why you should spare me," I said. "Anyway, don't you think you're just involved with Tom because you're lonely and feeling dislocated?"

Miranda shrugged. "Maybe. But I really like him. I think this is serious."

"Don't get too invested in it," I warned. "It might not last."

"It will," she said.

Although some of my European Politics classmates were unappealing, most of them were friendly and warm. Some of the time, even disgustingly sexist Rudolph could be quite bearable. François was fine when he wasn't following Miranda around, and Vincent was full of good cheer and loved to rush us off to pubs after class. Henry, though a know-it-all, was always more than willing to help other people who were having academic difficulties— if you didn't mind getting a lecture delivered in the tone of a military drill, you could learn an enormous amount from Henry. He patiently spent hours explaining the concept of corporatism to me one day when I confessed that I was floundering.

I also found several good friends among my classmates; Antonio, who was Italian, and Gavin, who was English, were both quiet, cheerful, generous, and good-natured. They organized dinners and parties for our class and always acted as peacemakers when others squabbled. Heinrich was a German medical doctor, wistful and homesick. Irish Nelson was friendly, pedantic, short, and round as a Weeble (remember Fisher-Price Weebles, the little egg-shaped creatures sold to the jingle, "Weebles Wobble but they don't fall down?"). He was amiable and knowledgeable. David was from Montreal and wanted to be a film maker. He loved dancing and art, and was always eager to go out for coffee or a drink. Mary and Emma had no personality at all and never spoke, but they smiled meekly when directly addressed, so I suppose that they were nice enough. Like my Marshall group, it wasn't long before all of us began to spend time together; we had a number of dinner parties, group lunches, and pub meetings.

The Statistical Methods class was taught by Paul, a rather sweet Politics D.Phil. student (at least, I thought he was sweet. Gavin couldn't stand him. "I hate these Old Etonian types." Gavin had been to a comprehensive school in Yorkshire before getting his BA at Oxford and although otherwise placid, he nursed a lively class resentment. I would never have pegged Paul for an Old Etonian; he seemed too dopey. Gavin assured me that dopiness was an infallible sign of an expensive public school. "Besides," he said irately, "he actually wears his old school tie to lectures!"). As far as I was concerned, Paul's only problem was that he couldn't teach to save his life. He lectured in a distracted monotone and covered himself with chalk dust. "Say we wanted to determine whether the English have higher IQs than the Scottish." (Why would we want to determine that?) "We would pick a sample of at least thirty and—"

After three weeks I stopped going to Statistical Methods. So did David and Miranda (the first signs that we were Bad Oxford Students already emerging). Everyone else kept going; they were funded by the Economic and Social Research Council, and taking statistics was a condition of their grants. This meant that I had to avoid Paul from then on, out of guilt, and this was tricky because he went to a lot of the same lectures that I went to. Luckily, he was so embarrassed himself by his own poor teaching that he never reproached me.

My other seminars were more interesting, because

they were participatory. More than anything else I enjoyed listening to people talk, and trying to get a sense, from that, of what they were like. I was continually looking around and telling myself with astonishment, "These are Oxford students. Those are Oxford dons. I am a graduate student at Oxford." The seminar on Comparative Political Institutions was taught by Hugh Ford and a don from All Souls College, while the seminar on European Integration was taught by two lecturers from St Antony's.

The only problem with the seminars was that I didn't have the foggiest idea what was going on. I had told Hugh Ford that I didn't know anything about European Politics, but I had expected that I would be able to follow classroom discussions. After all, I read the newspapers, and I thought that I was generally up on the major European issues. In high school I had taken two years of European history. In college I had taken courses in economics and political theory. I knew that I lacked a lot of basic facts: I couldn't have named the prime minister of Sweden; I had no notion of how the German electoral system worked; I could not elaborate on the provisions of the Treaty of Paris. But surely this was just a matter of filling in gaps in my knowledge. And I certainly expected that discussions would be in English.

Not so. I soon discovered that the arcanities of political science can only be discussed in a peculiar sort of jargon, many of its words borrowed from the world of science, computers, and economics. This means that the well-read lay-person will have no possible way of understanding what is going on. I sat and gaped as the seminar leaders and know-it-alls like Henry and Rudolph spoke of polarized pluralism, of transparent and opaque corporatism, of cleavages and freezing, centrifugal drives and consensualism, consociationalism and dipolar systems. I didn't know what they were talking about.

This was a problem, as seminars were two hours long. I have never spoken so little in seminars. Normally, I participate. I can usually think of at least two or three respectable questions or comments during the course of two hours. But here—I didn't know what was going on, I couldn't understand much of what was being said, and what little I could understand seemed completely uninteresting.

For the time being, it seemed only fair to assume that this was my problem, and not the program's. I am not always the world's most diligent student. I skip lectures, take infrequent and illegible notes, ignore reading that seems uninteresting, and put off essay-writing and studying until a day or so before exams and deadlines. Somehow I have always scraped by, but I do not have a long attention span when it comes to academics. Back at home, I would have immediately stopped attending seminars that were incomprehensible. But at Oxford—well, I was prepared to be humble, and assume that my lack of comprehension was my own fault. Sooner or later, I figured, I would begin to get my bearings. For now I would keep quiet and try to do all the reading.

This proved to be impossible. For the first week's seminar in Political Institutions, the syllabus listed eight books, seven in English and one in German, along with one article in French. Really. I asked Dr. Ford if the readings were listed in order of importance. "Not really," he said. "They're all about equally important."

Let it be said that I tried. I really did. I went to the Christ Church library first. According to the library's computer, several of the books were on the shelves. But when I looked, they were nowhere to be seen. I went to the Bodleian. Books at the Bodleian cannot be borrowed, but Hugh Ford had promised that relevant books would be placed on the shelves in the Politics, Philosophy, and

Economics reading room. None of the books were on the shelves. I asked the librarian how I could locate the missing books. She replied that four had been ordered for the PPE reading room, but that if they were not on the shelves they were either being read by someone else, had been stolen, or had been hidden. The remaining four books had unaccountably never been ordered. The Bodleian is not an open-stack library, so only books ordered to reading rooms are on shelves for all to see. If I wanted a book, I had to submit a written form. The librarian suggested that I order the four unordered books, but warned that it would take at least until the next day for the books to be located and brought to the reading room. I filled out the order slips. What choice did I have? She also recommended that I look around the room to see whether someone had left the other books out or was in the process of reading them.

There were about a hundred people in the reading room, each of whom nursed a stack of books six inches high. I realized that it would take hours for me to go around asking each person if they had seen the books I wanted. I did spot my classmate Henry, however, and sure enough, he had two of the books. He grudgingly allowed me one of them, but said that he couldn't find the others either. So I settled down and took notes for a few hours.

Ever try reading in a cavernous room containing a hundred other people? Some of them tapped their feet and rustled papers. Some whispered to friends. Some walked about, scanning the shelves, and noisily scraped footstools on the floor. The floor squeaked when anyone walked. The ceiling was high, and all sneezes and coughs echoed resoundingly. The lights were dim and cast strange shadows. The air smelled of stale sweat, wafted around by a chill breeze. Late night or weekend studying was not possible, as the library closed at 10 p.m., and was closed all day Sunday.

After two hours, I gave up and went to the bookstore, where I was able to buy two of the books by pledging my first-born son to Blackwell's. (Books in England are expensive, especially academic books. It is not unusual to spend £25 or £30 on a single book—about $50.) During the next few days, I tried to read them both. They were each five hundred pages long. I was simultaneously trying to read the ten books Hugh Ford had given me for my essay on the essential bi-polarity of French Politics, and write the essay.

When I wasn't trying to find books, read them, or write about them, I was busy rowing. In line with my policy of pretending that I was really going to be at Oxford for two years, I attended the first meeting of the quaintly named "Ladies' Boat Club" in the Junior Common Room. At Harvard, I had rowed for my house. House Crew was not very serious: it only lasted for six weeks in the spring, culminating in races at the beginning of May. The Charles River is wide and straight enough to remain uncrowded even with dozens of boats out, and May is a lovely warm time of year in Boston. You had to get up early, but other than that it was all very civilized. Although most houses did have a first, second, and third boat, it would never have occurred to anyone to care which boat they were in. Each house would make up crew T-shirts, but that was about it. House Crew was considered a sociable form of recreation, not a serious competitive sport. I foolishly assumed that college rowing would be the same at Oxford.

The "Captain of Boats" was a woman named Tiffany, who was nicknamed Taffy. Taffy was a strapping young woman who was reading medicine. "Rather jolly hockey-sticks," had been Jerome's verdict when I asked him to describe Taffy to me. I had responded to this elliptical statement with a bright "What?" During my first weeks at Oxford, "What?" and "Sorry?" were probably the two expressions I used most often.

I had introduced myself to Taffy at the freshers' drinks party, and when she heard that I had rowed before, she had told me to come to the meeting for non-novice rowers. Most English girls do not row in school, so very few first-year women have any previous experience. This put me in an unusual position: I was a new student, and therefore not part of a crew, but on the other hand I was not a novice. I felt out of place. Everyone else seemed to know each other. They had all rowed together the past year.

Taffy introduced me. "This is Rosa. She rowed at Harvard."

Everyone said, "Ooh!" This worried me.

"It's much less serious there, though," I protested feebly. "I mean, House Crew . . ." But it was too late.

"Rosa, we'll put you in the first boat for now," said Taffy.

"I really don't think I'm good enough," I said.

"Oh, don't worry, I'm sure you'll be better than any of us!" said Taffy kindly.

I seriously doubted that, but I was too embarrassed to protest anymore.

"I'd like us all to be doing at least four outings a week," continued Taffy, "with three sessions of heavy weights in between. I'll try to arrange coaches and coxes, all right? In a minute we'll break up into eights and set schedules for the week. But first Peggy's going to explain the sponsorship thing."

A light-skinned black woman stood up. She was

heavyset and smiling, and she wore a Dartmouth sweat-shirt. "OK, guys," she said. Her accent immediately identified her as a fellow American—the only one, apparently. "Here's the deal. This year the Christ Church Ladies Crews are being sponsored by Gatorade." Everyone except Taffy and myself looked blank. Peggy was breathless with enthusiasm. "That's this stuff," she explained, brandishing a packet of orange powder. "It's a high energy drink. It balances your electrolytes. It's American. Anyway I've persuaded them to sponsor us, and they'll be providing us all with free kit: splash top, cap, socks, Lycra all-in-one body suit, sweatshirts. They'll say Gatorade on one side, Christ Church on the other. I have got to say that they are *really* neat. The kit should be here in a few weeks. It was all designed by Gatorade's fashion consultant in Italy. And, they've sent us some Gatorade in advance as a gesture of good faith." She dragged an enormous vat from under the table. "So I thought we should all join together in a Gatorade toast!"

The Gatorade tasted disgusting. In summer camp, we called it bug juice. Everyone looked at Peggy and me, the two Americans. I shrugged apologetically. Cultural and commercial imperialism. "Yes, well. It's not very good. Never was."

No laughter. Just solemn looks. Everyone drank their Gatorade.

When people started to drift away, Peggy came up to me. Something about the way she walked and talked, all bossy beaming enthusiasm, reminded me of a former President of the PTA at my school. But I was grateful, because I had fallen prey to an unfamiliar feeling of shyness.

"I've been meaning to come say hi to you," said Peggy. "I've been hearing about you because you're the only other American woman here. It's all sort of weird at first, but you'll get used to it pretty soon." I wasn't so sure. Peggy, as if reading my mind, said, "No, really, I was totally confused when I got here. But I really like it now. Although—" She leaned closer as if to impart a secret. "One word of advice: don't bother with the GCR. I mean, *think JCR*. The graduates are a waste of your time. This is where it's happening. The undergraduates are much cooler."

I didn't know the appropriate response to this, so I said neutrally, "Yes, I've been planning to get involved in some JCR activities."

"Absolutely," said Peggy. "That's what you should do. I'll come meet you on Saturday for the first outing, OK, and then we'll all go down to the boathouse together."

"That would be fantastic," I said appreciatively.

"OK! See you soon!" With a bouncy wave Peggy was off.

On Saturday I met Peggy, then went with her to find the rest of the group. Most of the girls were wearing navy blue sweatpants that said "House" (a nickname for Christ Church deriving from the Latin *Aedes Christi,* House of Christ) in white letters along the leg. I felt unclothed and out of place in my shorts and plain gray sweatshirt. And I discovered something horrible: "Going down to the boathouse together" meant *jogging* down to the boathouse together.

I don't jog. I hate it. It is an idiotic form of exercise, bad for the knees, ankles, and shins. It's boring. It's tiring.

But no excuses. We were going to run the ¾ mile to the boathouse. On day one, I was not going to make a fuss.

The path to the river was muddy and slippery. The

102

cows, looking neolithic as they waggled their scaly horns at us through the fog, mooed tragically as we raced past. We ran panting over a very steep and muddy bridge (it was steep enough that walking down it was not really a viable choice; momentum and gravity forced a run) and on to the wide strip containing all the college boathouses. Christ Church's boathouse, a squat red-brick structure, was (naturally) last.

Getting the boat out of the boathouse was not too much trouble; to my surprise, I hadn't forgotten the routine. But rowing was another story. Almost as soon as we pushed off from the raft, I realized two things. One was that the actual language of rowing is different in England, and the other was that the technique is also different. In England I had to unlearn most of the rowing habits that I had so painfully learned in the US. In some ways this made it harder for me than if I had been starting to row from scratch: my mind was filled with knowledge of rowing techniques that my Christ Church coaches assured me were harmful. And although it's hard to make a certain set of motions become habit, it's even harder to lose that habit when you're told to.

The result? I had thought that I was a decent rower, but I barely survived that first outing. I couldn't figure it out. I was always out of time with everyone else. The mental and physical anguish caused by my constant effort to figure out what I was doing wrong exhausted me and made it even more difficult. There is nothing, but nothing, more humiliating than sitting in a boat with eight other people, and knowing that your mistakes are slowing the boat down and upsetting its balance. Especially when your mistakes are made obvious to everyone by the coach's continual criticisms.

At Oxford, the cox does little more than steer and shout commands. Most commentary is provided by the coach, usually another student, who bicycles along the tow-path on the bank of the river. There are two problems with this method: first, since cyclists have their eyes on the river, and not on oncoming traffic, bicycle pile-ups are frequent. And second, the rowers often cannot hear anything the coach says, as wind and the noise of other crews and their coaches tend to carry away most instructions. The Thames is narrow and winding around Oxford, and it's hard to do much continuous rowing because the river is generally clogged with boats, many of them moving into the bank to listen to their coaches.

I sat panting as fragments of incomprehensible instructions drifted my way from the bank. My brain was overflowing and I couldn't process everything. Which side was "stroke side?" In the US we said "port and starboard." Did the command "easy all" (or maybe it was "easy oar?") mean the same as the familiar shout, "Way 'nough?" Was "the blade" the whole oar, or just its spoon? What did "drop" mean? What were "quick hands?" Rarely have I felt so wretched. I was horribly embarrassed as Taffy looked back at me reproachfully. I think that she had misguidedly assumed, like many English people, that all Americans are extremely athletic.

Thank God for Peggy. She came to my rescue when we pulled up to the bank and the coach looked at me despairingly. "Rosa's *not* doing it wrong," I heard her say loyally from behind me. "She's doing it right, American-style. It's just a different technique here. She'll pick it up soon."

I did pick it up soon enough, but that was my last outing in the first VIII. The next week I was booted down to the second VIII (and, a term later, to the third VIII after I failed to attend the trials for the second VIII). I was a lot happier in a lower boat, and I soon regained my confidence. I picked up the jargon, and I ordered some House boat club "kit." (In theory, there would soon be free Gatorade kit for all, but somehow it just kept getting delayed. Peggy sent several heated letters). I learned to say "splash jacket" instead of anorak or shell, and to say "tracky bots" instead of sweatpants.

After a few weeks I was confident enough to say, "I hate jogging. Let's briskly *walk* to the boathouse." The undergraduates kept jogging but Antoinette and Ellen, the two other graduates in our boat, joined me in walking. In the boat, I realized that I wasn't the only one who frequently could neither hear nor comprehend our coach's shouted instructions. Our coach was a second-year student called Colin, and every time Colin said anything from the bank, at least two or three people would say, "What?" Moreover, after a few weeks I was rarely one of the people Colin corrected the most.

At Oxford, probably a third of all students row at one time or another. For most students, one or two terms of desultory rowing is enough; having learned the basics, they quit, on the sensible grounds that rowing is boring, painful, and extremely time-consuming. On top of that rowing often takes place before 8 a.m. on very cold mornings. Finally, there is not much glory in it. Only the top two or three college crews in Oxford receive any attention at all. The outside world focuses only on the Oxford University Boat Club's varsity crew, which races against Cambridge.

But there are always a few students who go down to the river in their first term at Oxford, and—never leave. Gluttons for punishment, they devote four or more hours a day to rowing and working out, in an usually vain effort to go from being the 36th best boat in Oxford to being the 35th, or (please God!) the 34th. Their hands are blistered and their thighs expand with rolls of muscle. They lose all their non-rowing friends because all they want to talk about is rowing. They huddle with fellow rowers in many college bars. They are called "boaties". Most other students consider them a sick, diseased lot.

Colin, our coach, was a prime example of a "boatie." He was a clean-cut public school boy, and he was addicted to rowing. Colin rowed stroke in the men's second VIII. He subbed in frequently for missing members of other crews. He coached a women's crew and two men's novice crews. He occasionally coxed. It was impossible to imagine him wearing anything other than a splash jacket. During quiet moments on the river, Ellen and I amused ourselves by speculating on whether Colin owned several splash jackets, or just one which was never washed.

Colin fascinated me. He was kind and dedicated. I thought he was attractive, but he seemed quite unable or unwilling to converse about subjects other than rowing. So I quizzed him about that. He had an older brother who was a star rower at Cambridge, and Colin was tremendously proud of him. He wished he could row in the men's first VIII, but he just wasn't big enough, although, he assured me, he had been doing weights every day for two hours and he was much bigger this year than last year. He was out at the river by 6 a.m., and there until long after dark, still valiantly struggling to coach a crew the whereabouts of which were marked only by feeble bicycle lights at the bow and stern.

As a coach, he was entirely devoted. Unfortunately his devotion was matched only by his inability to teach; his demonstrations and explanations left us all baffled. "You see you just—*pop* the blade in, right, just pop it, while resting your hands on your knees," Colin would shout to us, leaning his bicycle against a bush and hunkering down on the cold ground to demonstrate. "Right, and you should just *feel* it all come together . . ." We learned to nod politely and ignore him.

One cold early morning I found Colin sitting shivering on the steps of the boathouse. It was still dark, and there was thick frost covering the grass. His teeth were chattering and he blew his nose and coughed. He told me in a low, feverish monotone that he was going to sub for a rower in another crew. I looked at him as he sat there and sniffled.

"Colin, go home. You're ill."

"No, no, can't," he mumbled. "Got to row, promised. Got to be back here at eight anyway to coach. Mmm. Got to row, row . . ."

"You're a *wreck*, Colin. I think you're feverish. Look, cancel the outings. Or—I'll sub for you, I'll find someone else to coach your boats. You really should be home in bed."

But he just shivered and kept on mumbling, "Got to row. Got a shot at moving up to division one this year, really got a shot now, can't let it slip, lads doing well, got to row . . ."

I gave up.

I enjoyed rowing. I had no desire whatsoever to win races, or to race at all: I liked it for the exercise, and took great pleasure in gazing raptly at my growing muscles each day. It felt good to be getting in shape, for once. And rowing was a good way to get to know people, at least superficially. You might never learn anything about a fellow crew member other than her views on setting the boat or Colin's coaching ability, but at least you knew her name and had someone to wave at across the quad. By the end of the first term, I knew half the female undergraduates by sight, through rowing. And I had made a few friends, like Antoinette and Ellen.

Antoinette was half English, half French. She had a haughty air and an aristocratic accent; she had been brought up in London, Paris, and Rome. She was further distinguished because she went out with Winston, the Australian President of the GCR.

"I know the meaning of true love," she told me earnestly as we walked to the boathouse one day.

"Oh," I said. "Really."

She sniffed suspiciously. "Yes, really."

"What is it?" I asked.

Antoinette began an elegant discourse on art and music and the Sistine Chapel. "I am extremely fortunate," she concluded, brushing her sleek black hair off her forehead. "Throughout my life, I have been privileged to enjoy the most beautiful things in the world. Perhaps I should feel guilty. But I cannot!"

"Certainly not," I agreed, unsure of what this had to do with the meaning of love.

"And now, my fortune merely continues. I have Winston. He is perfect: a frontier prince, a noble savage. Isn't he wonderful?"

I blinked. "Yes, he certainly is."

Antoinette sighed. "You *must* come for tea sometime, Rosa."

Ellen was English and was doing a literature D.Phil. She was as conventional as Antoinette was exotic. She wore cardigans and long skirts. She had a peaches and cream complexion and a double-barrelled surname. Ellen looked like a goody-goody, but she had a devastating wit; and was fond of imitating Antoinette in her wilder flights of passion. "Oh, Winston," she'd sigh, looking around to make sure Antoinette was out of hearing. "You are my prince, my noble savage! Let me accompany you to the . . . the . . . the *Bush* of your native land, and help you civilize your countrymen! I, after all, have lived surrounded by beauty!" In truth, Ellen was very fond of Antoinette, and feared that she was too obsessed with Winston. "She'd hate it in Australia," she told me. "Just look at her. I'm afraid she's going to do something she'll regret." Ellen and I often had tea together after rowing.

That first term, once I got the hang of it, rowing was pure pleasure. There were no races until the winter term, so no great pressure to work very hard, and our schedules worked out so that we rarely rowed in the morning.

Rowing helped make me feel like I was a part of Christ Church, and not just a visitor. In my Christ Church splash jacket I felt like an old hand as I loitered with other crew members, waiting to get the boathouse key. In an odd way it almost embarrassed me. The porters now knew me by sight and said hello to me. Coming back from the boathouse, we usually returned to Christ Church through the Meadows Gate—the same gate through which tourists entered, after paying an admission fee. Each day we would stroll casually past a line of envious tourists, wave to the porter who grumpily collected their admission money (he always smiled at *us*), and walk brazenly right through the turnstile! I always felt that I should turn and apologize to the waiting tourists. I still couldn't accept my own right to just walk in, and I felt for all the world as though I were cutting in line. Alternately, I felt that I should offer to bring the tourists in as my guests, so that they could see Tom Quad for free. I wasn't sure the view was worth £2.

I also kept busy by singing in the choir. When I was in school, I liked to sing, but half the students only sang because they had to, and therefore only half-heartedly. Because the Christ Church College Choir was an unglorious volunteer choir, the only people who went were people like me who simply enjoyed singing. The standard was quite high, considering—everyone in the group read music, learned new songs quickly, and had a decent voice. This made practices a pleasure. I hadn't been part of a singing group in years and I enjoyed it now all the more.

That first term, we prepared songs for the College Corporate Communion, a service aimed towards students.

My atheistic upbringing put me at a disadvantage when it came to the Corporate Communion and similar occasions, because the Choir was frequently expected to lead in the singing of psalms. It was assumed that we had all been brought up in the Church of England and knew how to sing most psalms, and so we didn't bother to rehearse. To me, most psalms were not only unfamiliar but seemed mind-bogglingly similar to one another, and I couldn't sight-read well enough to make up for not knowing the melodies. I was reduced to mouthing the words and coming in a half-beat after everyone else. But at the Corporate Communion, the pleasure of reading the program more than compensated me for this minor humiliation. It was filled with unintentionally amusing lines, like the highly alliterative "The Christ Church College Choir will collect checks at the College Corporate Communion for the Chernobyl Children's Charity". Even the Ch-Ch-Chaplain could not read this without inadvertently spitting.

Our choir was politely *not* encouraged to sing at regular cathedral services. The previous year, the College Choir had sung one Evensong a week, and had apparently not done itself proud. It was a decent amateur choir, but needed more than a week to learn a new set of songs. So the Chaplain (Michael Jackson) had decided that we should only sing for other students, not for the general public. (I had had my tea with the Chaplain, out of curiosity. He was a very kind, shy young man, with a wife and small child. He made no mention at all of religion, for which I was grateful. So were his other guests, I think. They were almost all glum boys who were visibly aware of doing their duty. He seemed grateful in return that we had

110

actually attended his tea, and that some of us sang in the Choir. Such is the fate of a chaplain at a modern college.)

Singing at public services was left to the Cathedral Choir, a choir of men and boys attending the Christ Church Cathedral School on Brewer Street. The Cathedral School bordered St. Aldate's Quad, and several times a day the choir boys paraded past my window. In the afternoon they marched across the street wearing cricket whites or tiny rugby shirts, shrieking happily as they headed in an unruly line for the playing fields in the Meadows. Some of them were very young, only five or six. The oldest were about thirteen. To hear them shout, you wouldn't have guessed that they all had singing voices like angels. They sounded like any group of little boys. Shortly before evensong they marched out again, more dignified this time, in tiny little black gowns and strange angular caps. I thought they were adorable in their little uniforms, if sometimes a tad noisy. When they walked across the street, the littlest boys all held hands. I wondered when homophobia would set in and change all that.

PART THREE

DISILLUSIONMENT

CONTENT-FREE LEARNING

BY THE TIME my Political Institutions seminar rolled around again I had succeeded in reading about two hundred pages of two books. I had tried returning to the Bodleian to see if my ordered books had arrived, but only one had; the other three could not be found, said the librarian. I felt pitifully under-prepared for the seminar. Not surprisingly, I again found myself unable to follow most of the discussion. Henry and Rudolph spoke a good deal, and several other people made contributions. None of their contributions seemed particularly related to one another, but I still assumed that it was my ignorance that made it seem that way.

I had succeeded in writing my first essay for Hugh Ford, and after the seminar I went to his office for my tutorial.

"I really liked the footnotes in your essay," he told me.

"Oh," I said cautiously. I tried to remember if I had done anything more than just provide sources. I didn't think I had. "What did you like about them?"

"Well, I liked the way you told me what your sources were."

This struck me as another indication that Hugh Ford had low expectations of American students.

"I'm not sure that I deserve praise for noting the sources used," I told him. I had had to footnote papers since the age of thirteen. It was just one of the rules for all academic papers: name at upper left, number your pages, check punctuation and spelling, note all sources. "I mean, it's sort of unethical not to, isn't it? I couldn't very well *not* use footnotes in a paper of this sort."

His answer made me realize that I had misinterpreted his praise. He wasn't surprised that an *American* would use footnotes. He was surprised that *any* student would use footnotes. "Most of my students never note their sources," he said.

What kind of academic institution is this, I wondered?

Unfortunately, Dr. Ford did not admire the substance of my essay nearly as much as he admired my footnotes. In fact he looked positively queasy as he held it out to me.

I took it. Dr. Ford didn't say anything. He looked mournful. He stared at the ceiling. He coughed. He stared out the window. He sneezed. Finally, with evident effort, he focused his eyes on me.

"I blame myself," he began.

Uh-oh. "Please don't do that," I put in politely.

"No, no. It's my fault." He looked at me sadly, like a guilt-ridden and inadequate parent gazing upon his juvenile-delinquent child. (It was not to be for the last time.) "I can see that now. I left things too vague. I failed to provide you with an adequate framework. No structure with which to work." He gazed at the floor. He cleared his throat.

What was coming next, I wondered? A statement of allegiance to "ToughLove?"

"I was confused about exactly what sort of argument you were looking for," I admitted. In fact, my essay topic had struck me as profoundly uninteresting, a topic that allowed only one possible sort of essay: the unimaginative sort that simply rehashes all known facts and theories. But again, I was ready to believe that I had overlooked something or misunderstood something, and I waited for Dr Ford to explain what it was.

116

But he just murmured a few more apologetic words about letting me down, and gave me a remarkably similar assignment to do the following week. This time I was to address the question, "Does the theory of polarized pluralism adequately account for Italian politics since 1970?" As Italian politics was Ford's own field, I expected some "structure" and "framework" to be forthcoming, but none was. He gave me an encouraging little speech, saying that things would soon fall into place for me, and he handed me some books and sent me off.

I was also finding lectures frustrating. I was used to lectures that all built upon a particular theme, or that covered some particular time period. In other words, all the lectures in a series would bear some connection to all other lectures in a series, and each lecture would build upon the previous lecture. If you attended a history lecture on "Nineteenth-Century America," well—you would expect that each lecture would tell you a bit more, and that lectures would be ordered in some sensible manner. You wouldn't expect them to skip wildly from a statistical analysis of membership in abolitionist groups one week to an exegesis on the Gilded Age the next.

But that is just what lectures at Oxford—at least the ones in European Politics—seemed to do. Each lecture was given by a different lecturer. Each lecture was on a different subject. For example, here are the titles of the first three lectures given in a series called "The Party Systems of Western Europe:" Week one: "The effect of unification on the German party system." Week two: "France: a presidentialized party system?" Week three: "The failure of the SDP to bring about the realignment of the British party system in the 1980s."

Obviously, "Party Systems in Western Europe" was not really designed to teach students the basics about party systems. It was designed to showcase the research of particular faculty members and distinguished visitors. This was fine, but it left the students in the lurch. What most of us needed was a series of lectures explaining what was meant by party systems, how modern party systems developed, what parties existed in each country and how they had come to be, how different party systems affect the nature of political discourse and change. Only a handful of the M.Phil. students had any prior exposure to the study of comparative European politics. We didn't have enough background to gain anything from these highly focused lectures. And yet we were all told to attend them.

The more lectures I attended, the more it seemed clear that the lectures were not designed for students at all. They were a way for faculty members to keep up with one another and show off in front of one another. At each lecture, the speaker would go on for an hour, and then pause for half an hour of questions. The students virtually never asked questions. For most of us, it was hard to think of anything intelligent to say. Imagine going to a lecture on verb patterns in ancient Urdu. Even if you noted down every word, it would still be mighty hard to think of a question. There was just—no framework, no structure, as Hugh Ford might have said.

Even if a student had been able to come up with a good question, he or she found it hard to get called on. Faculty members seemed to be given preference. Lectures generally degenerated into nit-picky scholarly arguments between two or three dons. Questions from the floor took two basic forms: the "I will prove that you know less than I do" question and the "let's stroke each other" questions.

The first was typified by questions like "*Nnnn* Peter I'm sure we all find your analysis very intriguing"—this said by a thin gray-haired don as he rises, stretching languorously—"but are you familiar with the results of the Sardinian mayoral elections of 1932?"

The speaker would be forced to admit, through clenched teeth, that he was not just at that moment able to recall the exact details of the Sardinian mayoral races in 1932.

Gray-hair sits down again with a smug little smile. "*Nnnn* well I think perhaps if you refresh your memory of what was after all an important event, you may well find that it *nnnn* undermines your case a tad."

Then the "let's stroke each other" question. A brisk younger don rises. "Peter, I found your analysis remarkably enlightening and I am reminded of the time the King of Spain asked me to advise him on creating a new constitution. I gave him some suggestions based on an analysis similar to yours and perhaps you would care to tell us just what you now think of the situation in Spain, as I know that we'll both be at a government conference there next week."

After all interested faculty members had spoken up, one or two eager students would get a question in. These questions were invariably of the sort we came to call "Henry questions." In other words, big-league brown-nosing. In a stentorian voice, some student (often Henry himself; inevitably male) would rise and say, "Peter, I just wanted to say that I've enjoyed your talk and that I'm thinking of doing my dissertation on a particularly fascinating aspect of your work. Could you perhaps tell us a bit more about yourself and your views?"

After several weeks of seminars and lectures, I began to lose my feelings of awe and humility. They were replaced by feelings of incredulity and frustration.

My tutorials with Hugh Ford were all as inconclusive and baffling as my first tutorial had been. Ford never really seemed to like my essays, but on the other hand, he made no specific suggestions about how I could improve them. This was very frustrating for me. In the US, all college essays receive grades along with written comments. I was accustomed to getting a lot of feedback on my work. If Ford didn't like my essays, I wanted to know why, so that I could improve them. But Ford never exactly came out and said that my essays were no good. He just continued to hold them as though he held a dead fish in his hand, and he continued to sigh and say that he blamed himself.

It wasn't that I thought my essays were good. On the contrary. I was not proud of my essays; they were by no means showpieces of intelligence or scholarly wit. In fact, I genuinely thought that the essays I produced for Hugh Ford were far worse and far less interesting than any essays I had written in college. I thought that my essays were dry and stilted. But I also thought that the topics he gave me were dry and stilted. I would have preferred to write about things that interested me, but Ford never suggested that I pick my own topics. When I tentatively said that I would prefer to write on some different topics, he said I needed to get a grasp of the basics first, and he continued to give me highly specific assignments. So tutorials continued to be a source of what I suspect was mutual frustration. Ford couldn't understand why I didn't perform as expected, and I couldn't for the life of me figure out what he expected.

It had also become obvious that I was not the only student who had trouble finding the required books. One day, as we all walked to a coffee shop after our seminar, Miranda admitted that she couldn't find many either. We looked at each other, and did a quick poll of the other students. Of that week's reading, Henry, as ever more efficient than the rest of us, had found five books. Gavin had found three. Miranda and I had found two, in bookstores. Several people hadn't found any.

It was impossible not to come to one conclusion.

"So," I began. "I've, uh, been feeling a bit confused in our seminars, but I thought it was just me. I was wondering . . . has anyone else felt a bit confused?"

It was like opening the floodgates. Out poured a chorus of assents, everyone talking at once.

From Anne (petulantly): "I had *absolutely* no idea what was going on—"

From Vincent (querulously): "Ford is a nice fellow but he never makes sense. Chap needs a little bit of the old Four-fart logic in him."

From Heinrich (glumly): "The others are even worse sometimes. I'm spending my own money to be here and it's beginning to seem like a waste. I could be *earning* money in Germany."

From François (bewilderedly): "There seems to be no framework, no structure to this course. What are they meant to be teaching? What are we meant to be learning? Is it written down anywhere?"

From Antonio (apologetically): "I felt I had to say something in class but I couldn't think of anything since I hadn't been able to get any books—"

From David (exasperatedly): "Why do lectures always end in pompous arguments between faculty members?"

From Rudolph (contemptuously): "These people are fools. They know nothing."

And one lone dissenter, in a firm, military voice: "Personally, for my money, they're doing a fine job and I really can't see the difficulty." That was from Henry.

But aside from Henry, we all agreed that we were unhappy. Even the two women who never spoke nodded their agreement. Lectures, with rare exceptions, were tedious and irrelevant, and we resented the esoteric disputes between dons: most questions seemed designed to show off, rather than to advance the discussion constructively. Seminars were poorly planned and discussion was impossible, because none of us had enough shared know-ledge. Even if one person threw out an interesting comment, no one else had read the same books and therefore no one was capable of responding in a meaningful way. And the reading lists were too long anyway. No one could read ten books a week and write essays on top of that.

So began our mutiny. For weeks, we had each silently gotten more and more depressed. Our failure to understand lectures or read the books had left us each feeling inadequate. It was a great relief to discover that we were not alone. And if almost all of us felt the same way, didn't that mean that there was something fundamentally wrong with the program, and not just with us? It was liberating to realize that maybe I wasn't a thick-headed student—maybe Dr. Ford wasn't terribly good at explaining things. Only Henry and Gavin seemed unimpressed by this logic. Henry was unimpressed because he was finding everything quite easy to follow, thank you. "Don't be childish," he told us. "Did you come here to be spoon-fed? If you don't know the basics, go buy a textbook or something. We're graduate students, and we're presumed to be capable of figuring these things out for ourselves. I enjoy lectures—they give us a sense of what's going on in the field. Personally, I find them inspiring."

"That's fine, Henry," said Miranda, patiently. "You're lucky; you know more than we do. But this program was advertised as a *taught* course, not as a research degree. Shouldn't they try to *teach* us something? They accepted us into the program knowing full well that many of us have no background in this area. They don't need to do much—just go over the basics a little tiny bit. It wouldn't cost them anything and it would save us a lot of angst." She gestured around the room. "Surely it's not a good sign that more than three-quarters of us are lost and confused, six weeks into the term?"

I agreed. "Absolutely. Sink or swim is hardly a good educational technique."

Gavin, who had done his undergraduate work at Oxford, backed up Henry. "Look," he said, shrugging with embarrassment. He hated having to disagree with the group. "That's just the way it is here. You'll get used to it. It may not be ideal, but you can't change it, so there's no use getting upset. Things will get easier."

The rest of us ignored Gavin and Henry. We planned a meeting for the following day. Everyone was to come with ideas for improving the program. No one was to tell Hugh Ford, or anyone else on the faculty.

"It's important for us to have a unified set of demands first," said Antonio.

Henry snorted. "What do you think you're going to do, overthrow the faculty committee?"

"No," I said, "Antonio's right. Right now we're all upset and excited. If we spoke to Dr Ford now he'd just think we've gone crazy. We should think about it tonight, and then tomorrow try to come up with some specific suggestions about how things could be improved."

"All I'm saying," said Henry, "is that presenting some sort of—" his voice lowered contemptuously—"*manifesto* isn't going to do anything except make them all angry at you. What good would that do?"

Gavin nodded.

Miranda had been glaring at Henry for several minutes. She broke in. "Would you just *try* not to sound so damned arrogant all the time, Henry? If you don't like it you can present Ford with a separate manifesto urging him to kick the rest of us out."

At this point everyone began to talk at once again. Henry sniffed with irritation, and looked like he was considering challenging Miranda to a fistfight.

I didn't like the fact that we were already quarreling

with one another. With some difficulty, I managed to make myself heard: "Look, Henry's got a point. Whatever we do, we need to be tactful. It's a new program. Ford is doing his best and we don't want to hurt his feelings. He probably just doesn't realize that we're all a bit unhappy."

There was a murmur of agreement. We adjourned the discussion to the St Antony's bar.

The next day we met in an empty room at the Social Studies Faculty Centre. We sat around the table, notebooks open in front of us, and began to make a list of suggestions for how to improve the course.

We wanted our reading lists to be shorter, or at the least, we wanted to be told which two or three books would serve as the primary basis for the next week's discussion, so that we could all come to class with some shared background knowledge. We wanted all books to be put on reserve at the Bodleian, and we wanted Hugh Ford and the other seminar leaders (the only people who owned all the books) to make their copies available for us to read. We wanted short journal articles to be photocopied and given out in advance, because journal articles were usually even more difficult to track down than books—reading four journal articles generally entailed trips to four different libraries. As it was, we all agreed that we spent twice as much time trying to find articles and books as we did actually reading them.

We wanted lectures to be designed with students, not dons, in mind, and we wanted dons to talk less during question periods and students to be called on more. We wanted Ford, or someone, to try to sum up the purpose of the European Politics M.Phil. What was the point of the course? What skills or knowledge was it meant to impart? Exactly how was the curriculum going to be structured? How much flexibility would we have? What material would be tested on the qualifying exam? It was a taught course, after all; we thought it was reasonable to expect a little teaching.

We wanted to know why, in a course titled "European Politics and Society," we had seen nothing of "Society." Where was literature, the arts, political "culture?" We wanted to discuss the substance of European politics. What were the issues? How had these things become issues? What could be said about whether and how those issues might be resolved? We wanted more emphasis on history and less on the paradigms of political science; we thought it was pointless to discuss the organization of party systems without any reference to the substance of political discourse. (Miranda neatly summed up our attitude towards our seminars: she called it "content-free learning," a phrase that stuck.) We wanted more emphasis on Eastern Europe, instead of just Western Europe.

The M.Phil. in European Politics and Society was a new program, so we were willing to forgive Hugh Ford and the others for their shortcomings. But because it was a new program, we also thought that it wouldn't be too difficult to change things. Ford could hardly argue that the curriculum and teaching methods had worked in the past. The European Politics M.Phil., unlike virtually everything else at Oxford, had no past.

Once we had listed our suggestions, we argued about how to present them to Hugh Ford. Initially most of us had favored writing a formal letter, and presenting it to Dr Ford. But Gavin and Henry convinced us that this was a bad idea. "If you want to suggest improvements, go ahead," said Henry. "But don't forget that this isn't like the States. Students are not expected to make this kind of suggestion here. And if you alienate Ford and all the others, there goes your degree."

This was a chilling thought. In American universities, no one professor has that much power over a student. At most, one professor may be responsible for three or four of the thirty-odd course grade students have at the end of four years. At Oxford, one works with fewer people each year, and is unusually dependent on them for co-operation, support and letters of reference. Although final examinations (which are the sole determinant of degree quality) are marked at least in part by a board of external examiners, it is widely believed by Oxford students that one's tutor has a good deal of influence over one's examination performance. I don't know exactly how this influence is supposed to be wielded, but every student I have ever discussed this with insists that "the tutors decide in advance who should get a first." Whether or not this is true I have no idea. I doubt that it is true to the degree students think it is. On some level, however, the truth of the belief is irrelevant: what matters is that students believe, strongly, that tutors can determine who will do well and who will do poorly. This belief colors their actions and attitudes towards tutors and supervisors, and makes students far less willing to issue challenges or criticisms.

It breeds a form of schoolboy obedience: I once became exasperated with Rob, an English friend, for arriving an hour late to have lunch with me. Rob met my irritable questions with apologies. He said that his tutorial had gone on longer than he had expected it would. I had been standing in the rain for an hour and didn't find this an adequate excuse.

"Couldn't you have said, when it was clear that things were running late, 'I'm terribly sorry, Dr. Wright, but I have another appointment. Could I come in later today or tomorrow to continue this discussion?'"

Rob was not normally shy or unassertive, but he

looked shocked. "Oh, no, that would have been rude. It was a *tutorial*."

"Rob," I said, "you were late for a *lunch,* with me!"

Rob was twenty-five years old. He was finishing a D.Phil. in History. He couldn't imagine that he had the right to politely duck out of a meeting with his supervisor that had run late.

A few weeks after that, I invited Rob to come to Wales for the weekend with a group of friends. He agreed happily and all went well until he realized that going to Wales would require him to leave twenty minutes early from his Friday afternoon seminar. He said that perhaps he shouldn't come after all. This despite the fact that attendance at seminars, while strongly encouraged, is optional!

"Rob," I said firmly, "you are an adult. Go up to the man leading the seminar before it begins, and say that you're sorry but you'll have to leave twenty minutes early. I promise you, promise you, that he'll smile and say, 'That's no problem, thanks for letting me know.'"

Under duress, Rob reluctantly agreed to try this technique. When he finally emerged from his seminar, he ran panting to our rental car, leapt in, and said in astonishment, "You were right, he wasn't angry. He told me to have a good weekend."

Rob may have been an extreme case. But after Henry's threatening comment about Dr. Ford's control over our degrees, I could see that all of my European Politics classmates were regressing into schoolchildren: better not make teacher mad!

It was decided that it would be more diplomatic to present our suggestions to Dr. Ford informally. I worried about this tactic. As the veteran of similar battles at Harvard, I knew that there is lot to be said for having things in writing. That way all exchanges are on record and can't be as easily ignored or forgotten. But most people felt that we could trust Ford's good faith and his desire to improve the program.

We planned to announce at the next seminar that we wanted to have a meeting to discuss the course, but we were saved from having to do this by an announcement from Ford himself.

"I understand," he said, "that some of you are feeling a bit confused about the direction of the course." (We all looked at each other. Who told him? We looked at Henry, who cleared his throat.) "Why don't we have a meeting tomorrow to go over such things?"

Our mutiny began to die right then. Most people don't really want to rebel, and can summon up the courage to do so only for a short while. And most people are easily fobbed off with a gesture of good faith. By the end of the seminar, I could see things were coming apart. Several people commented that it was obvious that Dr Ford really wanted to make the program work, and that there was no reason to be too pressing with our demands. We had to give Ford time, breathing space, support.

At the meeting the next day, things disintegrated entirely. Only David and Miranda and I stuck to our original list of suggestions. Dr Ford listened, and agreed that things had been somewhat disorganized. He promised that everything would get better. He agreed that it was difficult for us to get the reading. He said that copyright laws made it difficult to photocopy articles for us. He reiterated that it was really impossible to say, in any week, that some books were more important than others. He agreed that more emphasis on history, culture, and Eastern Europe would be a good thing, but the core seminars couldn't cover everything.

"True," I responded, "but why assume that the core

seminars shouldn't cover those things at the expense of some of what's covered now? On what basis do you decide what is 'core' and what is peripheral?"

Ford nodded vaguely. "Quite, yes. It's always difficult." He suggested that, as talented and mature graduate students, we pursue interests not dealt with in the core seminars on our own time.

"What time?" objected David. "We each have so many essays and class presentations on top of the required seminar reading that there *is* no time left over to pursue our own interests."

"Mmm," said Dr. Ford sympathetically. "Yes, I do see that. Hmm. Well, just do your best, and I'm sure that everything will turn out well in the end."

He said that we had a number of good suggestions, and that he would see to it that those suggestions were made known to all other faculty members. He regretted that he was unable to say exactly what optional seminars would be available the next term, because that really depended on student interests and the availability of people to teach us. He further regretted that he couldn't really say what would be covered on the qualifying exam, but advised us to be ready for anything. He said he felt that our meeting had been extremely productive, and that he hoped we would be able to make this an ongoing discussion. He pointed out that most people at Oxford would not be prepared to take student suggestions into account, but that he felt strongly that students should be involved in the process of planning courses. He apologized that he couldn't stay and discuss the issue further, but he had to get to another meeting.

When he left the room I looked around at a sea of beatific smiles. Everyone seemed so pleased, so flattered.

"I think he really took us seriously," said Rudloph. "We presented our demands in a forceful manner and he really can't ignore them."

"*Can't* ignore them," I wailed. "But he just *did* ignore them!"

"He did not agree to change a single thing," agreed Miranda.

"Give the man a chance," said Vincent. "I think he really understood us."

"Can you say *co-optation*, children?" muttered David.

Ford *had* understood us, too well, and he had out-manoeuvered us. He had correctly seen that most of us would be satisfied with some attention and some flattery in lieu of some real changes. I wished that we had presented them with a letter, instead. But I knew it was hopeless; without the support of the rest of the class, David, Miranda, and I weren't going to change anything.

It wasn't that Ford was being deliberately manipulative. He was doing his best, by his lights. He was a busy man: in addition to his own teaching and the administrative demands of the European Politics program, he was also involved with College administration. He was a kind, conscientious man; he wanted the program to be successful, and he wanted his students to be happy and intellectually fulfilled. It was simply that he hadn't the time or the energy to make any fundamental changes. He was genuinely troubled, I think, by our mutinous behavior—but consciously or not, he realized that we were complaining about problems that went deeper than the European Politics program. We were complaining about the Oxford approach to teaching and learning, although not all of us realized it yet. Essentially, all Ford would or could do was to tell us, as Gavin had told us, to be patient: things would all become more clear as time went on.

THE SULKS

THE END OF our mutiny marked the end of the first phase of my year at Oxford. After the mutiny, I was no longer awed by Oxford. I was critical, and became steadily more so. Until our mutiny, I had tried as hard as I could to do well in my program. After the mutiny was·quelled by Ford's masterful tactics, I didn't really bother. I stopped going out of my way to get the reading. There was no point, really. The books didn't seem terribly relevant or interesting, and even if I read them, no one else would have, so meaningful class discussions were impossible. I stopped going to lectures. I didn't understand them anyway, and I had better things to do, like sleep late, read novels, and have tea with friends. I was so bored that I even went jogging with Antoinette, Ellen, and Peggy twice a week, despite my dislike of running. I wrote fewer and shorter essays, and Dr. Ford never objected. He may have been guiltily relieved.

I took to going out for coffee with David and Miranda after each seminar. We would sit around glumly and complain about our course. We sat drowning in self-pity and bad coffee.

"The people in this course," said David, "are very nice. But they're not very interesting. No, I mean it. Some of them are sweet, I like them. But *intellectual?* No. Not that I should complain. I'm brain-dead myself now. I haven't had an interesting thought in months."

"My brain is mush," agreed Miranda.

"Your brain is mush?" I said. "My brain is less than mush. I don't think my brain is *there* anymore. I did more intellectually demanding work in high school. This course is a waste of time."

We ordered more coffee.

"Rudolph is a scumbag," said Miranda. "Vincent is just weird. Henry is pompous and unbearable and he always interrupts women speakers. Anne is spoiled rotten. I will throw up if François follows me home one more time."

"Ford brings up Italian politics all the time," said David, "even when it's completely irrelevant."

"That's because it's the only thing he knows about."

"Professor Twedler, in our Institutions seminar, keeps telling us about advising foreign governments."

"They're all show-offs. But what do they have going for them? Nothing. Has Twedler ever written a book?"

"None of these people do any interesting research."

"None of these people do *any* research."

"Does *anyone* at Oxford do any research?"

"Not only that but they can't teach."

"Explain to me why we read the books we read. Explain to me why it took some guy five hundred pages to deduce that some political parties are large, some are small."

"Explain to me why these people can't write in English. What's the jargon for? Why say 'problematic?' What's wrong with plain old 'problem?' Why say 'optimal'? What's wrong with 'best'?"

"It makes people who don't know any better think that what they say is important."

"Explain to me why so many of the people we read think that their uninteresting theory becomes more impressive if they draw a little graph to illustrate it."

"It looks pretty. 'The fourth quadrant, at thirty-seven degrees, is the quadrant of secular/religious cleavage.'"

"You know, I could be making films now," said David. "Or putting together a dance troupe."

"I could be climbing mountains in Colorado," said Miranda. "Or living in Prague, actually doing something."

David leaned forward intensely. "Listen. You know, we don't have to be here. We could just leave. Go to Germany. Let's make a documentary about immigration."

"If we're not here, we have no money and no jobs."

We drank more coffee.

I wince to recall those long, self-indulgent discussions. There we were, three young, well-educated North Americans, at Oxford on mind-bogglingly generous scholarships. We had every advantage. And we couldn't find anything better to do than sit around and whine.

What was wrong with us?

I still don't know. We weren't happy to be sitting around and whining. We hated it. We were bitter; we thought that Oxford had somehow betrayed us.

All that I can say in our defense is that we weren't the only ones who felt that way. Virtually all of the foreign students I knew were unhappy. "What am I doing here?" was a frequently heard question. The 1992 presidential election was coming up in the United States; I began to idly dream of working for the Democratic campaign during the summer and not coming back to Oxford until after Election Day, halfway through the first term. And I began to think, well, why come back then? Why not just stay away altogether? Get a job . . . Maybe Bill Clinton (who had suddenly become Oxford's favorite son), would win. Maybe I should go work in Washington.

Every second week my Marshall class got together for tea, cookies, and therapy; a favorite topic was how dissatisfied we all were with our courses. At some point during the middle of the year, we realized that more than three-fourths of us had either switched courses, planned to switch courses, or had tried without success to switch courses. Most of us were disgruntled, and felt that the Marshall Commission should have warned us, somehow, and prepared us for Oxford more realistically. "I'm not saying I'm not grateful for the money," said Tom. "But they should have *warned* us that we were going to a third-rate academic institution."

I began to ask American friends if they would want their children to spend a few years at Oxford. Some typical responses elicited that year:

Richard (appalled): "Are you kidding?"

Justin (sarcastically): "Sure, why not? It would be good for them. If they could survive Oxford, they'd survive anything life could throw at them."

Natalie (facetiously): "Would I send my child to Oxford? Only if he'd been very, very bad. I'd hold it over his head as the ultimate punishment."

Janet (somberly): "Well, if my kids really wanted to come here, I guess I'd let them. I mean I wouldn't hide their passports or anything."

We were not an academically unmotivated group to begin with. On the contrary. Almost without exception we were students who had gotten As at excellent American universities. All of us enjoyed academic work and had many intellectual interests. Many of us planned to do further graduate work after leaving Oxford. We had arrived at Oxford expecting to find an atmosphere of intellectual excitement; instead we found almost unvarying mediocrity. We longed to be impressed and overawed by Oxford, and when Oxford failed to measure up, our bitterness was as great as our initial enthusiasm had been.

After a few months, our feelings about academic programs at Oxford ranged from lukewarm tolerance to hostility. We all had similar complaints. Some of our complaints had to do with the mundane and the trivial: for instance, we were frustrated by the lack of what we considered basic resources. We were used to having libraries open until 1 or 2 a.m., and we found it difficult to adjust to libraries that worked on restricted hours (for instance, most closed by 7 p.m., and often were closed at lunchtime, too). We were used to open-stack libraries, where browsing was part of research. We were used to having *access* to all libraries without having to get special permission every time we wanted to use the facilities at other colleges or departments. We were used to being able to borrow books. We were used to more computers, copy machines, and so on.

Obviously, it's not Oxford's fault that it can't afford better resources. To some extent, it's Margaret Thatcher's fault. But Oxford did not respond to funding cuts in an imaginative or efficient manner. The decentralized nature of the University means that scarce resources are not distributed well. Colleges jealously guard their own resources instead of sharing, and the result is that things are shabby all over and students suffer the most. Human resources are also not put to good use. In European Politics, for instance, two rival power centers, one at St. Antony's and one at Nuffield, compete for funding and prestige. Fellows at each college sometimes put on nearly identical lectures on one topic, while neither college offers any lectures on another equally important topic. Tutors were quick to bad-mouth rivals, and students were implicitly urged to choose sides.

We were also unhappy with the substance of our programs. A few students, doing D.Phils, complained that they saw their supervisors only infrequently and received little guidance or support. Many of the rest of us had the opposite complaint: we were rarely given the opportunity to do original research of our own, and many of us felt overwhelmed with marginally relevant busy-work. The European Politics program, for instance, was an odd combination of obsessive micromanagement and near total lack of macromanagement. In other words, there was no overall curriculum, no big theme about what it meant to study for a M.Phil. in European Politics. The big questions were entirely ignored. But the little questions were there in abundance. Why did the EDC collapse in the 1950s? What role did the European Parliament play in influencing the Maastricht Treaty?

At risk of over-generalizing, much teaching (for BAs and for taught graduate courses like the M.Phil. and the M.St.) at Oxford rests on the assumption that it is more important for students to learn a particular body of knowledge than for them to learn to do original research. At better universities in the US it is the opposite: on the whole more emphasis is placed on learning to think and do research than on learning a body of material. Thus, at Oxford, students are generally told to write essays on particular topics: describe this, discuss the flaws in this, compare this with that.

In the US this is much rarer. Instead, students are often simply told to think of a topic that interests them and go out and do research, with, of course, the support and assistance of the supervisor. Most Oxford under-graduates never do research (their tutor gives them a list of books to read instead) and never write essays of more than six or eight handwritten sides. When I was an undergraduate, most of my essays were research essays, and generally were from twelve to thirty typewritten pages. Most of the Americans I knew at Oxford agreed that they were writing on a lower level as graduate students than they had as undergraduates in the States.

I am not arguing that one system is obviously better than the other. The American system does indeed encourage students to think for themselves, and rewards individual motivation and curiosity. But the danger is that although students learn to think, they have little to think *about*. Several of my courses at Harvard were seminars requiring one long essay of twenty to forty pages, and no exams; this meant that one really only knew well the subject of one's own essay. Even in lecture-based courses, with a final exam, this was often the case.

For instance, I once took a course on the history of British Imperialism. I wrote a twenty-five-page research paper on the significance of the royal visit to Canada in 1939. I felt that the Canadian Prime Minister had skillfully used the royal visit to simultaneously shore up Canadian loyalty to Britain (on the eve of World War Two) and to assert Canadian political autonomy. My paper received a very good grade, and when the course was over I knew an enormous amount about Canadian-British relations in the 1930s. But I really couldn't have said much of anything about India, Australia, China, the West Indies—certainly, I had crammed for the final, and just scraped by with a decent grade. But I had literally spent only ten hours cramming, and promptly forgot everything except the royal visit to Canada.

Most English undergraduates know a lot more about their subject than most American undergraduates. English undergraduates who study British Imperial History usually know names, dates, and major authors like the back of their hands. They have to: they write short weekly essays on set subjects and are expected to recall this for an examination a year or two years later. My friend Rob had been shocked when I told him he could leave a seminar early. He was even more shocked when he plumbed the depths of my ignorance about British history.

"I know the broad outline," I told him defensively.

"But you don't know dates, battles, characters!" he said. "Didn't they teach that?"

"Probably they taught it," I said. "But that wasn't what was stressed. The *themes* were stressed more than the facts, I suppose."

"Themes." Rob rolled his eyes.

This was a major reason so many of us were unhappy. We were used to a broad, interdisciplinary approach. America's élite universities cherish the ideal of a "liberal" education; the concept was well expressed by Richard Levin, the President of Yale, in his inaugural address to freshmen:

> The purpose of liberal education is to develop the capacity for independent thought, rather than to acquire specific or "useful" knowledge . . . To equip students for public or community service is only one contribution that liberal education makes to the well-being of our nation and the wider world . . . a liberal education will prepare you to be thinking citizens for a lifetime . . . You enter an institution rich in the traditions of scholarship, abounding in the joys of learning. But a liberal education is not simply given to you. You must actively pursue it. Take every advantage of the treasures before you. The world is all before you, where to choose your place of rest.

We were bored silly by the Oxford approach to education. Our assignments seemed too narrow. We thought that curricula were rigid and old-fashioned. Not only were we not encouraged to go out and do research, we were only given very conventional ideas to work with. Tradition was in; innovation was out. Feminist criticism, social history, and most other arts disciplines less than thirty years old were not exactly in vogue at Oxford.

Compared to their American peers, British students are better educated, if education means knowing a subject through and through. But if education means knowing how to go beyond the basics, knowing how to learn on one's own, and knowing how to take an in-depth look at a subject and say something new about it, I think that Americans are somewhat better off. As *Washington Monthly* editor David Segal notes sardonically, British students, unlike Americans, are

> accepted into college to study one subject—and only one subject. Their advantage is they get to dig deeper in a narrow field and develop an expertise. The drawback is, they're bored. The academy becomes something like a salad bar where you can only help yourself to beans—which tends to make you very cynical about beans and sick of salad bars in general. The standard rap against American education is that it's superficial, and next to the British system, it's guilty as charged. But while the smattering approach to the curriculum may not lend itself to penetrating thought, it has the advantage of keeping the enthusiasm level high.

We were also frustrated to find that our complaints were largely ignored—and that was if we could figure out to whom we should complain. The shock of the student rebellions in the 1960s made American universities more responsive to student needs. By and large, American universities treat students as consumers, at worst, if not as fully-functioning adults. It is usually clear whom to go to for advice or to try to change something. And sometimes things *do* change in response to student input. Most of us recalled good, easy-going relationships with professors who didn't hesitate to invite groups of students home for dinner or out for lunch. At Oxford a common subject among American students was the difficulty of establishing a collegial relationship with tutors.

American universities are more student-centered because of America's very size. About half of American high-school students go on to one of the several thousand colleges in the US. If students don't like Harvard, they can go to Yale, or Stanford, or Berkeley, or any of twenty other equally good and equally respected universities. This means that universities can't just rest on their laurels; they have to convince students that they offer something better than all the others. But in England, a more class-bound society where only fifteen percent of school-leavers go on to higher education, Oxford and Cambridge are so much more prestigious than other universities that they exercise a virtual monopoly. You don't like Oxbridge? Tough luck. This means that unlike other British universities, Oxford and Cambridge have not been forced to change with the times. Most curricula have changed little in the last few decades. Rules from the eighteenth century are still on the books. And as far as administration goes, lines of authority are far from clear. Oxford, with its many semi-autonomous colleges, resembles nothing so much as medieval Germany, filled with jealous squabbling princes and dozens of petty fiefdoms.

Feelings of disappointment and frustration were widespread among foreign students, particularly among Americans. In a survey commissioned by Rhodes House in 1992, about two thousand former Rhodes Scholars, of all nationalities, described their Oxford days. In a preliminary tabulation of results, twenty-one percent rated the quality of teaching at Oxford average; fourteen percent described it as bad or very bad. Twenty-two percent rated university supervision only average, with twenty-one percent claiming it was bad or very bad. Twenty-three percent rated college academic staff average, thirteen percent responded with bad or very bad. About half rated libraries, equipment, and facilities average to very bad. Twenty-three percent had switched courses, and a quarter reported problems with their programs.

One might dispute the notion that this proves something about Oxford, by asserting that there's nothing wrong with "average." But isn't there? This is *Oxford* we're talking about, arguably the world's most famous and prestigious university. Shouldn't Oxford be better than just "average?" Should fourteen percent or so of Rhodes Scholars rate it as bad or very bad?

The survey had a response rate of only fifty-five percent. It seems reasonable to surmise that the fifty-five percent who responded had more positive feelings towards Oxford and the Rhodes than the forty-five percent who didn't bother. This would suggest that actual Rhodes scholar dissatisfaction with Oxford may be higher than the survey results alone would indicate.

I suspect that when the final survey results are released, they will be even more damning. Younger graduates and current students will likely be more severe than older graduates; their views will not yet be colored by nostalgia. And it will be interesting to see the results broken down by nationality. Here too, I suspect that Americans will be more dissatisfied with Oxford than Rhodes Scholars from other countries.

I remember a conversation I had once with a former Rhodes Scholar. He had gone to a Rhodes reunion, but had left after the first few hours. "It was too depressing," he told me. "First, everyone said 'Hey, how's it going!' Then everyone would talk about jobs. Then about families. Then there would be a silence. Then everyone would start talking about how miserable they'd been at Oxford. I decided it was all too depressing, so I left early."

There is a long history of dissatisfied Americans at Oxford, from the fictional Steele in James Childer's *Laurel and Straw* to the otherwise Anglophilic writers Henry James and T. S. Eliot. Steele, an early Rhodes Scholar, eventually finds himself so put off by Oxford pretensions that he can't avoid violence: "Almost before the last syllable was out of the Englishman's mouth, Steele sunk his fist into it." Henry James wrote that a stay at the University was "tainted with that Oxford priggery which is not one of the things I enjoy most." Eliot is reported to have said that although Oxford was all right, he didn't really like being dead.

None of us hated Oxford *all* the time. Even in European Politics, despite my overall disenchantment with the program and the material, I found a few dons I admired and liked: William Wallace stood out for his witty and insightful writing and his cheerful demeanor. Anne Deighton often managed to pull together the threads of a discussion in an enlightening way, and she gently chastised Henry when he began to sound too pompous. (Once, when Henry interrupted a woman's tentative comments for the third time, Anne Deighton laughed, and said wryly, "Sorry, Emma, if you want to speak in this seminar you can't afford to think first. I suppose that's why women speak so much less than men in seminars—they think before they open their mouths.") And Vincent Wright was such a good teacher that he managed to provoke lively discussion about even the deadliest of topics.

My friends also found some things to admire. Every now and then someone would report a fascinating lecture, a brilliant teacher, a wonderful project, a great seminar discussion. But these shining moments were rare. We were left to wonder why so many people still came to Oxford from all over the world, and why we had, from our first breaths, learnt to think of Oxford with awe and respect. Andre Schiffrin, an American who spent two years at Cambridge several decades ago, recalls being told by a visiting American historian, "Obviously some kind of learning process goes on here, but I'll be damned if I know what it is."

I couldn't figure out the academic learning process, either. So I opted out. I did little work, dreamed vaguely of leaving and never coming back, and devoted myself to my social life. One nice thing about Oxford is that if you don't want to do any work, no one will really make you. (This was a clue to just what the learning process was, but I didn't figure it out until it was too late to do me any good, at least in European Politics.) I stopped going to lectures. I stopped writing essays for Hugh Ford, and he stopped asking for essays. I suppose he figured that it was really my problem. I was happy to agree. It was easy for me to agree: I had a bachelor's degree, and I didn't want to be an academic. What did I care how well I did in the European Politics M.Phil.?

I rowed. I sang. I read a lot of novels. Within a month, novels took up more space on my shelves than did course books. I had long conversations in my kitchen with Peter, bemoaning the paucity of mountains in England, the wan, pale faces of the English, the sadly unimaginative food, and the early closing hours of all pubs. I saw a lot of movies and tried every restaurant in town. I explored pubs. I went to parties with my classmates from European Politics. I went to parties in the Christ Church GCR, noisy dance parties where the floor shook under our feet. The parties were just like parties in the US: cheap wine, everyone struggling to be witty and charming, squabbles over whose musical tastes should prevail. I got to know the two young men who had sat across from me that first night in Hall: Neal, a computer scientist from Ireland, and Bill, a boxer from Liverpool. They were both friendly and easy-going, nothing like my alarming initial impression of them.

Things did settle into a routine. Of course. I stopped waking up and being astonished to find myself at Oxford.

I had a number of dinner parties, cramming ten or so people into my room in St Aldate's. I hosted a dance party. I had lengthy teas every afternoon. My life seemed to divide into three overlapping worlds: friends from my course, friends from College, and friends from America. Friends were increasingly my refuge; I was angry at Oxford for disappointing me academically, but I was unceasingly grateful that the Oxford name had attracted so many interesting graduate students, of all nationalities. I wasn't wildly happy, but I was reasonably content.

Most of my fellow foreign students seemed to be doing the same thing: trying hard not to let their academic disappointment interfere with their ability to enjoy the other aspects of their life. My old friend Justin was an exception. He had been becoming more and more extreme in his condemnations of Oxford. We all had become more extreme, I suppose, but Justin, by virtue of having spent a lonely junior year there before getting a Rhodes, had gotten a head start on hating Oxford. He had come back, he said, in order to prove to himself that he could conquer Oxford—or somehow get revenge. But he didn't seem to be having much luck with that project. Like the rest of us, he was finding it difficult to do the work he had come to Oxford to do. His supervisors, he said, were obstructive.

He switched courses. The new department was obstructive. Justin sulked. He allowed his unhappiness at Oxford to seep over into all other parts of his life. He was quarrelsome. He was quick to puncture other people's illusions and mock their affectations. People began to avoid him.

He seemed bent on alienating everyone. He went around like Holden Caulfield, telling anyone who would listen that we were all "phonies," smooth manners covering up essentially false or empty characters. He was bitterly unhappy himself, and couldn't understand how other sensitive people might manage to go through life with even marginally greater equanimity. *Ergo:* we were all insensitive louts.

For a while he exempted me from his criticisms. But not for long. I had been getting more impatient with him for a while; he was so angry at everything and everyone that I found it hard to spend time with him. I finally tried arguing with him. "Justin, I'm disappointed by Oxford too, but I really think you're not giving it, or anyone, a chance. You expect them to be awful, so you behave provocatively, and so they are awful. Maybe bullies bloodied your nose in junior high school—but remember, you practically dared them to. You wouldn't leave them alone. Try cheering up—people may get nicer." But Justin wasn't having any of it, and accused me, not without some justification, of shallow psychologizing. From then on he made it clear that he included me on his list of phonies. He told me this in several irate letters. I made the error of replying seriously to the first few notes; which merely provoked a further stream of accusing missives about false consciousness and hypocritical attitudes.

Oddly enough, by mid-November Justin also began to wear silk scarves knotted at the neck. He took to handing out little cards which has his name on them: *Justin Dietz, Esq.* It was said by some that he frequently drank vast quantities of sherry; it was suggested by others that he felt an obscure kinship with Oscar Wilde.

His affectations were not without a substantial degree of self-mockery. I remembered his bitter words about "upper-class snots." At the beginning of the year, he had said that he both resented Oxford and longed to be fully accepted by Oxford. He had also predicted that he would never be accepted by Oxford or by the larger world that Oxford represented to him.

I think he was right, but I also think that his prophecy was deliberately self-fulfilling. Oxford fills some Americans with a peculiar form of self-hatred, and Justin, with his stubborn and pugnacious personality, was an easy victim. Justin was introspective enough to recognize this, but too fatalistic to do anything but give in to it. He was afraid that the world would mock him and be unkind to him, and rather than fear the worst, he avoided the suspense by manufacturing the worst himself. He created a self-image that was impossible for others to like. It made him feel miserable, but at least he was in control.

Score: Oxford Myth 1, Americans 0.

At about this time I was invited to a dinner party by Julietta, a large woman from Rome with dyed red hair and a thunderingly raucous laugh. Like me, she was a graduate student at Christ Church. I had chatted with her at a number of parties, and I was flattered when she stopped to talk to me in the GCR computer room.

"R-rrosa," warbled Julietta huskily. "Arrre you bissy on Frriday?"

"No, I don't think so," I said, looking up with relief from the essay I was writing on the EC's agricultural policy.

"Then you musst come to a leetle deener party of mine."

I agreed with pleasure. Julietta slapped me hard on the shoulder and laughed fiendishly. "Good. We will have a good time!"

On Friday night, I dressed with care. Most of Julietta's friends were English, and I didn't know any of them well. I was nervous: despite the comfortable GCR parties and the friendliness of everyone I had met, I was still somewhat intimidated socially. I was afraid of making some sort of horrible British dinner party *faux pas*.

Despite my fears, everything went well for the first hour or two. Until the dessert.

The dessert was fruit cocktail: little bits of banana, apple, and mandarin orange floating in a gooey liquid. I was deep in polite conversation with the dour-faced philosophy D.Phil. student on my right: we were discussing his dissertation, which apparently stood on its head the previous two centuries of British philosophy. "Oh, really, that's very clever," I said encouragingly. I glanced around the table, searching for conversational help.

Just then, a juicy lump of orange sailed across the room. It flew gracefully between the chandelier and the ceiling and hit Julietta square in the forehead, landing with a gentle squelch. "Oooh!" she squealed. Juice ran down the bridge of her nose. She contorted her face in an effort to lick the juice off her nose, achieving an almost Gorgonlike state.

"I *kill* you, Tommy!" She gave a deep belly laugh, and scooped up a banana. It landed on Tommy's head. With a goofy grin he picked it out of his hair and threw it back, wiping his sticky fingers on his Blues blazer.

"Heh, heh," I said weakly, turning to the philosophy student. "Julietta and Tommy must be old friends, huh?"

"Mmm," he replied. "Rather." He looked disapproving.

I smiled gamely around the table. What's a little bit of fruit among friends, after all? A brief volley of bananas and then it would stop, with laughing apologies and disclaimers. Really rather sweet, wasn't it? It was good to see a group of graduate students, undoubtedly tense about dissertations, exams, and funding, unwind a bit.

But it didn't stop. Instead it escalated until fruit was flying all over the room. Goo dripped from the ceiling. I pushed my chair back out of the line of fire, and turned to ask my philosophy student whether food fights like this were a common occurrence in the Christ Church Graduate Common Room. But he was busy scooping up some thick *bleu* cheese dressing from his salad bowl and lobbing it at the woman sitting opposite him. The glob of *bleu* cheese landed on her shoulder. She lunged at him, brandishing the burnt end of a cork, and smeared black ash all over his face.

Soon the room was bedlam. Twelve people leapt around, giggling, shrieking and overturning furniture, attacking each other with *bleu* cheese-laden *crudités* and little pieces of fruit salad. The glowering men in the portraits on the wall were not exempt: one dignified but unlucky fellow in military dress had a hunk of banana over his ear. Under my feet, the carpet was sticky and wet. Wine was being poured down the throat of a woman held down in her chair by two men, and some of the men began to sing rugby songs about the sexual predilections of students at a rival college.

I stood by the door, trying to keep a tolerant and amused smile on my face. Was there something wrong with me? Would a normal person have rushed happily into the fray, perhaps daringly signalling a new round by

148

tossing a plate at the wall? Was I missing some crucial "fun gene?" Maybe it was just that they were drunk and I was sober, a bad cold having prevented me from drinking much.

But whatever the reason, I was horrified and disgusted, not least because Ralph, the kindly GCR steward, would have to clean up the mess the next day. But I was a guest, and I knew no one in the room at all well. It seemed ungrateful to act ostentatiously disgusted. On the other hand, everyday rules of etiquette seemed to have been laid aside long since. I kept smiling grimly, hoping that no one would notice me and that the food fight would stop.

"Having fun?" asked the man standing next to me. It was Tommy. He had cork on his face and a large piece of banana in his hair.

"Well, I guess I'm not too big on food fights," I said, trying not to sound like a prude. "All in all mud wrestling seems cleaner, you know? I think I'd rather mud wrestle than be in a food fight."

Tommy swayed ominously in my direction. "We could arrange a little mud wrestling, you and I," he leered, clamping a sticky hand on my arm.

"No thanks," I said, squeamishly detaching his hand.

It was only 11:15, but I couldn't take it any longer. I slipped out the door and walked with relief into the cool air of Tom Quad.

Needless to say, this dinner party added yet another complication to my social life. Not only was there Justin's odd behavior and unfriendly notes; I now had to avoid Julietta, my food-fight hostess. I ran into her the day after the dinner party, and blurted out a forced apology for leaving so early. She cackled and gave me what I took to be a hostile look. From then on I was too embarrassed to speak to her, and ducked around corners whenever I heard her approaching.

At the beginning of the year, I had known almost no one. Now I sometimes felt that I knew too many people. Oxford seemed to have shrunk. I began to feel claustrophobic. The Marshall and Rhodes crowd was too gossipy; at Christ Church the same old faces were always there at lunch and at dinner. I wanted to be in a big country again.

I Join the Élite, Briefly

ONE DAY SHORTLY after this I found a small envelope in my pigeon-hole at the porters' lodge. It contained a red card, which said: "The Cardinals request the honour of your company at cocktails. Friday, 8 p.m. in the McKenna Room, Christ Church. Black tie. A guest may be brought."

There was no indication of who had sent the card, and I had no idea who or what the Cardinals might be. A species of bird? A baseball team? An organization of Roman Catholic clergymen?

None of these seemed too likely. I decided to ask around.

"Did you get this card?" I asked Peter.

"No. No one ever invites me to cocktail parties. The English are so antisocial. Why do you think I don't have a girlfriend? So, who are the Cardinals?"

I asked an undergraduate with whom I rowed. "Ooh," she said. "The Cardinals. Aren't they some kind of exclusive dining society?"

They couldn't be that exclusive, I thought, if they had invited me. But I was intrigued. Apparently I had met some of the "right" people at Christ Church. I just didn't know who they were.

I have always been opposed to all-male clubs. As a rule, I do not think that women should go to parties given to all-male clubs; it only lends them legitimacy. But I was curious. I wanted to go to the Cardinals. I had read

Brideshead; and I wanted a glimpse into what I imagined—despite food fights and other evidence to the contrary—might be a world of elegance, refinement, and wit. I wanted to see what an exclusive Oxford drinking society was like.

If possible, I told myself, I wanted to subvert it from within. (A rationalization? Probably. But I still remember the glee I felt when a female friend and I challenged some members of an all-male Harvard final club to a game of pool. We beat them, badly, three games in a row. The looks on their faces made feeling the tiniest bit un-p.c. well worth it.) By this time, I had lost my hope of academic gain, and I had also lost my unqualified awe of Oxford. I was by now looking upon my time at Oxford as anthropological field-work. I wanted to be there to witness the odd customs and rites of the last days of English élitism.

I recalled an anecdote about the late great American critic, Edmund Wilson. Sir Isaiah Berlin, showing him around on a visit to Oxford, offered to take Wilson to eat in a restaurant rather than in a college. Wilson preferred dining in college:

> He said he wished to plumb the depths of old, decayed, conservative English academic life in its death throes—I remember his words: "It can't be long now," he said ominously. "I think we're in at the kill."

Wilson was wrong: "old, decayed, conservative English academic life" isn't dead yet, although most would say it's surely dying. And it has the allure, for some people, of an injured but still venomous rattlesnake: witness Justin's doomed attempt to court it.

Like Wilson, I wanted to witness its decline, but I

didn't intend to get bitten. I invited Miranda to come with me on Friday night and provide moral support. ("You want me to come with you to a *what?*" she said. "What am I going to tell Tom? 'Oh, sorry, I have to go hob-nob with the lads at the House?'") I wore the black cocktail dress that I had bought with my mother after hours of searching in Lord and Taylor's, in anticipation of just such an occasion.

The McKenna Room was dim and partly filled with well-dressed young men and women, all of whom looked like undergraduates. Most of them looked nervous. Some of them looked terrified. Miranda and I seemed to be the only graduates and the only Americans. To my relief, I soon recognized Owen, who occasionally coxed for our boat. Owen was extremely tall and thin, and could often be seen drifting gracefully around Tom Quad, a silk scarf draped dashingly around his neck. He was part of the *faux Brideshead* set in college. (He was rumored to have arrived in Hall on his first night in Christ Church carrying a teddy bear. I think this must be apocryphal.)

Owen welcomed us and got us each a drink. "Hello, ladies! Welcome, welcome . . ." Ralph, the Graduate Common Room butler, was serving the drinks.

"Hello, Rosa," said Ralph, and winked at me. I winked back, praying that Ralph did not know I had been present at Julietta's dinner party, the one that left the GCR in such a state.

I struck up a conversation with Frank, a beefy young man I had seen around the boathouse. The conversation didn't go too well. He asked me what I studied. I asked him what he studied.

"Law," he said.

"Oh, I know a graduate who's doing a second BA in law," I told him. "Jerome, he's the one who plays tennis."

153

"Oh, sure, Jerome. Yeah. Jerome's got a brain as big as a planet," said Frank.

I thought about this. "Which planet?"

Frank looked at me strangely. "You know, like a planet, like, *big,* planets are big."

"Sure," I agreed, "but some planets are bigger than others."

Frank looked surprised.

This line of conversation was going nowhere. It was interrupted by the appearance of Tommy, Julietta's friend, last seen clutching a bit of burnt cork and covered with bits of fruit. Today he was drunkenly clutching a teapot. I tried to duck but it was too late. I scanned his clothes, searching for left-over bits of food, and he grabbed my shoulder.

"You were nice to me," he said accusingly, "but now you're not. You've broken my heart."

"Really, I doubt that," I told him crossly. "Why do you have a teapot?"

He straightened up and said, in an aggrieved tone, "Madam, this teapot is my own." He bowed, and departed.

I grabbed Miranda's arm and we turned to Owen, who had materialized again by my side.

"Entertaining chap, Tommy," said Owen.

I said, with my most charming smile, "Tell me about the Cardinals, Owen. Is it a new group?"

Owen looked gratified at my interest. "Well, Cardinals was originally founded in the last century but the group folded in the 1920s. It's just recently been resurrected here."

"What do the Cardinals do each term?" I asked.

"We have a few cocktail parties, like this—" Owen gestured modestly around the room. "Then at the end of term we have a big bang-up dinner for members. But—"

he was apologetic—"I'm afraid that the dinner is only for *chaps*."

Miranda and I looked at one another. Miranda smiled sweetly at Owen. "When you resurrected the Cardinals after seventy years, how come you couldn't just resurrect it with *women* in it?"

"Why—" Owen looked taken aback. He gave us an appalled smile. "Why, I'm afraid—I'm afraid that's just not *done!*"

Miranda and I looked at each other, astonished. "That's just not done" was the sort of thing English people always said in old television movies. Now here was an actual, real life Oxford student saying it. It was almost too good to be true.

Owen fled shortly after this exchange, and Miranda and I figured that we had just blown our one and only chance to be admitted to the upper echelons of Oxford society. It turned out, though, that the upper echelons wanted us. (Well, not the *upper* upper echelons—I never saw those.) Owen was not only not offended by our irreverent attitude, he actually invited us back. This is one advantage of being an American at Oxford. People *expect* you to say foolish and inappropriate things. English students are too easily pegged by their peers: their class background is easily detected, and they have to behave well. Americans, almost by definition, have no class, at least as far as the English are concerned. They're just— *Americans*. So they're allowed to do more or less whatever they want.

I was not unduly flattered to discover that a rash of invitations to similar events followed my début at the Cardinals' drinks party. I knew that it wasn't my distinctive charm, elegant clothing, or refined social graces. It was just that I happened to be female, and for all intents and purposes single. There is a dire shortage of women at

Oxford, and available women quickly find themselves inundated with invitations from all-male drinking societies. Within two weeks I had been issued invitations to the Stoics, the Monarchists, the Nondescripts, and to Vincent's, the Blues club. (Do these guys share their mailing lists? Is that how the British establishment survives, through one big shared mailing list?) I was even invited to the Beaglers' Ball. The Stoics got me on their invitation list and didn't take me off the whole year, even though I only went to two events. Every two weeks, I'd get a poison-pen letter from Justin and yet another invitation to a Stoics party. It got to be irritating, like receiving multiple copies of the Land's End catalogue.

I turned down the invitation to the Beaglers' Ball, sponsored though it was by the alluringly named Christ Church and Farley Hill Beagling Society (they even had a special letter-head). This was partly because going seemed to involve staying in a hotel with a rower who publicly wore his Lycra all-in-ones far too much of the time, and partly because it turned out that I wouldn't get to see the actual beagles. Also, I couldn't drum up a lot of respect for beagling. I have a beagle at home, and—sorry, beaglers—watching a bunch of grown men dressed in silly outfits chasing around after a pack of beagles (who themselves chase a false scent) struck me as a pretty silly thing to do.

I went to the Stoics a few times. The Stoics were not all from Christ Church, like the Cardinals, but there were many Christ Church people among them. The ubiquitous and willowy Owen was there, as were several graduate students. I noticed Jerome, and also Neal and Bill, the two men who had been so silent my first night in Hall. Julietta, my food-fight hostess, was there in a pink tulle ball gown, so I had to hide in the cloakroom until she moved into another room. Also Mark, the American who had snapped at Mrs Edgerton, and Andrew Blake.

Andrew Blake deserves a description. He was a Rhodes who had graduated from Princeton in 1987. He had aroused dislike amongst his Princeton classmates by announcing freshman year that he planned to win a Rhodes, and he took up rowing to further that goal. He wrote his senior thesis on the intellectual influences on Cecil Rhodes' thought. Anglophilic to the bone, Andrew's way of handling Oxford was to try to become English. He became more English than the English. He wore waistcoats and cravats. (He had had a special waistcoat with the Stoics' colors on it made for himself, presumably at great expense.) The minute his D.Phil. came through he changed the nameplate on his door to read "*Dr* Andrew Blake." Andrew was friendly and jovial to all, but he remained an object of mild disdain to most of his peers. He also, I fear, had a large and handsome blond head, with the emphasis on *large*. His enemies called him Dr. Bighead. His friends called him Rugby Ball.

He was very popular with a certain group of English students, including Owen—perhaps his affectations were flattering to them. When his back was turned, they spoke of him condescendingly, seeming to regard him as a sort of mascot.

Andrew took an approach common to many Americans at Oxford. He out-Englished the English. In this he was not unlike Justin, but Andrew, I think, had the good fortune to be slightly less intelligent than Justin. His affectations were not self-mocking. People laughed at him, but he didn't frighten them away.

Justin couldn't help fearing that the English were somehow better than Americans. Andrew Blake was sure of it, so he shamelessly shed his American traits. But some

Americans went to the opposite extreme, wearing baseball caps, watching the Superbowl, eating at McDonald's, and trying to pretend they had never left home. My friend Parker, who grew up in rural Arizona, used an aggressive variation on this tactic. Whenever Parker felt irritated by someone he viewed as a little English twit, he'd lean down, look the offending piece of chicken shit in the eye, and say in a low, dangerous drawl: "Ever wrestled a bear to death with your own two hands?"

As far as I know they don't actually have any bears in Arizona. But Parker was part American Indian. He stood six foot five and weighed about 230 lbs, so no one ever called him on this. (It wasn't always a bear. Sometimes it was a deer shot on the run with a bow and arrow.) Parker became an object of fear and veneration at Magdalen College, where he rose to dizzying heights of power in the MCR (the Middle Common Room).

I'm not sure which strategy, if any, leads to happiness, since I tried to follow the narrow and winding middle path. I never watched the Superbowl. I didn't go to McDonald's much, and I did occasionally go to dining society parties and other haunts of the self-hating Americans. But I not infrequently found myself bridling at the snooty anti-Americanism of many English people at Oxford. I was once informed by a supercilious undergraduate that the movie *Wayne's World*, a transatlantic hit, had been "highly interesting, and amusing for what its popularity said about American tastes." *American* tastes, I thought? *Wayne's World* was a joke—it was a deliberate parody of American pop culture. My English friend didn't seem to get the joke. I reminded him that it wasn't Oxford's five hundred American students who had kept the cinema full three weeks in a row. In my opinion, the popularity of *Wayne's World* said a lot about the tastes of the English viewing public.

Similarly, I often heard English people complain about the presence of McDonald's, Pizza Hut, and Kentucky Fried Chicken in the sacred groves of academe. Oxford, they felt, was somehow contaminated by these disgusting tumors of the American consumer society. But again, it wasn't Oxford's five hundred Americans who kept these places in business—it was the English. England is not a Third World country, unable to resist the impredations of the powerful and culturally imperialist US. England is filled with American fast food, American blue jeans, and American movies because many English young people *prefer* the American articles to their English counterparts. And strangely, the very people who most often railed against American cultural imperialism were usually the very ones who tried to dress like James Dean and who rushed off to the States for holidays at every opportunity.

In many ways I preferred people like Tina the Veg Girl, the one who ate only raw veggies and went around claiming to be American. She carried the English affection for American pop culture to its logical extreme. No bad faith for Tina: she didn't try to pretend a contempt for America that she didn't feel. (On the other hand, she was crazy.)

The Stoics were unusual in that they counted two Americans as members. Most exclusive Oxford societies didn't welcome American men, although women of any race, nationality, or creed were more than welcome.

The Stoics' colors were blue and gold. These colors shone from Neal and Bill's bow ties, and from Andrew's waistcoat. In keeping with the attractive color scheme, the Stoics served watery blue and gold drinks. Neither one was very good. At least the Cardinals had managed wine. I was surprised by the watery quality of the drinks, because it was widely known that most drinking societies made members go through some ghastly alcoholic initiation ritual.

My flatmate Peter, despite his claim that no one ever invited him out, had been urged to join another drinking society, the Nondescripts. The Nondescripts, jocularly known as the "Nondies", was a society open to Christ Church men who played at least two college sports and otherwise met with the approval of the "lads". Peter played cricket and occasionally turned out for second team rugby matches, and he seemed to know a lot of the sporting types in College.

One night I had some American friends from London visiting in my room when there was a loud knock on the door. It was Peter, clad in a dinner jacket, reeling slightly.

"Rosa!" he said boisterously. "Good, you're still up. Thought I'd come for a chat." He noticed my friends and waved vaguely at them. "Oh, company. How nice!"

"Peter, this is Kevin, Joe, Erik, Patrick, Ellen."

"Nice to meet you all. A party I see! Good. Love parties. Not enough of 'em in this rotten country."

I looked at him dubiously. He swayed happily then sat down. "Have you been to a party, Peter?"

"Ummmf, yes, Nondescripts, fine—fine chaps all. Lots to drink. Made me drink port from—a shoe. Port from a shoe, that's it."

My American friends exchanged glances.

'Yes," repeated Peter, "a shoe full." He put his head in his hands.

"Do you feel OK, Peter?"

"Oh yes," he said. "Had a lot to drink, that's all."

Then he began, very daintily, to throw up on the carpet.

"Oh, damn," I said. We all leapt up. He moaned apologies as three of the men grabbed him and carried him through the hall to the toilet. The rest of us leapt for water, towels, disinfectant. I was embarrassed—my friends had just come for dessert and here they were, saddled with a vomiting stranger. I called Jerome. He was reliable and kind-hearted, and he was friendly with Peter. He came over quickly and took on the disagreeable task of keeping Peter company in the bathroom. My friends helped clean the carpet in my room, and then left. "Honestly," I said. "Don't think that Oxford is always like this."

"Oh yes," they agreed, backing away. "Sure."

When they were gone I checked up on Peter. Jerome had put him into his bed, with the rubbish bin by his side. Peter was mumbling semi-coherently by now. He could hardly look at me. "I'm so embarrassed," he groaned. "So sorry, Rosa. Your floor . . . your friends . . ."

"Peter, *why* did you want to be a member of the Nondescripts? You hate drinking societies!"

"I wasn't going to go," explained Peter woefully, "but I ran into Mark and Peggy and they told me it was an *honor*."

"That was terrible of Mark," I said crossly. "He turned down the offer of membership in the Stoics because he didn't want to go through the initiation."

Peter picked up on this with alacrity. "I wasn't going to go. He told me to. It's his fault. Oh, I hate Mark! I'm never going back. I *hate* Mark!"

He continued to murmur this to himself as Jerome and I tiptoed out to clean the bathroom.

Peter remained contrite for several weeks afterwards, and as far as I know he never did go back to the Nondescripts.

There were other all-male drinking and dining societies that were much more exclusive, like the Bullingdon, with which I had no contact. Jerome was invited to join a mysterious organization called "P." "P" stood for "pineapple", and a favorite P after-dinner game involved having members guess the number of spines on a pineapple. P was so very special and secret that members were not supposed to utter its name to the uninitiate. It was rather more high-falutin' than the Stoics or the Cardinals, and counted several dons as members, including a prominent historian who had been made a life peer. P was a bastion of British clubbiness; Jerome had presumably been invited to join because in some circles South Africans were still considered good colonials and good sportsmen.

Mark was also invited to join (he did, since they didn't require an initiation ritual involving the consumption of dangerous quantities of alcohol). The prominent historian nearly blackballed Mark, commenting that if there were any people he hated more than graduate students, it had to be American graduate students. But Mark presumably didn't know this, and was pleased by the invitation. He rewarded P with a fair amount of loyalty. I once asked Mark how his dinner at P had gone, and he looked at me in mock horror.

"Sshh," he said. "You're not supposed to know about it. Who told you? No one's supposed to say anything." Then he laughed. "It's absurd," he said. "We played charades."

Mark took Oxford seriously. He wasn't at all like Andrew Blake (he of the oversized head and the Stoics' waistcoat). He didn't put on an act. But he remained filled with a certain reverence towards Oxford. He was critical of Oxford in many ways, laughed at it in many ways— but he took it seriously, and expected Oxford to take him seriously in return. He was in his second year of graduate work when I arrived at Christ Church, and during the course of the year he became a good friend. He was a little older than most of us; he had worked for a few years before coming to Christ Church on a Rhodes. He seemed even older than his years. This was partly because of his looks—he was tall and rather patrician looking, and dressed more formally than most students. This, in turn, was partly because of his job. Mark was affiliated with Christ Church, but he was also the Dean at Oriel College.

How he became dean I'm not sure. Mark had been a resident advisor when he was an undergraduate in the US. At Oriel, the dean was not unlike a resident advisor. The dean was the junior administrator who was in charge of discipline for the undergraduates. And the undergraduates at Oriel were a rowdy lot. Mark seemed to enjoy his job, which gave him membership in the Oriel Senior Common Room. He would regale us sometimes with stories of his occasionally obstreperous colleagues in the SCR, but on the whole he took being dean as seriously as he took his academic work. He conscientiously tried to get help, instead of mere punishment, for undergraduate miscreants. That was rarely easy. Oxford has far too few counseling resources, and for the most part undergraduate alcoholics and anorexics are either ignored or sent home as being beyond hope.

Mark found this extremely frustrating, and he told me that it was hard not to get discouraged at times. "I'm just the fall guy," he said. "The Warden agrees with everything I say but he won't back me up. I spend most of my time tilting at windmills—arguing with indifferent dons or being laughed at by drunken undergraduates."

One night in Hall, Mark, Antoinette, Ellen, Peggy, and I were discussing whether or not universities ought to be *in loco parentis* to students with regard to alcohol. Peggy said she didn't think it was the universities' job to keep students from drinking. Mark snapped at her angrily: this would inevitably cause student alcoholism. "Bollocks," said Ellen succinctly. Trying to ease the situation, I laughed, and said, "Come on, Mark, you're acting as though Peggy had suggested that each incoming freshman ought to be personally handed a vodka bottle by the Dean!"

Mark stood up. "Fine. Laugh. You don't take this seriously. I do. I don't want to continue this conversation." And we stomped off, refusing to listen to our protests.

The next day, I got an apologetic note from Mark. "I'm terribly sorry," he wrote, "to have left so rudely. I was very upset about the way Oriel was handling the case of a student alcoholic—they just weren't interested in accepting that they had a responsibility to get him any help. I was taking it all very personally, although none of you could have known this, and my feelings about this colored my response to Peggy's argument. Please accept my apologies; I'm also writing to Peggy, Ellen, and Antoinette."

I could hardly blame Mark for being upset when I considered the atmosphere at Oriel College. It would have tried the patience of a saint. At Oriel, the lads rule. Rowing successes of the Oriel boats are followed by a ritual boat-burning, and then a bacchanalian "bump-supper," held in Hall at the College's expense. The alcohol flows freely; victorious crews throw a bit of food, stomp on the tables, and sing obscene songs: "At the end of the day, Oriel men will be on top, and Oriel women will be spreading their legs." It is traditional to roast one's friends by singing: "John's a horse's ass, he is a horse's penis, he sucks a horse's penis . . ." Another celebratory song of the Oriel crews went like this:

> We're quick at the catch, and quicker at the snatch
> We're fast at the wind, we take them from behind
> When we come in a rush we know we'll be in the bush
> We like to win and we like to stuff it in

164

Even if it's choppy we know we won't go floppy
When we come up the stream all the women start to cream
You can see from our ratio we really like fellatio!

Mark and his Assistant Dean, an English graduate student called Anne, tried to convince the College that it was their responsibility to tell the high-spirited rowers that such drunken, sexually threatening antics were inappropriate at college-wide functions. But the Oriel powers-that-be felt that boys will be boys. So the money of British taxpayers continues to fund such dinners.

The day after the first regatta of the year, Mark and Anne came by for coffee. "What really appalled me at last night's celebratory dinner," said Mark, "was that you had all these drunken obscenities, you had broken bottles, food all over the floor, people walking on the tables. And in the mean time, you have these *children*—local fifteen- and sixteen-year-olds—who are serving the food and drink and mopping up the mess. What on earth must they think?"

"Charles Dickens, where are you when we need you?" I asked.

"It's true," said Mark. "These little waifs from Blackbird Leys cleaning up after these drunken louts. And this isn't a private club or anything—this is a college subsidized in large part by the British taxpayers."

I asked Anne how widespread such behavior was amongst Oxford undergraduates.

"Pretty widespread," she answered. "I was at New College, and I was a totally unreconstructed undergraduate myself. I honestly couldn't see anything wrong with the fact that I couldn't leave my room during certain hours because the boys were playing hockey in the halls using piles of stolen women's underwear as goals. It was only when a woman was sexually assaulted in College that I stopped to think about what sort of atmosphere was created by that behavior."

Anne and Mark did their best to foster a more civilized and mutually respectful atmosphere at Oriel, but it was a lost cause. What can you really do, at a place where college students have to be warned, in writing, not to engage in acts of violence or vandalism to celebrate rowing successes? Shouldn't that go without saying? I don't think Oxford, home of lost causes as it once was, deserved Anne and Mark.

"When I got to Oxford, I assumed that I would go straight to law school after I finished, or maybe go into business, and eventually be a big success and make a lot of money," Mark told me. "That's what everyone in my family has always done, and that's what I was encouraged to do, as a child. But being here has made me reconsider a lot of my assumptions. That privileged world was something I used to take for granted and admire. But now I think I want to do something different."

"Like what?" I asked.

"Go into educational policy, maybe, or psychology. The combination of obnoxiousness and neediness that I see in undergraduates every day has shaken me up a lot."

After a number of parties given by all-male drinking societies, I concluded that men are a pretty foolish lot. Going out regularly, wearing black tie, and getting drunk enough to vomit isn't that appealing; I couldn't imagine women voluntarily doing anything similar. A male acquaintance once told me a story about a drunken evening. I won't repeat it in detail here; but suffice it to say that it involved a bucket placed in the middle of a table, to collect the quantities of vomit spewed up by partying hockey players. I've told this story to many men, all of whom profess to find it amusing. I've also told this story to many women, all of whom look revolted and ask me why I had to share that story with them.

But my relatively high opinion of the maturity of female Oxford students was shattered when I heard about the Misdemeanours. The Misdemeanours is a Christ Church drinking society for women. It was the female equivalent of the Nondescripts, and those in the know called it "Misdies," to match "Nondies." Peggy, my American friend who rowed for the women's first VIII, was invited to become a member.

Americans don't usually make it into anything approaching the Oxford social élite, but Peggy was an exception to this rule, as to virtually every other rule. Peggy went everywhere and did everything. She was a Rhodes Scholar from Dartmouth College. Her mother was black, and her father was a prominent white Atlanta lawyer. Peggy managed to be active both in numerous organizations for African-American women and in the Daughters of the Confederacy, without any apparent cognitive dissonance. She was bossy, friendly, and astonishingly ambitious: during my first year she managed to befriend the Vice-Chancellor of Oxford, get invited to a Thanksgiving bash hosted by the Commander of NATO Forces in Europe, and have dinner with the Prince of Wales. She seemed to be a close friend of numerous American university presidents. Well-known corporate raiders sent her postcards. She had several prestigious job offers and was deferred at two excellent American medical schools. She was likeable, energetic, and bubbling over with ideas and opinions, and she frequently began sentences with the statement, "When I'm rich and famous someday—and I *will* be rich and famous someday—this is what I'm going to do." She would say this with a merry laugh, but no one ever doubted that she was serious, or that she would, eventually, become rich and famous.

I rarely saw Peggy for more than a few minutes at a time; she was always rushing off to her next activity. People spent a lot of time wondering how she managed to be so successful. I don't know, but I think it was her basic kind-heartedness and good humor, despite her bluster. She also had ability to enter into superficial but vaguely conspiratorial relationships with people, managing always to convey the impression that you were the very person she really wanted to talk to, if only she didn't have to run off: "I would just *love* to talk to you more, but I *really* have to go. But let's *definitely* get together and really *talk,* soon! Bye! Got to run!"

Peggy cornered me at the Christ Church winter ball. She was encased in a tight green satin dress. "Rosa!" she exclaimed. "I have *got* to talk to you!"

"Hi, Peggy. What's up?"

She edged close to me, and hissed, "You won't *believe* what happened at a party the other night."

"What party?"

"*Shh!* I really shouldn't say."

I shrugged. I knew that with a build-up like this, Peggy might or might not actually tell me anything. "Well, if it's private, maybe you shouldn't tell me."

"It was *really* incredible. You won't believe it. I mean, I am twenty-four *years old!* I just couldn't believe it."

"Mmm-hmm." I glanced around the room. I strongly suspected that Peggy was not really going to tell me anything.

But I was wrong. Perhaps because she saw my attention wander, Peggy said, "It was at the Misdemeanours party. Really decadent!" She laughed, then followed my gaze around the room, and added irrelevantly, "You know there are just *no* good-looking men here. I would settle down if I could, but there are just *no* good men."

"So what was the party like?"

"Do you think my dress looks OK? You see, my problem is that I—" she lowered her voice still further— "I have *a big bust.* I'm afraid my dress is too tight."

"You look fine. Tell me about the party."

"I *mean* that about settling down. *You* know—*tick tick tick!*"

"*What?*"

"Sometimes I hear that *biological clock!*"

"Peggy—" I rolled my eyes. "You've got a few years yet."

"Oh, I'm only kidding. I'm a spring chicken really."

Finally, after a number of further detours, Peggy got back to the Misdemeanours. She swore me to silence ("I'm only telling this to *you*, Rosa," she said disingenuously). This is what she told me:

The Misdemeanours had a party to which all members were required to bring a male guest. Drinks were served, and after everyone was properly sloshed, the games began. In one game, the names of barnyard animals were written on slips of paper. Two slips were marked "cow", two "pig", and so on. Then slips were distributed randomly to women and to men—i.e. there was a male cow and a female cow, a male pig and a female pig. The lights were then turned out and everyone got down on all fours and began to crawl around, making the noise of their assigned animal. Moo, oink. The object of the game was to locate one's counterpart of the opposite sex, and then, as Peggy put it, to "snog".

Another game involved the men lying flat on their backs on the floor. The lights out, the women, barefoot, would run around the room. The men would attempt to tackle a woman dashing by, and to pull her down to the floor. And snog. An amusing rape-simulation game.

For once, Peggy had me hooked. I gaped at her. "You're not serious," I said. "Peggy, that was the kind of game I played when I was thirteen. Only we were more innocent. We didn't snog. We exchanged chaste kisses. Like in spin the bottle. Don't tell me this was done by twenty-year-olds. Don't tell me that a group of *women* thought this up."

By this time, though, Peggy was obviously thinking ahead to her next activity. "Rosa, I *agree completely*. I felt *very* uncomfortable, so I left. And I *would* really like to talk about this more with you, because it's *very* interesting and I've *really* enjoyed our chat, but it's going to have to be some other *time*. I really *have* to go talk to Ellen now." And she went racing off.

She left me flabbergasted. I found it hard to believe that college students couldn't think of better forms of social interaction. But her story fit well with what I had observed myself: most college bops were followed the next day by a good deal of gossip about who had drunkenly snogged whom the previous night. "She snogged three people! And did you see Luke with Anne?" A few undergraduates seemed to be involved in long-term relationships, but for many students, social life centered around alcohol, snogging, and the occasional two-week affair.

And the double standard lived and thrived: one unfortunate woman was said to have "snogged" five people at a boat club bop. Men who snogged five women were clapped on the back and congratulated by their mates, but poor Sarah was treated to a "joking" paragraph in the College gossip sheet, which was distributed to all rooms a few days later: "Sarah the Queen of Boats was recently diagnosed with a serious venereal disease. All male rowers are advised to have themselves tested at the Radcliffe Infirmary." In the US, this would have qualified as sexual harassment. At Christ Church, it just provoked sniggers from the men, and anxious sympathy from most women—they knew that with one misstep, it could be their name next time around.

Not that I never behaved like this myself. I did—when I was fourteen or fifteen. High-school social life centered around illicit beer parties and gossip about who was fooling around with whom in the bushes. This is what happens when people discover the opposite sex for the very first time. But by the time I got to college, I and most other people had outgrown this stage. Certainly, we drank beer and fooled around—but in the age of AIDS, "responsibility," "commitment," "friendship," and "mutual respect" were our bywords. At least in theory. If anything, my generation of college students was criticized by our parents' generation (in college in the 60s) for being too serious, too pragmatic, too adult too soon.

Some might argue that while the above may be true of most students at top universities like Harvard and Yale, it is certainly not true of many less academically élite American universities. This may be so; some universities in the US are notorious for beer swilling fraternity-dominated social life. But I think it's reasonable to compare Oxford to the academically *best* universities in America, not the average universities. After all, Oxford views itself as certainly the best university in Britain, and possibly the best university in the world. It should therefore have to stand comparison with the best universities of other countries.

Why, then, were the brightest young minds in England engaged in such juvenile forms of decadence? I asked my friend Rob. He shrugged. "I did that myself as an undergraduate. You have to remember that the average Oxford undergraduate, particularly at a place like Christ Church, has been to a single-sex boarding school. Most undergraduates have never before had the chance to interact socially with their peers of the opposite sex, and they've never really been allowed to drink before. So they get here and they go crazy. It's like a feeding frenzy. They just haven't yet learned to relate to one another in a relaxed and mature way. Almost all Americans go to coeducational schools, so they have a head start on the English when it comes to social maturity. English undergraduates are usually more articulate than American undergraduates, but a lot less socially mature."

The frantic pace of undergraduate social life seemed far removed from life in St. Aldate's Quad, among the graduates. Many graduates were involved in a serious relationship, and parties tended to be a lot more sedate. But St. Aldate's had one thing in common with the rest of Christ Church, and that was its total lack of privacy. Everyone in the quad was aware of one's comings and goings, and of the comings and goings of all frequent visitors.

In early December I started going out with Jerome. Since he lived in the next staircase over, I ran into him a lot when I visited Jonah or went to use the pay phone. But I had never spent much time with him. If anything, Jerome usually seemed eager to keep our conversations short. I was bewildered by his behavior—he seemed friendly, but he often terminated conversations abruptly.

One night I went to a party given by Frank, the law student I had met at Cardinals. Jerome was there, as were a number of other students reading law at Christ Church. Frank was a star rower, and his walls were covered with "blades," or oars, he had won with the Christ Church first VIII.

After a while, Jerome drifted over. "Did you have a nice time when your boyfriend visited?" he asked.

"Boyfriend?" I said blankly.

"That tall guy. Isn't he your boyfriend?"

"Oh . . ." I knew what Jerome meant. My former boyfriend had visited the week before. We were trying to figure out if we should go out again. We hadn't really made any progress.

"Sort of," I told Jerome. "His visit was a bit difficult."

"Oh," he said.

We walked for a while longer, and I suggested we have tea sometime. He agreed. Tea turned into a drink, and the following week he invited me to dinner.

I was nervous. Before getting to Oxford, I had been going out with one man for two years. My dating skills were rusty. I tried on ten outfits before finally settling on black jeans and a purple velvet shirt. As soon as Jerome came by, I decided that this outfit was a disaster. Luckily, Jerome didn't seem to notice my self-consciousness, and our dinner was a success. We had a slightly tipsy four-hour conversation about our families, politics, favorite books, ambitions.

After dinner, we walked back to St. Aldate's. When we reached the quad, awkwardness set in. We giggled a bit and looked at our watches. Finally, I said, "If you'd like to come up, I can give you some tea."

"That's a good idea," Jerome said with relief.

But once the tea was made, the awkwardness returned. Jerome paced around, picking up books, reading a sentence at random, and putting them down again. I told inane stories. I didn't want him to leave. Occasionally our eyes met, and we laughed anxiously. We both paced back and forth, too nervous to sit still.

"How tall are you?" I asked. It was 2 a.m. No progress had been made in any direction.

"Six feet," he told me. "How tall are you?"

"Five foot five."

"Really? Let me see." He walked towards me and I spun around with my back to him. I'm not sure why, but I think I had some idea that my height could be better seen from behind. I wasn't thinking straight.

It seemed to me then that there was a long pause. Finally Jerome said softly, "Turn around."

I did, and he put his arms around me and pressed his forehead to mine.

"You know," he said, "I think you're really only five four and three-fourths."

The next day, I said, "Jerome, for a long time I thought maybe you didn't like me. You always seemed eager to end our conversations."

He shrugged. "No . . . but I thought you had a boyfriend. I thought there was no point getting to know you well. But when I spoke to you at Frank's party, I realized I had been wrong."

"So here we are."

"Here we are."

At first things were very tentative between us. I wasn't sure that I wanted to get into another serious relationship, particularly not with a man who would probably want to go off and live in South Africa at some point. Jerome had similar doubts, and by unspoken agreement we tried to keep our new relationship quiet.

This was not easy. Oxford is a small place; the second time Jerome and I went out to dinner together we ran into four people we knew on the way, all of whom chortled and said, "Oh ho, a date!" Jerome and I had many mutual friends, and within a few days everyone seemed at least to suspect something. When we went into Hall for dinner, we were greeted with winks and nudges. I got a note from Mark, decorated with little holly leaves, asking, "Is it true that you and Jerome are having a *passionate affair?*" Various friends took to popping round in the evenings, just to check up on us. It was like living in a city full of chaperones.

The vacation was about to begin, and although I was sorry to leave Jerome, I was glad to be escaping the hothouse atmosphere of Christ Church.

The shops were filled with Christmas music by now. I turned down an invitation to an undergraduate Christmas party ("Get Down in Santa's Grotto—Horny Reindeer—Lizzers says 'If you're early I'll snog you'— Timmers says 'Get slayed in my sleigh.'"). I went to a lovely carol service in the cathedral, and to the special Christmas dinner in Hall. I ended up sitting next to the Chaplain. We didn't have much to talk about, so we talked about the food, which, Christmas or no, was as terrible as ever. There was just more of it than usual. The nice thing was that the dessert came with fresh cream. The Chaplain explained that the cows in the Meadows had been milked to provide the cream. This isn't as bad as what happens at Magdalen College—Magdalen keeps deer in its parks. The deer are very tame through being fed by tourists. Half of them are albino, through generations of deer in-breeding. When the parks become over-populated with deer, some are shot and eaten at High Table. The Chaplain told me an apocryphal story he had once heard about an American student, who, upon hearing this, said, "And when the High Table gets too crowded, do they shoot some dons and feed them to the deer?"

No such luck, I thought.

A HIATUS

AND THEN IT was vacation.

That's another amazing thing about Oxford. Most of the year is vacation. There are three eight-week terms, separated by a six-week vacation at Christmas, a six-week vacation at Easter, and a three-month summer holiday. The American academic year is about two months longer; Harvard's Christmas break lasted less than two weeks. I didn't know what to do with six weeks off. It was too short a time to get a job, but too long of a time to do nothing. In theory, I think, the idea was that I would remain in Oxford and read all about European Politics. But I knew no one who planned to stay. And I wasn't sure that I could stand Oxford for even five minutes longer than necessary.

I spent my winter vacation in a state of mild misery and near total confusion. Everyone I met said, "So how's Oxford? I envy you! You must be having such a wonderful, wonderful experience!" After trying several times, and failing, to explain that I was disappointed by Oxford, I gave up; people refused to believe me. When I said, "Well, actually, Oxford's not all it's made out to be," they just thought I was being modest. Finally I just started to provide the expected answer: yes, absolutely, Oxford was wonderful, yes, I just *love* those English accents, so sophisticated!

Feeling guilty about lying, I retreated to the Career Services Office at Harvard, and spent a long time thinking about working for political campaigns. I thought about never going back to Oxford. I thought about going back but leaving at the end of the year.

Jerome was in South Africa with his family. I didn't know his telephone number. I didn't know if he would still want to go out with me when the six-week vacation was over. I didn't know if I would want to go out with him. I didn't know what to do with my life.

I spent Christmas with my family in Key West, Florida. I thought of becoming a social drop-out and living forever on the beaches of Key West. I would set up a stand at Mallory Pier and sell hand-painted T-shirts to Japanese tourists.

I talked to a lot of College friends and caught up on what my non-Oxford peers were doing. One guy I knew had been elected mayor of a town of ninety thousand people. Another guy had had a play produced on Broadway. A friend in law school had gotten accepted as clerk for a Supreme Court judge. Another friend had written a novel.

I began to suspect that I was mentally retarded. Everyone else seemed to be wildly happy and successful, and what did I have to show? Nothing. "Well, I've really read a lot of good fiction this year, and I actually learned how to cook pork chops."

I moped from room to room. My parents shook their heads in exasperation.

Most things seemed the same when I got back to Oxford. Shortly before the vacation, a construction crew had begun to tear up St. Aldate's. When I returned, the street was still torn up. Every day the construction crew tore up some bits of pavement. The next day they replaced the same bits of pavement, for no apparent reason. They used pneumatic drills beginning at 7 a.m., and the dust generated came through my window and made me cough. Everything in my room became coated by a fine layer of silt.

My seminars were still frustrating. Tina the Veg Girl still shoveled down plates of raw carrots in Hall and still took everyone else's salad portions. Colin the Boatie still wore nothing but a splash jacket. Andrew Blake still had a very big head. As for my flatmates, Peter wanted to talk about the dismal weather and people he had encountered while visiting relatives in Derbyshire. And Ian was as furtive as ever. He made me think of a Barbara Pym character in war-time London.

I had become very curious about Ian. This was because I had noticed that he didn't keep his butter in the fridge. Instead, he kept it in a china dish, which he locked inside a cabinet. I thought this was odd. I worried that his butter would go rancid. And I thought locking the cabinet was sort of paranoid. I wasn't going to steal his rancid butter. But the truly odd thing was that while he did not refrigerate the butter itself, he did refrigerate empty foil butter wrappers. Every time I took my butter out (of the fridge, where I very sensibly kept it), two or three greasy foil butter wrappers fluttered to the floor. I squeamishly replaced them. This became a compelling mystery. Why did Ian save butter wrappers? Why keep them in the fridge, when the actual butter was in the cabinet? For some reason, perhaps because Ian seemed so like a war orphan, furtive and hungry at a time of rationing, I envisioned him hoarding bits of foil from the butter wrappers to send to munitions factories, in aid of the war effort.

I continued to go out with Jerome. That too made me feel a tiny bit fonder of Oxford. If Jerome was there, and he liked it, how bad could it be?

Jerome and I took long walks in the cold mist, to Port

Meadow, along the river, through the University Parks. Usually it was raining; we would walk until our shoes made squishing noises, then stop at pubs to dry off and have a snack. My memory of Oxford is in part a physical memory. When I think of those walks, I think of mist, of the smell of damp earth, the sound of gravel underfoot. Occasionally the sun would come out in the afternoon. Oxford is far enough north that there is never light directly overhead, and the long light caught treetops and spires dramatically. Sometimes I felt delirious with happiness. I knew that Jerome and I were going to have a difficult time if our relationship was going to last. We came from different cultures and, worse, different continents. But as we wandered along under our big black umbrellas, it wasn't hard to push such worries away. Oxford is a good place for romance.

Sort of. Or, as everyone said that year (thanks to *Wayne's World*), "*Not.*" The only difficulty was that the scout who cleaned Jerome's staircase was very fond of Jerome. She liked to come in and chat with him in the mornings. She never knocked at his door first, just bursting in. This was embarrassing; Jerome would leap up as we heard the dooknob turn, and position himself squarely in front of the door. ("No overnight guests." Most scouts didn't mind overlooking overnight guests if students were discreet, but as a general rule, scouts make it clear that if they actually *see* an overnight guest, they'll have to report it. Then, who knows? It's off to the dungeon . . .) I would cower in the closet, waiting the agonizingly long time it took the scout to inquire after Jerome's health and inform him of the symptoms of her younger nephew's bad case of flu. "I am like a mother to Jerome," she hissed warningly to me once when she saw me in the hall on my return from the shower.

I went to the Rhodes Ball with Jerome. This was a

relatively small and cheap affair, tickets going for a mere £40, instead of the £90 it cost to go to the Christ Church Ball, which was on the same night. But security was tight. Ticket purchasers had to send in photographs of themselves and their dates, and were issued small photo admission tickets. Perhaps the organizers of the ball thought that vast hordes would try to gate crash. I thought this was a bit overly optimistic: somehow I couldn't imagine all the people of Oxford not lucky enough to have a Rhodes Scholarship or date a Rhodes Scholar loitering furtively outside Rhodes House in the hopes of sneaking in. But possibly the Ball Committee asked for photos for security reasons. Rhodes Scholars, as a group, are not known for their modesty. A friend told me that the Rhodes Trust sends new American Rhodes Scholars to England on two separate planes—that way, even if one plane crashes or is hijacked, only half of the Rhodes Scholars will be in jeopardy.

Needless to say, in the end the ball organizers couldn't sell all the tickets. They had so many left over the week before the ball that they were forced to advertise amongst non-Rhodes. In an effort to minimize the disruption, they only invited Americans from one caste down, like those on Marshall Scholarships.

The ball took place in Rhodes House, lights dimmed for the occasion. The ill-chosen theme for the evening was "Arabian Nights;" this was indicated by the thick incense fumes swirling everywhere, the awful music, and the pita bread scattered around the tables. A large female Rhodes Scholar from Stanford unwisely chose to belly dance, much to the merriment of the crowd. After a while a guy who I'd known vaguely at Harvard approached me, ignoring Jerome, and suggested that we get married and breed a race of super children. I declined. After a while Jerome and I left.

We got back to Christ Church in time to run into people leaving the ball there. They didn't seem to have gotten their money's worth any more than we had; in fact, they were even less happy, as many of the events at the Christ Church ball had been outdoors. They informed us that free ice-cream wasn't worth much when the temperature was below freezing. The ball had been OK, they said, but hardly worth a hundred quid per ticket.

After the Ball, I got sick three times in a row. Each time, a head cold moved to my chest and settled in to stay. Maybe it was the long walk back from Rhodes House. Maybe it was the dust from the construction across the street. Each time, I went to the doctor. Each time, he listened to me cough, winced, and handed me a prescription for some antibiotics. (The National Health Service is just amazing, if you ask me. I mean, I'm sure it's not that great if you want a hip replacement or something. But if you have the flu, it's terrific. At home, each of those visits would have cost about $150. The antibiotics would have cost about $40 on top of that. The first time I got a prescription, the doctor actually apologized to me: "I'm afraid the prescription fee has just gone up," he said. "You'll have to pay £3.70 instead of £3.45." I giggled. Only £3.70?)

The third time I got sick I asked the doctor what could be wrong with me. I hadn't been sick so much in years. He glared at me as if I had touched upon a sore point.

"You are ill," he said, "because Oxford is a bog. A *bog!* Just look at those disgusting rivers."

"Oh!" I said. I wasn't sure of the medical accuracy of this theory.

"There are only two good universities in this country," the doctor continued, still glaring at me, "Oxford and Cambridge. And they are both—in *bogs!*"

PART FOUR

INSIGHT

Class, Hierarchy,
and Apathy

MY CONSTANT ILLNESS didn't help my singing voice. This was a shame, because the choir season, if there can be said to be such a thing, was heating up. We sang at a church service in Long Compton, a too cute to be true town in the Cotswolds. We sang at someone's wedding. We even planned to sing for Evensong again.

Then something happened which sent the choir into a flurry. The Chaplain, who had not previously been known for his radical ideas, came up with a suggestion. He thought that we should go sing at a church service in Blackbird Leys, and he communicated this suggestion to Jane and Patrick, the two undergraduates who coordinated the choir.

Blackbird Leys is a working-class part of Oxford. Shortly before I arrived at Oxford, it made the news as a locus of angry youth rioting. It was not a part of town that students frequented.

Jane resentfully informed the choir of the Chaplain's idea. "I don't know why," she said, "but he seems to think it would be good for us to go sing in Blackbird Leys."

There was a chorus of moans from the soprano section and irate noises from the basses. "Blackbird Leys! Why?"

"I really can't understand it," said Jane crossly. "He has some idea that it would be a positive community gesture."

"We'll get beaten up," complained a skinny male alto.

185

"I had a friend whose car was broken into there," added a tenor.

"Well," said Jane, "I don't like it either. But the Chaplain's rather keen on it so I don't see how we can say no."

"I bet they won't like it if we sing to them in Latin," whined a soprano with a nervous giggle.

"I hardly think that they would be able to appreciate it," agreed Patrick.

I was flabbergasted. "Are these people for real?" I asked Ellen, who also sung in the choir.

She shrugged. "Regrettably."

As an undergraduate, I had spent most of my non-class hours working on various community service projects. Not infrequently, that meant spending time in "bad" parts of Boston, at tenant meetings, hospitals, schools. The bad parts of Boston are a lot worse than the bad parts of Oxford. During the years I was in college, Boston alone had an annual homicide rate about ten times that of all Britain. I have no doubt at all that many middle-class undergraduates were frightened at the prospect of going into Roxbury and Dorchester, into neighborhoods infested with drugs, guns, and gangs. But most of the undergraduates I knew felt a healthy shame about admitting this, and readily agreed that any anti-student feeling in those poverty-stricken areas was understandable. We saw it as an obligation to try to build bridges with the community beyond the university, and to work with community organizations as much as possible.

We were very concerned that public service not be tinged with *noblesse oblige*. As college students, we had some particular skills and resources to offer, but the assumption was that we also had a lot to learn. We went into communities to put our skills at the disposal of those communities, not to tell people how to run their lives. If someone had suggested singing at a Roxbury church service, the only objections raised would have been from people who feared that such a move might seem condescending: "Hello, lesser mortals, this is your lucky Sunday. We've come to show you how we *educated* people sing hymns!"

But no one in the Christ Church choir raised this objection. The only worries people had were about getting beaten up and mocked, or about the folly of wasting our tuneful voices and Latin hymns on the ignorant masses. The Chaplain insisted, though, and one cold Sunday morning we found ourselves on a bus to Blackbird Leys. Looking around, I saw a sea of set faces and stiff upper lips. Several people ostentatiously transferred their wallets to inner pockets as we entered the church, as if the congregation might be full of pickpockets.

We were greeted warmly by the local vicar. The church was spacious, modern, and bright; light streamed through a skylight. On the walls children's artwork was displayed. A large sign said "peace" in several languages, including Hebrew, and a colorful mural behind the altar depicted a joyous multi-racial crowd following along after Christ. The crowd contained blacks, whites, Indian women in saris, Asian peasants in broad hats, Arabs in flowing robes. Christ himself was an indeterminate tan.

The mural was perhaps a bit optimistic, as the people who slowly filled the pews were mostly white. A few ancient black people also tottered in. Most of the people attending were over the age of forty, with a fair sprinkling of the wheelchair-bound elderly. They all beamed at us as we stood to one side, rehearsing.

As I have said, I am not ordinarily sentimental about religion. But I was enormously touched by the artwork and the smiles on the faces of the congregation. This was a church that genuinely seemed committed to breaking down barriers between different races and classes. They deserved better than to be sung to by a supercilious group of students who kept one hand on their wallets at all times.

Our singing received thunderous applause, and after the service we were given coffee and donuts. Many people thanked us for coming. Finally we left for the bus stop. It was very cold out, and we stood huddled and shivering. A strange shyness seemed to have come over the group. People surreptitiously put their wallets back in outer pockets.

"Well," said Jane brusquely. "I suppose that wasn't so bad."

There were some embarrassed murmurs. No, it was agreed. Blackbird Leys really hadn't been all that bad.

In America, class is a secret. Americans try to play down class, and become embarrassed if they are forced to acknowledge class differences. Many Americans insist that "class" is a meaningless concept: all there is is money, of which some people have more than others. But in England class differences, though far less profound than they used to be, are readily acknowledged by everyone.

I was continually surprised by the seriousness and lack of embarrassment with which people at Oxford spoke of class differences. I once heard an acquaintance describe another student as "the girl with the common accent." My friend Rob was amazed when I struck up a conversation with the young man behind the counter at the newsagents. "Bit of yob, wasn't he?" he said dismissively.

The upper class has little use for the working class and for those who consciously reject Oxford and all it represents—and, needless to say, most working-class and ordinary middle-class people have little use for the posh

Oxford swots, regarding Oxford as a bit of a joke—a not very funny and not very relevant joke. While I was in England, I met many people who had no connection to Oxford: a Kentish miner and his family, a London art student, an Islington rock musician, a graduate student/ taxi driver at the University of Sussex. Most of them greeted all mention of Oxford with a contemptuous roll of the eyes.

Of course, there are always some people who long for what they haven't got, even while the thing they don't have becomes in creasingly socially irrelevant. I was very surprised when an undergraduate told me that Owen, he of the Cardinals and silk scarf fame, had actually gone to a comprehensive school in Manchester. I had started coxing for a men's boat in addition to rowing with a women's boat, and I found the members of my crew an invaluable source of gossip.

"Owen tells people he went to Harrow," said Matt, my informant, as we walked to the boathouse. "But really his father's a lorry driver."

"*Really?*" Owen had certainly managed to convince me that he was the inheritor of centuries of snobbish Oxford tradition.

"Yes. The stupid thing is," said Matt, "that no one would care if he was honest. You know James Turner and Bert Cheever? They both went to the same school Owen went to, and everyone likes them."

But then he more or less contradicted himself. "Anyway, although Owen is a good actor, if you put him up next to the genuine upper-class article, like Sebastian Blackstone, it's easy to see who's the real thing. Anyone could tell the difference. Owen just can't cut it."

Yes: no one might *care* if Owen admitted his working-class roots. But, as Matt said, everyone at Christ Church would *notice*, except ignorant Americans like me, and put

Owen into a little box in their brains: "Working Class but Nice." Why not just "Nice"? I felt sorry for Owen, of whom I was rather fond. Despite his affectations, Owen was unfailingly interested, cheerful, and friendly, and continued to be friendly to me despite the fact that I teased him whenever he made some particularly élitist remark. Hearing that Owen himself was fighting to be accepted by a world from which he felt excluded made me understand his posing a little more.

No, one couldn't ever detach oneself from one's origins. This was why I was glad to be an American, outside of the English class system by birth. At Oxford—certainly at Christ Church—those within the class system were constantly being judged, and not infrequently found lacking.

It could be argued that the English have a healthier attitude towards class than do Americans. At least the English are honest enough to admit their fears and their snobbishness. Deep down, Americans know that class differences exist—but they deny it, even to themselves. Still, America remains a more egalitarian country. Lines between classes are blurrier and more flexible; the national myth of social mobility is more than just a myth. And it seems to me that Americans make more effort than do upper-middle-class English people to break down hierarchies of all sorts.

Certainly, few students at Oxford seemed interested in working to eradicate class differences. Admittedly, Christ Church is probably Oxford's most self-consciously conservative college. Things are slightly better, I'm told, at colleges like Balliol and Wadham. But even outside of Christ Church, public service, so widespread and institutionalized at American universities, was rare. Few Oxford students seemed to involve themselves in community activities other than the occasional charity drive. The

Oxford Student, a student government publication, admits that "the record of Oxford students for providing social services has long been something of an embarrassment" when compared even to other British universities. One of the few Oxford-based tutoring programs for local children had been founded by my American friend, Mark.

When I was an undergraduate, about two-thirds of my fellow students were involved in some form of community service; the public service organization was by far the largest student group on campus. One year, seventy percent of students signed a petition supporting the union drive among Harvard's clerical and technical workers. Somehow I couldn't imagine something similar happening at the Oxford of 1992. Political action, common even at a moderate American university like Harvard, was rare; Oxford, after twelve years of Tory government, seemed mired in apathy and indifference.

I had been moved by the multi-racial crowd depicted in the mural at the Blackbird Leys church. It was the first time I had seen something like that at Oxford. The Town/Gown split can hardly be overstated; back in central Oxford, among the spires and pristine quads, no one points out that the portraits on the walls are all of white men, just as few people point out that the students in the colleges are mostly white and mostly male. At that small community church, in Blackbird Leys, they seemed at least to realize that there might be some other, better way to organize a society. Yes, it was unsophisticated, perhaps—but it was honest and earnest and hopeful.

This, to some extent, is cultural difference between England and America. Americans prize earnestness. Recall our national heroes: George Washington saying, "Father, I cannot tell a lie;" Horatio Alger's innumerable poor boys succeeding by dint of hard work and honest ambition. Americans believe in good and evil, and we are charmed by lack of sophistication and naïvety. "Hey there! How are you?" and "You have a nice day now!" are the hallmarks of our national culture. I'm OK, you're OK. Let's all join hands for a moments here, folks.

Try saying "You have a real nice day now!" to an upper-class Oxford type. One can imagine the sneer of horror. Within University circles, such a display of naïve hopefulness as the Blackbird Leys mural would be frowned upon as embarrassing and in poor taste. How unsophisticated! How terribly *naff*! Only the lower classes show their emotions and enthusiasms in such a vulgar way!

Three cheers for the lower classes, then. Most of the Oxford students I met made it clear from their behavior that they prized wit over earnestness. Passion is to be avoided; intellectual and political passions are sources of shame, not pride, and wise students hide all such passions from their peers.

I remember one particular article in an Oxford student newspaper. It was about life in an Oxford emergency homeless shelter, written by a young man who did volunteer work there. I have worked in shelters myself, and I know how difficult such work can be. It can be frustrating and shocking, and heart-breaking. But although I am sure the author of this article was a decent, kind young man, possessing a normal share of human empathy, you'd never have known it from what he wrote. From the first paragraph:

Doody is typical of Oxford's more senior homeless people, his two shifty sidekicks never far away, in anticipation of their colleague's acquiring enough money for their next bottle of cheap sherry. Would that they were so supervisory at bath-times. Alas not. The task instead falls to one of the staff at

Oxford Night Shelter . . . If ever a man deserved
recognition in the Honours List, it is the misfortunate
chap who has to bath Doody [*sic*]. For he is, without a doubt, the single smelliest creature I have
ever encountered. A boatie's armpit is fresh by
comparison . . .

Hell, yes, let's all have a good chuckle at the expense
of the homeless. For after all, as the author of this article
uproariously concludes, volunteering in a shelter is "certainly the best night's entertainment in Oxford." When I
finished reading this article, I was nearly speechless with
anger and disgust. A homeless shelter is a place filled with
people, not zoo animals. The homeless are not living on
the streets for our amusement. They are there because
something—alcoholism, mental illness, long-term unem-
ployment—has gone tragically wrong with their lives.

As my anger faded, I began to feel sorry for the author
of the article. What sort of culture makes talented, fortunate young people feel that they should be ashamed of their
desire to do some good for society? The tone taken in that
article was not exceptional; instead, it was typical of nearly
all student articles on "serious" subjects. Student writers
seemed to feel that they had to somehow "make up" for
their gaucheness in raising a serious subject. Adopting a
snide tone was the technique most writers chose. The
subtext of the article on homelessness was about fear: fear
of being mocked, fear of being seen as a "wet," fear of not
being one of the lads.

I felt sympathetic towards the young man struggling
to find a socially acceptable way to talk about his work
with Oxford's homeless population. The fact that he
bothered to work in a shelter at all is testimony to a
relatively unusual generosity of spirit. But my feeling of
disgust remained; I hope that if he reads over his article

some day many years in the future, he will have the good grace to be ashamed. (I was glad to note, over the following weeks, that I was not the only person offended by the tone of this article; several undergraduates wrote into the *Oxford Student* to complain.)

This upper-middle-class British fear of showing undue interest or passion is also evident in the attitude of most undergraduates towards academic work. Once on the way to Gatwick Airport, I overheard two young American men talking. From their conversation, I learned that they were students in Stanford University's Oxford program. They were sturdy and athletic looking; they wore jeans and baseball caps. They were asking each other about their academic interests. One said, "Yeah, well, I'm really looking forward to next term. There are a bunch of really cool courses in the history department that I want to take." I thought to myself: somehow that is a uniquely American thing to say.

I have never heard Oxford undergraduates speak of academic work to their peers with the same serious (if inarticulate) interest displayed by the young man from Stanford. American friends at other colleges said the same thing. When I was an undergraduate, dining hall conversations were frequently about work: "God, I'm writing this term paper on Kant, it's pretty neat, but some of the stuff he says is *so* ridiculous, I mean, he says—" Or politics: "How can you *possibly* say that the SALT II treaty was unimportant? Why, it was obviously the most *crucial* moment in arms control history!" This can be irritating, of course, particularly as much of it is mere posturing— but I think the sense of enthusiasm is genuine, if the expertise is often sham.

Mike, an English friend of mine who had done his

undergraduate work at Harvard, related a telling anecdote. His parents had flown from England to visit him during his senior year. They took him and his roommates out to dinner at one of Harvard Square's many Chinese restaurants. After the meal, his mother wondered out loud: "Why do you think it is that there are so many Chinese restaurants around Boston?" It was the sort of idle, not to be taken seriously question that would evoke, in Oxford circles, a wise "Hmm . . ." from listeners, or perhaps a jest, followed by a rapid change of subject. But all five American roommates (none of them of Chinese ancestry, none of them experts on Boston immigration patterns) simultaneously burst out with theories:

"Well, when you consider that there was probably a surge of immigration here because New York was already over-saturated with Chinese restaurants—"

"It could be that Chinese food is cheap and students can afford it, and Boston is a college town—"

"It's not that there are so many *Chinese* restaurants. There are so many of *all* kinds of restaurant, and that may be because—"

And so on. Mike's parents burst out laughing. "This typical of you Americans," they told his roommates. "You always need to have an opinion about everything, even things that you know nothing about."

There was a sequel to this episode. Mike, in Oxford to do graduate work, told this story to a group of friends, some English, some American. When he had finished speaking, there was laughter, somewhat sheepish on the Americans' part. Then there was a short silence. And then, unable to keep quiet anymore, all the Americans present burst into—guess what?—enthusiastic and ignorant explanations about just why there were so many Chinese restaurants in Boston.

I blushed when Mike told me this story. It's true:

sometimes you have to actually gag young, educated Americans to make them shut up. As every upper-middle-class English person will testify with a roll of the eyes, Americans talk too much, about everything. We talk about our problems. We talk about our pets and our parents and our love lives. We talk about the books we're reading. We talk about politics and restaurants. We love a good argument. It can be wearying, self-centered and intrusive. But it's evidence of the fact that young Americans expect there to be answers, and expect to find those answers. And they expect their opinions to be respected.

In *Zuleika Dobson,* Max Beerbohm calls Oxford "that lotus-land which saps the will-power, the power of action . . . it gives, above all, that . . . suavity of manner which comes from a conviction that nothing matters." Simon Schama, who taught at Oxford but has since gone on to join Harvard's history department, seems to agree; he attributes the difference in intellectual attitudes between Americans and the British to the British devotion to irony: "Irony is an almost mandatory part of the British education. There's almost no irony in American education. American students believe there's an answer to everything. British students believe there are no answers to anything. This prepares the British student to be indifferent to anything other than having a good time." Work is a chore; it isn't cool to say that it actually *interests* you. Don't question, don't assert, don't argue. The stiff upper lip reigns. If you can't manage effortless superiority, go for irony, juvenile pranks, and black tie mediocrity instead.

But I don't think Schama's explanation goes far enough. Thomas de Quincey was more blunt than Schama or Beerbohm. He found his contemporaries at Oxford to be "juvenile, unintellectual, and commonplace." At Oxford, for the most part students are treated like children. They respond like sulky adolescents, putting on an

"I'm too cool to care" pose. Undergraduates plan elaborate practical jokes to relieve the boredom of tutorials. David Segal, now an editor at the *Washington Monthly*, recalls a British undergraduate friend's technique: her tutor appeared so uninterested in her essays that she tested him by randomly inserting the word "ferret" at inappropriate times in essays. He didn't appear to notice. She began liberally to sprinkle "ferret" through her essays until her sentences were completely meaningless: "The problem ferret is that the Romantics ferret ferret could not countenance ferret . . .' Her tutor still didn't comment.

Most of the undergraduates I spoke to seemed to view deans and tutors with the same mixture of resentment and indifference felt by high-school students towards their teachers. And like high-school students, Oxford students rarely try to change anything about their environment, instead assuming that it's hopeless. They tolerate it because they also assume that it's temporary—in three years, they'll be gone. A poem by Louis MacNeice expresses this sense of hopelessness and resignation well:

> . . . *certainly it was fun while it lasted* . . .
> *But in case you should think my education was wasted*
> > *I hasten to explain*
> *That having once been to the University of Oxford*
> > *You can never really again*
> *Believe anything that anyone says and that of course is an asset*
> > *In a world like ours;*
> *Why bother to water a garden*
> > *That is planted with paper flowers?*

I remembered my surprise, in the first term, at my classmate Gavin's response to our mutinous complaints about European Politics. "That's just the way it is here," he had explained, not without regret. "You just have to get used to it." As an Oxford undergraduate, Gavin had already learned this lesson. Be deferential. Don't complain, but don't reward those in power with any enthusiasm.

This tradition of deference grated on me. The assumption at Oxford seemed to be that the world should be taken as it is. Class differences exist and can never be entirely over-ridden. Power differences exist. But if you are a good boy or girl and obey, then maybe someday you will be on top of the heap yourself. You can make people put on gowns in order to come and see you. And that is the most that one can hope for from life.

I was used to something different. At most American universities, students are treated more respectfully. Too respectfully, many Oxford dons would assert. When I was an undergraduate, for instance, students were encouraged to critique courses; every term, students fill out course evaluation forms, which are analyzed and compiled by a student office funded by the University. The results are published, and faculty members frequently change their teaching methods in response to student comments. Administrators hold "round-table discussions" with students to evaluate academic and disciplinary policies. Needless to say, student input is sometimes ignored—but at least lip service is paid to the idea that students should *have* some input. In the US, students generally call tutors and seminar leaders by their first names. At Oxford, a common complaint among Americans was about the difficulty in establishing collegial relationships with faculty members. Christ Church's rule about wearing gowns when consulting the Censor would not have lasted five minutes at Harvard—it would have been rightly ridiculed as the exercise of power for power's sake.

As American universities go, Harvard is considered

alienating and hierarchical. But as another Harvard alumnus commented after a year at Oxford, Oxford makes Harvard look radically egalitarian. This same alumnus recalled a joke about Oxford life that rang true for him: A student asks a don a question. The don draws himself up huffily, replying, "If you have to ask, it's obvious that you don't know," and stomps off.

That rang true for me as well. As an undergraduate, I was active in student politics and spent much of my time in disputes with the administration. But for the most part I was always taken seriously by professors and deans. I may be viewing things through the rosy lens of hindsight, but I recall Harvard as a place characterized by an essential community of interest between students, administrators, and faculty members. The message from those with power to the students was: this university belongs to all of us. We are older and probably wiser, but essentially we are all equals; someday you will take our places. In anticipation of that, we will treat you respectfully.

At Harvard I was taken seriously when I was a callow eighteen-year-old undergraduate. Arriving at Oxford four years later, with a bachelor's degree and a good deal of work experience behind me, I was treated like a child. Questions and complaints were greeted with the same indifference. At best, that indifference was polite; at worst, it was extremely rude. If you have to ask, it's obvious that you don't know.

And naturally, we all tend to act as we are expected to act. At Harvard, students behaved rather well. Treated respectfully by the authorities, students rewarded those authorities with respect, and generally were respectful of their peers as well. To the unsympathetic eye, I am sure that we often seemed ridiculous. We took ourselves so seriously. We held meetings, debated issues that really had little to do with us, passed resolutions, organized protests. We debated curriculum changes with a degree of passion usually reserved for major world events.

At Oxford, treated like children, most students respond in one of two ways. They act either like humble children or like resentful children. I don't say this condescendingly, because in many ways I behaved like a child myself for much of my first year at Oxford. And I behaved like a resentful child. When our academic mutiny failed, I didn't do anything constructive. I just gave up and sulked, and sought to avoid and ridicule my academic obligations.

REGRESSION

I TOOK ADVANTAGE of my constant illness to skip as many seminars as possible. David, Miranda, and I tried to introduce a note of juvenile jollity into seminars by playing little jokes. David and I had to do a presentation on corporatism for one seminar. We took the opportunity to illustrate our belief that most of the little graphs and illustrations in our books were meaningless. We created a lovely computerized "visual aid" for our presentation. It was based on a small drawing of a compass. It had beautiful arrows, little angle notations, delicate arcs. We argued, *à la* Montesquieu, that the degree of corporatism in a country was related to the country's longitudinal and latitudinal position. We "proved" this with the formular $E=Mc^2$ and some statistical gobbledygook. We drew handsome sea monsters and pirate ships in distant ocean quadrants of our drawing.

This was greeted with such glee by our classmates that, encouraged, we continued to pull similar stunts. (For those conscientious academics who are disturbed by this: yes, we did grudgingly do genuine presentations as well, after the laughter died down.) One presentation on the decline of the power of cabinet governments in Europe was introduced in the following way:

> *This cabinet is formed of gold*
> *And pearl and crystal shining bright,*

And within it opens into a world
And a little lovely moony night.
                Blake

Long, long ago, when men were men and dinosaurs stalked the earth, the Cabinets reigned supreme over Western Europe. In their glory days every Cabinet opened into a world and a little lovely moony night. Cabinets were decisive, powerful, brave: thus Henley, in lines learnt even today by children all the world over, wrote, "I am the master of my fate, I am the Cabinet of my soul." It seemed that the age of golden Cabinets would never end.

And so on, through to the decline of Cabinet government, expressed poetically in Walt Whitman's tear-jerker, "Oh Cabinet! My Cabinet! . . . I with mournful tread/Walk the deck my cabinet lies/fallen cold and dead."

Luckily, Hugh Ford was a kind-hearted man. He just thanked us for livening things up. He continued to treat me like a delinquent child for whom he could not quite give up hope, for sentimental reasons. He tactfully ignored the fact that I had taken to inserting childish little sentences into my essays: "In an effort to make this essay as dull as possible, I shall now enumerate the main points in favor of the recent EC budgetary changes . . ." Like the undergraduate who tried to use the word "ferret" as many times as possible in her essays, I had reached a point of such deadly boredom that I would do virtually anything to liven things up. Frequently I seemed to actually hear tiny whimpers of agony from inside my head, as my remaining brain cells expired one by one. Ferret Ferret.

Ford advised me to start thinking about what seminars I wanted to take as my elective seminars, and to start thinking about my thesis. I looked at the list of options and privately decided that I was interested in none of them. But I still hoped, with increasing desperation, that I would eventually be able to think of something interesting on which to do my thesis.

The previous term, Hugh Ford had promised that he would arrange for us to take language classes in order to improve our command of other EC languages. Nothing happened on this in Michaelmas term, but in Hilary term Ford announced that we could take either French or German. I already knew some French, so I decided to learn German, as did Miranda and Nelson. To my surprise, we were joined by one other student—my unhappy friend Justin. He was taking German in order to read Hegel in the original, he informed me. He was convinced that his supervisor was another obstructive obnoxious twit. He was sick of being told what to do, so he had decided to switch thesis topics, and supervisors, for the fourth time.

"Oh," I said dubiously. "Good. Well, I hope things work out this time. And Hegel in the original—that should be, uh, really interesting."

"Certainly," said Justin, looking at me suspiciously. "He's a genius. Unlike most people around here."

The classes were taught by a woman named Helke. She was German, and she resembled a repressed nineteenth-century school-marm. She was tall and stoop-shouldered, with the startled eyes and awkward grace of a gazelle. She was extremely well-meaning and very strict. She gave homework every day, and scolded us severely when we made errors or neglected our work. She treated us all like ten-year-olds. Naturally we all began to act like ten-year-olds.

Miranda, Nelson, and I regressed into Good Little Children. We giggled, did our homework, and shamelessly buttered up Helke. We obediently completed absurd assignments. We used verb flash cards. We drew our family trees. We cut out magazine photographs of our favorite foods. "*Schwester, Mutter, Tante,*" we caroled in unison. We acted out little scenes.

It was boring, but the homework was not terribly demanding—it only took up about an hour a week. Miranda and I liked Helke. We became teacher's pets. We skipped happily into class with Nelson and urged Helke to tell us stories about Germany.

But Justin, not surprisingly, didn't like Helke at all. He had been getting grimmer and grimmer since Christmas. He began to speak of leaving Oxford. He would get a job with the BBC and produce an exposé of Oxford's pretensions.

Miranda had little patience with his attitude. I had *no* patience—I was thoroughly fed up with the critical little notes from Justin that continued to arrive in the mail at regular intervals. Miranda and I were reasonably content to stay at Oxford ourselves. Miranda didn't like the course, but she wanted to work on Eastern European policy, so the M.Phil. would be useful to her. And like me, she had a boyfriend at Oxford: Tom. ("I told you it would last," she said reproachfully when she told me that she and Tom were moving in together.) Tom wanted to stay on for D.Phil., and Miranda wanted to stay in order to be with him. So she was determined to get along as happily as she could. So was I. I was working on this book, and I was willing to endure all sorts of idiocy for the sake of being able to tell a good tale at some later point. And spending time with Jerome had cheered me up unmeasurably. But Justin had no one to stay for, and no real project. "Revenge on Oxford" was not a very satisfying reason to stay.

The weather got colder and everything else stayed the same. Justin got more and more dour and depressed. Miranda and I regressed into teacher's pets; he regressed into a Problem Child.

In his sour state of mind, Helke was just too much. He resented her intrusive and imperious commands. He didn't want to be treated like a ten-year-old. He refused to make a family tree. He rarely did his homework. Every day in class, the first thing we did was go over the homework, taking turns answering the questions out loud. Miranda, Nelson and I excelled at this. Helke beamed proudly at us. Justin never did his homework, and would try to work out answers on the spot, at which, naturally, he rarely succeeded: German isn't something that just comes to you. Miranda and I tried to hold our notebooks open so that he could read our answers, but a stubborn pride kept him from using that means of keeping the peace. Helke would scold. "Justin, you are very bad! You must do your homework!" He would look down and mutter rudely to himself.

He was surly during exercises. "*Möchten Sie Weiner Schnitzel?*" Helke would ask cheerily.

"I hate weiner schnitzel," Justin would growl, in English.

Helke would scold him again. "You are being disruptive, Justin."

Justin began to attribute to her all of the negative traits of the German nation. He took to blaming her, only partly tongue in cheek, for the Holocaust. He would goose-step into class singing "*Deutschland, Deutschland über Alles*" under his breath. He pointedly perused articles on the rise of German neo-Nazi fascism during class. He saluted Helke with a straight arm when leaving. He loudly asserted that she didn't appreciate the finer points of Hegel.

Miranda and I remonstrated with him.

"Come on, Justin. She's doing her best, give her a break."

"That class is stupid," he said stubbornly. "She's a

proto-fascist. How the hell is learning to order *tea* in a restaurant supposed to help me read Hegel?"

We tried a different tack. "Justin, we know you can do the homework. Please do it, for our sake. It's embarrassing for us when Helke scolds you."

He laughed. "*Embarrassing?*" He was not at all chastened. "It's not my problem if you two are willing to sacrifice your intellectual development in order to keep the peace. Go ahead, do it—you'll make good politicians someday, you're so good at dissembling."

I rolled my eyes. "Cut the crap, Justin. I mean, just leave it—this isn't junior high, and Helke is not a bully."

He shrugged. "So? I'm more honest than you are. I can't take this place. You think it's doing Helke a favor to hide that from her? You know you think this class is idiotic, too. You're just better at being phoney."

It was impossible not to rise to the provocation. "Justin," I said furiously, "ever heard of politeness? Make the best of a bad bargain. You think that rudeness is a good quality, because it more *honestly* expresses your true feelings. Do you wonder why people react to you badly?"

"The truth hurts," he replied with satisfaction. But perhaps my words had had some small impact, because he went on: "Fine, have it your way. I'll be nice. I can be a politician too."

He did improve, temporarily. But within a week he was backsliding. One day he arrived late. Helke scolded him. "Sorry," he muttered. He hadn't done his homework. He made no attempt to participate in class. Helke scolded more. Finally Justin stood up.

"I'm sorry,' he said. "I have to leave now."

Helke blew up. "Justin, you come late, you don't participate, you leave in the middle. You are disrupting this class. Why do you come at all?"

"You're right, I'm really sorry. But this is just a waste of my time. I won't come again." He stormed out the door.

Miranda and I shrugged helplessly. "It's not you," we told Helke. "He's just having a really bad time right now."

"He feels terrible about it, though," I told Helke dishonestly.

Justin never came back to German. Miranda and I told him he should go apologize to Helke, but he said that he wouldn't. "Apologize? Let me tell you, everyone at this institution ought to be apologizing to *me*."

"Justin's so *angry*," Miranda told me privately. "I thought he'd get better after Christmas, but he's just gotten worse. When I talk to him, I either get furious at him or I start agreeing with him and I get depressed myself. Everything he says makes sense, in some slightly insane way. But you can only spend so long sitting around feeling sorry for yourself. Eventually you just have to do something, or cheer up anyway."

I agreed. Justin's behavior, extreme as it was, had held up a mirror to my own. Looking at him, I was forced to ask myself if my behavior was really different in kind, rather than in degree, from his. And I had to conclude that it wasn't. But just like Justin, I had responded to my sense of academic disappointment by resentfully giving up. I had deliberately tried not to think about my academic life. But by nature I'm a fairly restless, optimistic person; I couldn't stand to sulk for the next year and a half.

It was February; the year was half over. It was by now more than apparent that Oxford was not going to fall over itself to please me. A year before I had thought to myself, if I get a fellowship to Oxford, all of my problems will disappear. And they had—but as soon as I got to Oxford they came racing back. Oxford was not the magic solution it had seemed to be. Instead, it was a real, fallible place, filled with real, fallible people. In a lot of ways I didn't much like it. I spent my first term being disappointed over and over. But this didn't mean I should resign myself to being disappointed for ever. This term it was time to take things into my own hands, before I became, in the words of another American Oxonian, utterly "addled by tedium." If my seminars stubbornly refused to yield up anything interesting, I was going to damn well *squeeze* them until something interesting emerged.

I started by thinking about possible thesis topics. I realized that I simply did not want to do a traditional political science analysis of something or other. By now I had gotten my footing and learned the jargon, and I didn't like it. I thought that the approach of the program was far too narrow; looking at political changes without reference to broader cultural patterns was next to meaningless. I didn't want to analyze levels of electoral volatility, or utilize survey data to determine the exact correlation betweeen region and vote. I was interested primarily in people and in ideas. What makes people behave as they do? What motivates people? What kinds of things will people make sacrifices for? Why and how do these things change over time? Can people be persuaded to change their most fundamental loyalties?

I thought of a possible thesis topic one day when I was reading the *International Herald Tribune,* that slim news-paper so beloved of Americans abroad. It looks just like the *New York Times*. I was reading an article about EuroDisney, which was, at the time, the subject of much controversy. Every European intellectual seemed to be raging against the destructive and insidious effects of the American pop-culture invasion. One Parisian was quoted as saying, huffily, that the values of Walt Disney were just "not European."

I was struck by this. Last time I had checked, the nations of Europe were busy quarreling about the Maastricht Treaty. Saying that something was "not European" implied that there were other things that *were* European. So what were they? And was it only French intellectuals who thought that some things were "European," as opposed to just French, or English, or German or Italian?

Thinking about this, I became interested in the broader question of European cultural identity. For economic and political integration to succeed, does a region need to have a common culture? To what degree? Does such a common culture currently exist within the European Community? Is it likely that such a common culture can be created? What efforts have the EC culture ministers made to create such a common culture? To what extent have those efforts been successful? Can European nationalism be eradicated? To what extent is it likely that any pan-European culture will be more negative than positive, an identity based more on what Europe isn't (Third World, American, Japanese) than on what it is?

I told Hugh Ford that I was interested in this. He looked relieved to discover that I was interested in *something,* but he was pessimistic about its viability as a thesis topic.

"You'd have to narrow it down a lot," he said.

"Sure, definitely," I agreed.

"And I really can't think who would be able to supervise such a thesis. It's more—really it's more literary and theoretical, if you know what I mean."

I did. But I was optimistic about finding someone to supervise the thesis. After all, it seemed to me that the questions that interested me were at the very core of "European Politics and Society."

But Hugh Ford was right. I spoke to several people in the Politics faculty. They all shook their heads, some sympathetically, some impatiently. No, they could not supervise such a thesis.

Finally Hugh Ford suggested that I talk to James Lane, a European Literature tutor he knew at another college. He said that Lane might be able to shadow-supervise me.

Lane was charming and welcoming when I dropped by to see him. Fascinating questions, he said. More people ought to do research on such things. He would certainly be prepared to assist in any way he could. He gave me suggestions about things to read. Finally I thanked him and stood up. "I appreciate your help," I said.

"Not at all, not at all." He rubbed his hands. "As I said I'm pleased that you're interested in this. I think that cultural issues are of enormous importance to politics."

"Yes," I said ruefully, "but I'm afraid that the Politics faculty doesn't exactly cherish that idea."

"Mmm, mmm," he said, batting his eyelashes. "Whenever you need a little cherishing, just come right back here!"

I left.

The winter term was drawing to a close, and I hadn't been very successful in coming up with someone to supervise my thesis. I had gone to see William Wallace and Anne Deighton, both of whom had been sympathetic and encouraging. But neither of them seemed to feel particularly enthusiastic about my topic. It was too broad, too fuzzy, too literary. Perhaps, suggested Anne Deighton, I should focus on the challenges to national identity posed by immigration. Wallace agreed that I needed more focus and more empirical data. Their comments were reasonable—after all, I was studying political science, not cultural history or anthropology or literature. But although I took the point, this simply made me realize that perhaps I didn't really *want* to be studying political science.

Moreover, every time I looked over the list of optional subjects to study in the next two terms, I got depressed. I had already taken the two required subjects, European Integration and Political Institutions. To get my degree, I also had to pick two other subjects from an approved list, and take examinations in those subjects the next spring. But I didn't want to take EC Law, or Governments of East Central Europe. I didn't want to take International Economics, or the Political Economy of Western Europe, Japan and the United States. I didn't want to take a seminar on the Goverments of France, Germany, Italy, and the UK. Because if the required seminars I had already taken were any indication of general seminar quality within the department, all of these seminars were going to be pretty dismal.

It wasn't that I couldn't think of anything interesting that came under the heading, "European Politics and Society." I could think of many fascinating subjects: the history of the idea of Europe, the effect of nationalism on the integration process, the impact of technological changes on political processes. I could easily go on. But within the M.Phil. course, most of these subjects were treated only in a cursory manner, if at all, and there was little scope for deviation from the formal curriculum.

There wasn't anything technically *wrong* with the curriculum. It was, I suppose, respectable enough as a political science curriculum. It was just profoundly unimaginative and narrow, with no room for an interdisciplinary approach. As an undergraduate, I had been in an interdisciplinary concentration, History and Literature. I was used to looking at issues from an interdisciplinary point of view. For instance, one seminar that I enjoyed as an undergraduate was on the tradition of American dissent. Technically, the seminar was offered under the auspices of the English department, but our readings ranged from autobiographies and sermons to novels, historical analyses, and political tracts. Needless to say, I learned far more that way than I would have if the seminar had been purely historical in its bent.

It's interesting to compare some of the course titles from my undergraduate years with seminar titles from European Politics. As an undergraduate, I took a few basic introductory courses: Principles of Economics, Major British Writers, History of Political Theory, History of Early National America, and so on. But I also took such courses as Dissent in America, the Literature of Social Reflection, the Concept of Consent in Philosophy and Literature, The Social Impact of Technology in America, the "Woman Question" in Victorian England. All of these courses drew on the traditions of several different disciplines: history, literature, philosophy and history of science, political theory, philosophy, sociology, anthropology.

Compare these to the European Politics seminar offerings. The Government and Politics of Place X. The Economics of Y. Social Policies in Z. As far as the European Politics curriculum was concerned, history began at the end of World War Two. Popular culture was irrelevant. Literature didn't exist.

I am not arguing that it is not important to learn about the Economics of Y and the Social Policies of Z. It is. Branching out into other disciplines is primarily valuable for students who have first obtained a solid understanding of the content and theoretical tenets of their own discipline. My objection to the European Politics curriculum was that there was very little room to branch out and go beyond the bounds of traditional political science. And this was a shame, because the most innovative work is usually that which goes beyond and cuts across the traditional boundaries.

And the most interesting work. By the end of the second term, I had, however reluctantly, acquired a decent grasp of the basics. I was capable of blathering on endlessly about the relations between the EC Commission and Council. I could explain the development and limitations of the European Parliament. I knew what was important about the Treaty of Rome and the Yaounde Conference. I understood the sordid history of EC agricultural policy. I knew the history of the Exchange Rate Mechanism. I could assess the impact of Cold War policies on the development of the European Community. I could discuss patterns of electoral volatility in Europe, and the decline of the Social Democratic Party in Britain. I knew all about the electoral fortunes of the Italian Communist Party. I could explain the relationship between social democracy and corporatist structures. I could compare the judicial systems of France, Germany, Italy, and the UK. I was glad I knew this, but I was bored silly.

It's like learning a language. One learns a language for purely instrumental reasons, not out of a deep love for memorizing vocabulary and grammar rules. The only point of memorizing such tedious things is to enable oneself to do something more interesting down the line— read foreign literature, or converse with interesting people. In European Politics, I was prepared to learn the basics, but I wanted to move beyond the basics as quickly as possible. The trouble was that the European Politics curriculum never really got away from the grammar and vocabulary.

I began to play with the idea of switching from the

M.Phil. to the M.Litt., a master's degree requiring no coursework or exams, only a thesis. Somehow I was going to find a way to study something interesting. If I could find someone to supervise my thesis, I would be happy enough to putter along and write, provided I didn't have to slog my way through the dreary optional subjects and take Finals. But the qualifying examination was coming up, and it struck me that it might be better to keep quiet about this idea until after the qualifying exam. Hugh Ford might not welcome the idea of my switching to the M.Litt., and I would be in a stronger position if I approached him after passing the qualifying exam.

The qualifying exam was set for the day after the Easter vacation. It was a depressing time: the Tories had just squeaked through in the British general election, and many people saw this as a bad sign for the upcoming US election. Conservatives seemed set for world domination. To cheer ourselves up, Jerome and I traveled for part of the vacation. We spent two weeks getting lost all over Greece; to save money, we had gone before the start of the tourist season proper. This meant no maps and no tourist information services. Finally, exhausted and befuddled, we stumbled back to Oxford, and I settled in to cram for the qualifying exam. I studied and studied for five days, breaking only for meals and to take long damp walks with Jerome, during which I raged and stamped my feet repeatedly about the idiocies of the European Politics curriculum. The pass level was set to be Beta++, or the equivalent of an upper second. I had no idea what that meant, and this made me nervous, never having taken an Oxford exam before. Hugh Ford had tried to explain the grading system to us:

"Well, there's apha triple plus, then alpha double plus,

then alpha plus. After that there's alpha/beta and then beta/alpha, followed by beta triple plus, beta double plus, beta plus, beta/gamma, gamma/beta, gamma triple plus—"

Miranda interrupted. "Why bother? How can anyone possibly distinguish between an alpha/beta paper and an beta/alpha paper?"

Hugh Ford shrugged disconsolately. "I don't know." He then reiterated his concern that Miranda, David, and I, as American students, might be unfamiliar with the concept of a three-hour essay examination. We again reassured him that we had taken several dozen three-hour essay exams during our college careers. He again appeared surprised.

"Honestly," muttered Miranda. "He thinks we're stupid. What does he think goes on at places like Harvard and Stanford? Ten-minute multiple choice quizzes? My work at Stanford was six times harder and more intellectually stimulating than anything I've done here."

As we left the class, David sighed. "What am I doing here? Why am I taking this exam? I'm not even interested in this subject!"

"Neither am I," I told him, "neither am I."

The qualifying exam was an official University exam, and that meant that we had to wear *sub fusc* and sit the papers at the Examination Schools building. We all sat nervously in our gowns and dark clothes. No one wanted to risk breaking some petty rule. There is a well-known Oxford story about an undergraduate who thought himself cleverer than the examiners. He appeared at Schools wearing *sub fusc*, at the appointed hour for his first exam. He went up to the Proctors, the University's officers, pointing to a copy of the University statutes, and demanded a glass of ale. Apparently there is still an obscure statute on the books requiring students at Finals to be provided with ale upon request. The Proctors grudgingly complied and managed to produce some ale, and the smug undergraduate, sipping his ale, went to his desk and went to work. The next day, when he arrived for his second exam, the Proctors were ready for him. They pointed to the statute requiring examinees to wear a sword to examinations, and kicked him out for failing to wear his sword. Since one failed exam leads to no degree being awarded, that was the end of him.

Bearing his fate in mind, we offered no funny business. Sitting in our *sub fusc,* it all seemed like a game, not like an exam. But the minute the question papers were passed out, that changed. Hugh Ford's worries notwithstanding, it was an exam like any other exam. I felt the usual rush of adrenalin as I surveyed the questions. I stared at the questions for about five minutes, and then I began to write.

Three hours later we all burst chattering out of the building. I thought that I had done reasonably well. Nothing stellar, perhaps, but I was sure I was solid on two questions and probably OK on the third. Most people seemed to feel the same way. Only David looked miserable.

"I blew it," he whispered in my ear. "I only answered two questions."

I looked at him, shocked. "David, why?"

He shrugged unhappily. His eyes were wider and bluer than usual. He looked sick. "I don't know. I got rattled. I just spent a really long time on my first essay, way too long, and it was a good essay. But then I didn't have time to finish. I really blew it."

"Well," I said reassuringly, "it'll probably be OK anyway. You know they have the power to retest you in June. They know you're sharp, and it's a new program. They don't want to lose anyone. The worst that'll happen is that they'll make you try again in June."

"I don't know," said David. "I really don't know."

It occurred to me suddenly that maybe David didn't really *want* to pass the exam. He wanted to go home. He was a good student, though, and for all his talk about film making, he couldn't quite bring himself to just get up and go. Like me, like most Americans at Oxford, he was an over-achiever. His super-ego was too strong to let him quit something halfway through, no matter how little he liked it. But if he failed the exam, his decision would be made for him.

"You don't really want to be given another chance, do you," I said.

He looked at me in surprise, and then he grinned weakly. "I was going to say, 'Of course I do!' But no, I guess in some ways I don't. I just want out of here, ignominiously if necessary. I hate this program."

I laughed. "You know what? So do I. Maybe we should both switch out. But I'll tell you something. If we get out, we're going to have to get out voluntarily. Because I really don't think that Hugh Ford is going to let anyone fail. He needs people, David. This program is his baby, he can't afford to lose any of us. He'll find a way to pass you if he has to doctor the results."

David laughed at this. "I can just see Hugh Ford breaking into the University offices, late at night, doctoring the exam results. Poor guy."

We all went to a pub to celebrate the end of the exam. David drank pint after pint. He waxed lyrical about how much he liked Hugh Ford, deep down. He suggested that Miranda and I take tap dancing lessons with him. Finally, Miranda and I shepherded him home. When he had gone inside, Miranda looked at me. "David's in a bad way. I almost hope, for his sake, that they won't let him resit that exam. He really ought to get out of Oxford."

RUGBY

I WENT TO an unusual dinner party a few days after the qualifying exam. It was not, this time, unusual because it ended in a food fight—on the contrary, it was remarkably decorous. It was unusual because both undergraduates and graduates were present. The dinner was given by a second-year law undergraduate named Colette. She was from a wealthy French family. She was bright, plump, voluble, and ambitious, and she wanted to find an "older man."

"I am so sick of undergraduate men," she informed me sadly. "So immature—not like in France! I must get to know more graduates."

To that end she sent out embossed invitations announcing her dinner party to three or four undergraduate pals and a carefully chosen group of graduate targets. Dress was to be "smart." I strongly suspect that I only made it onto the guest list through Jerome. I didn't know Colette well and didn't want to go to the dinner, particularly because the invitation I received was addressed to "Rosie." But Jerome, who knew Colette through law tutorials, thought we should go; after all, he pointed out, several good friends of ours among the graduates were also going. Complaining bitterly, I put on a skirt.

Colette had outdone herself. Her room was sparklingly clean, and lit only by candles. Desks had been pulled together to form a table large enough for sixteen. The guests were obediently wearing smart clothes; most men wore jackets and ties. There was much effusive European-style cheek-kissing.

Seats were assigned. To my irritation I noted that Colette had placed Jerome at her right, while I was down near the other end of the table. I made the best of it by chatting with my neighbors. On my right was an American woman from South Carolina, called Ashley. ("My mother was just so in *love* with Ashley Wilkes from *Gone With the Wind* that she decided to name her first child Ashley, even if it was a girl, which of course I *was!*") She was a big fan of George Bush ("He's very patrician looking."). My conversation with her didn't last long, because it soon became apparent that she had little interest in anything other than her coming-out party and her possessions. All exchanges rapidly got back around to those subjects.

"Could you pass the salt?" I would ask.

"Sure," she'd say with a delighted smile. "Here you go. It's *so* important that things have just the right amount of salt, don't you agree? *That* was the one thing that went wrong at my débutante ball. The caterers just put so much *salt* on everything. My mother was awfully upset, you can imagine . . ."

When I couldn't stand this anymore, I turned to the people sitting across from me, an undergraduate couple I knew only vaguely. Unfortunately, they weren't a big improvement. Emma and Eddie were cheerful, attractive, friendly, rich, and capable only of the most breathtakingly dull conversation. They were extremely popular among the undergraduates.

Emma must have been impressed by the new heights of vapidity I managed to reach in my conversation with her, because over dessert she said, "You row, don't you, Rosie?"

Rosie was clearly the name by which I was to be known. "Yes," I agreed cautiously.

"Such a lot of fun, isn't it?" Emma asked brightly.

"Oh, *brilliant* fun," I affirmed, unconsciously imitating her speech style.

"Would you be willing to play women's rugby for Christ Church?"

"Rugby?"

"It's new for women this year. The boys don't really think we'll do it. Oh, the boys are *so* silly! But we *can* do it. I'm sure rugby can't be that difficult. *Please* say you'll play. We need one more girl."

"Is it tackle?"

"Don't worry, the boys will teach us to tackle. Think—you can practice tackling all sorts of big horny men!"

"I've no doubt that I'll be able to knock them to the ground," I agreed.

"If you play rugby with us," Emma added enticingly, "you can come to Misdemeanours! You'll have your two sports. You'd have such a wonderful time. We play the *best* drinking games."

"I don't dare come to Misdies," I told her. "I don't want to have to snog my barnyard animal mate."

Emma looked delighted. "Yes, that's our favorite game!"

"No thanks."

"At least try rugby. Let me give your name to Jane Thorpe, she's captaining it."

I shrugged. "OK. Why not?"

That was how I became a member of the Christ Church Women's Rugby first team. There were only nine of us on the team; women's games, at the college level, were played with sides of seven people. Jane Thorpe and Emma had tried to recruit a few more players by putting up signs in the lodge: "Try Women's Rugby! Horny Male

Coaches!" but for some reason this failed to draw the expected mob of women. As usual, I was the only American and the only graduate. The other women on the team were mostly from the popular, sporty set who made up the core of the Misdemeanours. They were highly visible in the college bar, and they almost all rowed or played another sport as well.

None of us had played rugby before. It is primarily a male sport. It resembles American football but no protective padding is worn. Our first few practices ended when we all collapsed, giggling. The "boys," volunteers from the men's rugby team, tried to teach us to tackle. It seemed a bit rude to knock a female acquaintance to the ground, so for the first few practices we were somewhat tentative about our tackling. This led to ludicrous situations in which would-be tacklees jogged in slow motion through the mud while ineffective tacklers clung pathetically to their legs. The men thought this was even funnier than we did. "Oooh," Eddie, one of our coaches, would chortle, in falsetto. "I can't play *now,* girls, I've got a split end! I have to go *home* and condition my *hair!*"

When Eddie was tackled, he'd lie in the mud, feigning tears. "*Ja-ane!* You hurt me! You broke my *finger*nail!"

I tackled Eddie very hard the next time around. I was not averse to the idea of inducing genuine tears. I aimed for his groin.

This raillery did not seem to bother any of the other women. I gave up blaming Eddie; he was, after all, only doing what all the women present seemed to expect him to do. The other women staunchly defended our right to play a boys' game when male passersby jeered: "You pretty girls playing rugby? I'll be careful not to mess with you!" But that was as far as feminism went.

If ever anyone suffered from false consciousness, it was these women.

When we practised the scrum, which involves a lot of bodily contact, Emma whispered, "Oooh, isn't this kind of *lesby*?" and everyone giggled.

Sexist insults from the men were laughed off. Jane Thorpe took some of the worst sallies. She was slightly overweight and one day Eddie, looking her up and down, said, "Nice *leggings,* Jane."

"Oh, they're so ugly, I know," she said, too quickly. "My mother got them for me."

To which Eddie chivalrously replied, "She must have bought them for you when you were a little *thinner,* eh Jane?"

Jane blinked, hurt. But she recovered quickly, and giggled, "Oh, *Eddie,* you're too much."

During our matches, Jane was also the object of much "good-natured" male humor. As she jogged by the group of Christ Church students assembled to cheer us on, hoarse shouts followed her: "Steroid test for number five! Is that a man or a woman?!"

I found it difficult to understand. Here was a group of undoubtedly bright young women. Yet they continually put up with condescending and obnoxious comments from the men. And it wasn't only around the men that they censored themselves. Their self-censorship was so strict that I never heard them discuss anything other than men, parties, and food, even when none of the "boys" were around. Get them together at one of our post-practice teas, and the conversation went like this:

"I am *so* tired. I didn't get to sleep until four."

"Oh, were you at Charlie's party?"

"Was I at Charlie's? I was the one who had to stick my *fingers* down Charlie's *throat* to make him vomit so he wouldn't choke when he went to sleep."

"Disgusting!"

"God, I am a *cow*. Why are you letting me eat so much, Emma? You know I'm too fat!"

"We're all such cows. God."

"It was *such* good fun at Charlie's, though."

"Except when Owen and Tom were drinking scotch through a *funnel*, they took the funnel and poured scotch right over my *head*. I said, that is *not* very impressive, boys."

"Emma, can we go to the boys' rugby dinner piss-up?"

"We should get to go, we're rugby players too. But I told Eddie, if it will make people mad, we won't go."

I had been, as usual, on the periphery of the discussion. I didn't have much to contribute, never having had scotch poured on my head and never having stuffed my fingers down someone's throat to induce vomiting. As the oldest by a couple of years, I was treated rather gently by the other girls, like an antique that ought not to be handled roughly. They tactfully refrained from asking what my decorous social life was like among the dinosaurs. They occasionally invited me to their parties, on what they by now knew to be the safe assumption that I wouldn't show up. I had made my position fairly clear during one early conversation about parties that ended in group vomiting: I had risen to go, saying, "My, you undergraduates lead such exciting lives. Nothing so exciting ever happens among the graduates." This earned me some slightly chastened, uneasy laughter.

When I happened to meet Jane or Emma or Kate or any of my other teammates outside of the group, they were substantially more serious. Some of these women will probably never change: at the age of twenty, their self-esteem was permanently squashed flat, their vapidity already engrained. But most of them, I hope and believe, won't always be like that. Most of them will graduate, get the interesting jobs that their Oxford degrees will open to them, and become sophisticated, tough, funny, and probably feminist women.

In the meantime, they were patently too bright to be wasting their brains chatting about vomit induction and thinking up new drinking games. It seemed such a waste, such a shame. The world is a more interesting and better place than that. When they were alone, did they think this too?

I frequently felt like shaking them, and saying, "Come on, are you for real? Surely you're not this idiotic all the time. What are you afraid of? Losing the 'admiration' of the boys? Who needs that sort of admiration? Admit it! Admit that you're too smart for this!"

But I'm sure it would only have frightened them. I remembered a conversation with some undergraduate women the previous term. For some reason I had said, "Of course I'm a feminist." They had all looked at me as though I had said, "Of course, I'm really a Martian."

Obviously, not all undergraduates were like my rugby and rowing friends. There were many hard-working, conscientious undergraduates who disliked the laddish, boorish dominant culture as much as I did, undergraduates like my European Politics friend Gavin must have been, and like the two English students with whom I shared a flat the following year. I took up women's cricket for a brief time, and met a completely different group of undergraduates. ("That's because cricket's a gentleman's sport," said Phil, our cricket coach, when I told him this. "Rowers are louts, and ruggers are worse.") The cricketers were mostly freshers, and they seemed thoughtful, considerate, and good natured. Perhaps this was *because* they were freshers; they hadn't yet learned that they were supposed to act ironic and indifferent to everything except parties.

But unfortunately, the dominant culture was just that. It was the noisy, sporty types who prevailed in the College bar and who shouted down motions they disliked at JCR meetings. Even in the library, whispers, paper planes, and low hoots often made it difficult to work. So the more conscientious undergraduates kept to themselves and didn't challenge the College's social culture, any more than most of them dared to challenge the academic assumptions that prevailed.

One night after "rugby drinks" in the buttery, I turned to Frank, the big young man who had told me, at the Cardinals, that Jerome had "a brain as big as a planet," while declining to specify which planet.

"Frank," I said, "you're a man of the nineties. Do you consider yourself a feminist?"

"Uh, what?" said Frank, from behind his pint. "Uh, feminine? Do I consider myself feminine?"

"No, a *feminist*."

"Uh, no? Maybe? Uh, why?"

"Never mind."

"Hey, *look*," said Frank in loud excited voice, pointing out into the hall at a nervous looking boy with thick glasses and a long scarf. "Look! A genuine Oxford *spod!* Hey, and another spod!" The boy was followed by an owlish, scowling girl with long straight hair and an arm full of books. "Spods! They're all over!"

I turned to Eddie. "How about you, Eddie? Are you a feminist?"

Eddie twinkled at me. "Well, I wouldn't say that, but I believe in equal rights, of course. It's just that I think men and women are *different*, you know, men are better at certain things—"

"Like rugby," I suggested.

"Well, right, although up to a point I think it's brilliant that you girls are giving it a go. I just think that in general women should stick to what they do best, and men should stay with what they're good at. I mean," he added generously, "it would be silly for men to try to be professional nurses, or cooks."

There was a girl sitting beside me who I hadn't seen before. I gathered that she was someone's flatmate. She seemed to have been watching me, so I introduced myself.

"You're a graduate?" she asked. "I've never seen you around."

"That's because I'm a loser," I explained.

She blushed. "No, I don't mean that. I was listening to what you were saying, about feminism. I think that if you're at Christ Church, you sort of have to be a feminist, don't you?"

I looked at her with surprise. "Yes, I would think so, but no one else here seems to agree."

"Well," she said hesitantly. "It's just easier not to rock the boat. Did you read the *Oxford Student* today?"

I nodded.

"There was a letter, maybe you read it, from a woman who went to a JCR meeting at St Edmund Hall, trying to convince them to subscribe to a new Oxford women's magazine. The meeting was packed with male hecklers. She said it was an incredibly threatening atmosphere. Well, who needs that? It's easier not to say anything. Especially at places like Teddy Hall and Christ Church, where there's such a male culture. I know that's not good, but I do that too."

She shrugged and made a face. "It's a small college. It's incestuous. People aren't used to being with the opposite sex, and lots of boys, by the time they get out of their public school, think women exist just to cook and sweep the floors. Or sleep with them. You know—people have lots of one-night stands, and everyone knows everyone here." She gestured around the table. "I'm only in my second year, but I know that pretty much all the girls here have slept with pretty much all the boys here. Once or twice. That doesn't really help female bonding—everyone's after the same boys. And you still have to get on with everyone for three years. No one wants to risk making a fuss."

And, shooting me a last, apologetic look, she got up and went over to Eddie. I heard her say, "Eddie, don't get too pissed now, remember we're going to Owen's room and he's got all that wine still. We'll get pissed there."

"Bloody hell!" cried Eddie with enthusiasm, leaping up. "Let's go!"

My informant was quite correct: for most students at Oxford, and for women in particular, making waves just wasn't worth it. It was a sure recipe for social death. Consider the context: many colleges are filled with overtly sexist and élitist secret societies. Vincent's, the all-male Blues club, politely reminds members that women are not allowed in the club during weekday lunchtimes. What budding sportsman, eager for social acceptance, will challenge that? What woman eager to befriend a Blue will make a fuss? At Christ Church, the Nondescripts punish members who fail to come to parties with a female guest. Lone men are "sconced," forced to rapidly down several drinks, watched by a hooting crowd. The Disciples, an all-male Magdalen dining society, writes sexism into their constitution: "At least one meeting per term shall be a dinner where members must be accompanied by a non-feminist female . . . the President shall discreetly award cigars to the members who have brought the horniest females." At Keble, a similar society was formally banned by the College, but only after a dinner was followed by a sexual assault on a female guest.

Also at Keble, women who objected to a women's drinking society, along the lines of Christ Church's Misdemeanours, were told that they were "nothing but a bunch of bloody lesbians." At Merton, where the male-female ratio is 3:1, female graduate students wanted to change the MCR constitution to mandate the election of a "Women's Officer." Men objecting to the proposed change told newspapers that the debate was an example of women "just needing a good fuck to get over their problems." In Christ Church JCR, a poster announcing a lunch for College women was defaced repeatedly; each time it went up, some witty soul scrawled ". . . are not intelligent" next to the word "women."

In a culture which often explicitly condones the objectification of women, and in which social acceptance is predicated upon not criticizing the *status quo,* it's little wonder that most undergraduates internalize the prevailing mores. And those who don't rarely risk voicing their objections. In the 1920s, Oxford "hearties" broke up the rooms of aesthetes. Seventy years later, a vaguely threatening aura still lingers. Most unconventional or progressive undergraduates, like my feminist informant, decide that discretion is the better part of valor.

My rugby experiences had their positive side, however. They reinforced my feeling that I was indeed part of the College community, in however peripheral a way. And I enjoyed my first real moment of sporting glory. This was because, to my enormous surprise, I proved to be rather good at rugby. I was a tomboy and a fighter as a little girl, and perhaps this left me with some residual skill at tackling people. In our first match, I scored a try (the rugby term for a touchdown, or goal). A lot of the men's rugby team had turned out to cheer us on, and when I jogged back to our side, I was greeted with enthusiastic hugs and congratulations from everyone.

However critical I was of the Oxford social scene, the undergraduates I met were, almost without exception, bright, friendly, welcoming, and kind to me. They seemed rather less kind to one another. I liked most of the undergraduates I met; I wished them well. Most of all I hoped that they would change and flourish once they got out of Oxford. I just didn't want to spend all that much time with them until then. Socially and intellectually, I frequently thought that they suffered from a form of arrested development. Given the hierarchical, deferential tradition into which they had been born, they weren't doing too badly. I was glad not to be in their shoes, but if I were in their shoes I'm sure I'd be no different.

THE SWITCH

IN EARLY MAY the weather became unexpectedly, unseasonably lovely. There were flowers everywhere and the sun shone. People lay out on the grass and hosted garden parties with strawberries and champagne. I turned down an invitation to an undergraduate party ("Bare your body at Emma and Kate's Bare Necessities party—only one item of clothing per person after 9 p.m."). After a few days of heat the streets were sticky, the air fetid with diesel fumes. I dreamed of beaches, the scent of suntan oil, the texture of hot white sand.

I took a blanket and went to lie down in Christ Church Meadows. All around me echoed the shrieks of fourteen-year-old Italian schoolchildren on holiday. They raced around, throwing balls, pulling one another's hair, dropping garbage in their wake.

I could have avoided the tourists by sunbathing in the Dean's Garden, which was open only to Christ Church members. But if I had gone there I'd have had to be sociable, and chat with other students. The Meadows were devoid of Christ Church students, because no one else was willing to run the gauntlet of foreign teeny-boppers. I was glad of this: I didn't want to meet anyone who knew me, because I wanted to be undisturbed in order to think seriously about my future. More particularly, I wanted to think hard about Oxford, and decide if there was any way to salvage my Oxford academic career.

By now, I had a clear sense of what I disliked about

Oxford. I was unimpressed by Oxford's educational philosophy, by the quality of resources, and by the general atmosphere.

Theoretically, basing undergraduate education upon the tutorial offers students the opportunity of working closely with an older mentor. Occasionally the experience lives up to the hype—but too often, tutorials are a dismal flop, in which both don and student only barely manage to hide from one another their mutual lack of interest in the question under discussion. Little learning and less teaching goes on. Original research is not rewarded, because student achievement is recognized only through exam performance. Students can go beyond the set curriculum if they wish to, but few have the motivation. As exams are on set subjects, original research is only a detour. Thus, there is no incentive for students to dig deeper. Ideally, of course, all students would dig deeper out of simple love of learning; some people, indeed, maintain that the rewards of going beyond what is required are all the greater when one does it of one's own accord, and not out of the need for a good mark. This is probably true. But unfortunately, very few of us are sufficiently motivated to go beyond what is required, when we receive no recognition for doing so. With no incentive to do original research, essays all too often become an exercise in regurgitating information.

To the extent that graduate education also relies upon tutorials the same problems are encountered. Only graduates pursuing research degrees instead of "taught" courses can avoid these problems, and they are plagued by problems of their own—usually a frustrating lack of guidance and support.

For both graduates and undergraduates, seminars and lectures tend to suffer from a lack of direction. As lectures and seminars are not formally linked to tutorials, students frequently cannot see their relevance. The optional nature of lectures and seminars means that lecturers have no particular sense of responsibility towards students. They will never know of, and never be held responsible for, students' poor exam performance. This creates a lack of accountability. There is no regular or mechanized student feedback about lecture and seminar quality, so dons have no incentive to improve their teaching skills.

And the general quality of teaching is dismally low. I cannot count the number of lectures I attended in which the lecturer, seated and therefore invisible to all but those in the front row, droned on inaudibly while students in the back of the room quietly read the newspaper or wrote notes back and forth. The smug Oxford assumption seems to be that all Oxford dons are automatically capable of communicating their subject to students. But teaching does not come naturally to the academically gifted; it is a skill, like any other, that can be taught. And at Oxford it is not taught. Obviously good teaching depends to some extent upon intangibles, but there are certain basics which anyone can learn: lecturers should vary their tone, make eye contact with the audience, stand up while lecturing, speak audibly, make sure lectures have a clear organizational structure, and encourage students to ask questions about points that are not clear. I have also sat through many agonizing two-hour seminars at Oxford, in which the seminar leaders gazed dreamily into space during long, torturous silences, making no effort to guide the discussion into productive avenues.

The Finals system for undergraduates strikes me as particularly criminal. First of all it discourages creative deviation from the set curriculum: there is no institutionalized recognition for students who have taken the trouble to go beyond the basics and pursue their own intellectual interests. It creates very narrow students. Undergraduates have begun to specialize even before arriving at Oxford, and once they matriculate, there is no possibility of their doing substantive work outside of their own field. A salad bar of beans. Thus, Oxford produces scientists who haven't read a work of literature since they were fifteen, language students who know nothing of history, law students who know nothing of politics.

In the United States, most élite universities cherish the ideal of a "liberal" education: during their four years at college, students should gain an in-depth knowledge of a particular subject, but should also gain a sense of the diversity of knowledge, of the methods and philosophies of fields other than their own. This is caricatured by the phrase, "students should learn a little about a lot and a lot about a little". For this reason, students do not choose a "major" subject until after at least a year, and most colleges have distribution requirements: students must take courses in the sciences, arts, and social sciences, regardless of their own area of specialization. This leads to students with a good deal of superficial knowledge—but I think it also leads to students with broad sympathies and interests, and a sense of the excitement of learning.

The second problem with the Finals system is that too much rests on a few exams. Three years' worth of work is evaluated on the basis of a week's examination perform-ance. There is no mercy for poor exam takers or for those who simply had a rough week. Every year, a few students crack under the pressure, ending up in psychiatric care—I knew two people myself whose Finals were disrupted by nervous breakdowns. There are occasional suicides. Less dramatically, an undergraduate can do nothing but work for three long years, only to find that the luck of the draw goes against him at the last minute—he may discover that the questions on the exam are unexpected, or that his exam essays are treated more harshly than his tutorial essays ever were. Students unfortunate enough to have had weak or incompetent tutors pay the price when exams come round. And degree quality determines career opportunities and funding for graduate work.

The level of resources at Oxford is also shockingly low. The computer facilities are comparable to those available at American universities a decade ago. Students are themselves responsible for using the JCR budget to acquire and maintain things like photocopying machines and pay telephones (college rooms almost never have private telephones). The libraries are atrocious. They are open only during limited hours, they lack the facilities for lap-top computer users, they are perennially short-staffed and short on books. The cataloguing system is from the Dark Ages.

I would not complain about this if the problem was simply that Oxford is poor, and is still reeling from Thatcherite budget cuts. The cuts left Oxford *poorer,* but not poor. The problem is that Oxford does not utilize economies of scale. For instance, each college has its own library, creating a situation in which there are about thirty undergraduate libraries, all of which are inadequate and have only a tiny portion of the holdings of a respectable American college library. Some colleges are richer than others, so their students are lucky enough to have slightly less inadequate libraries. If colleges were to share facilities instead of duplicating inadequate resources, all students would be better off. The same is true of housing, computers, and sports facilities. Some colleges can afford to house undergraduates for all three years; others send them out into costly and run-down local housing after only one year in college. Christ Church boasts the finest cricket pitch and tennis courts in Oxford. Half the time the Christ Church courts are empty, while other colleges suffer through waterlogged, uneven fields and a perennial shortage of equipment.

Similarly, when money *is* spent, it is often lavished on unnecessary luxuries. Colleges boast of their wine cellars and the food served up at High Table. Rooms in the college quads are given to dons and emeritus college members, and sit empty much of the time when they could be used as student housing or as office space for student groups. In Christ Church, with its ecclesiastical traditions, a number of church officials have rooms, or whole apartments, in College. One canon has two sizeable apartments; he and his family live in one, and he rents the other out to graduate students, using rooms provided by the College to cut a tidy personal profit.

Rich colleges give wildly generous travel grants to students with dubious projects. I know because I benefited from such a travel grant myself—I wanted to visit South Africa, and I concocted a rather questionable research plan. I went to see the Censor, and asked what the College travel grant application procedure was: should I write a proposal, submit a bibliography, a research plan, a budget? Get a supporting letter from my supervisor? The Censor brushed my questions away: "Oh, don't bother, we'll give you some money, we know you. You don't need to give us a proposal or anything." A week later I got the check in the mail.

Margaret Thatcher hoped that cutting off the flow of cash would force Oxford to adapt to the twentieth century. She hoped that Oxford would be forced to rationalize its structure, rethink its spending priorities, and develop creative ways of raising money from private sources, as most American universities have had to do for a century or so. Although I firmly believe that the government ought to be responsible for funding higher education, I think

Thatcher's goal was to some extent laudable—Oxford *is* in dire need of rationalization. Unfortunately, the funding cuts created some unintended consequences, as such abrupt cuts always do—the result of the cuts was that Oxford blundered on unaltered, and students suffered from increasingly uneven resources. One frustrated don, trying to make it easier for his students to get access to libraries throughout the University, told me that change just wasn't possible: "Oxford has no center. It's made up of dozens of colleges and departments, all doing their own thing. In the middle, where the center ought to be, there's just an empty hole, a power vacuum. There's nowhere for change to start."

Each college jealously guards its resources and autonomy. Academic standards also suffer as a result of this. The widely differing prestige of the colleges means that some colleges can attract better dons and brighter students. Undergraduates receive tutoring mostly from tutors in their own college, and a student unfortunate enough to end up at a college that is weak in his or her field can be condemned to three years of inadequate supervision. Again, this can place some students at a serious competitive disadvantage when Finals roll around. Each college chooses which students to admit, and there is no well-articulated University-wide commitment to certain admissions standards. (Much less is there any University-wide commitment to admitting a racially, sexually, and socioeconomically diverse class.) In theory, student admissions applications are sent on to four colleges of the student's choice before going into the general pool. But in reality, not all colleges bother—sometimes applications rejected by the first choice college will be immediately tossed into the general pool, simply because the applicant's first choice college couldn't be bothered to pass the application on to the applicant's second choice.

The admissions process is haphazard and plagued by a near total lack of accountability. Its flaws are representative of a broader problem. Virtually *everything* at Oxford seems to be done in a lazy and slipshod manner, leaving the observer with the distinct impression that whatever good comes out of Oxford comes by accident, not by design. If some students manage to be happy and intellectually productive, it is despite Oxford, not because of it. Most students and many dons simply give up, faced with such an arbitrary and opaque process. Simon Schama says that irony is the essence of British education. Could it not be that this irony is a defense against caring, when understanding the system—much less changing it—seems so fruitless?

But this may be too kind. Too many Oxonians seem to take refuge within a sense of complacency that goes well beyond ironic resignation. Why doesn't Oxford change? A little soul-searching on the part of those who run the university might go a long way, but it rarely seems to occur to anyone to contemplate change. For instance, Oxford's basic approach to undergraduate education has not changed one iota for a century. To be sure, the content of courses has changed a bit, and a few new options have been added. But the tutorial system, leading to Finals at the end of three years, has remained in place, unquestioned. Yet few people will defend the Finals system. Even Cambridge doesn't base everything on one set of exams. Virtually everyone I've ever spoken to, students and faculty, agree that such a system is unnecessarily harsh and impossible to justify. Too much depends on too little. Far too much rests on a short week of examinations, and exam results are not necessarily an accurate valuation of a student's ability. But no one has tried to change it.

Similarly, most people agree that state school students,

women, and minorities are under-represented among Oxford students. People from the latter two categories are drastically under-represented on the Oxford faculties; women make up only 3.1 percent of professors, and only 14.1 percent of all academic staff. To change this, Oxford colleges and faculties would have to make a conscious, concerted effort to rethink recruitment methods and assessment methods. But this seems to be low on the agenda for change. A few highly motivated students do an excellent job of trying to encourage more "non-traditional" applicants through the student-initiated "target schools" scheme. But with little institutional support, there are obvious limits to how much they can do.

It is true that major changes in the academic structure of Oxford or in its admissions policies would be disruptive, frightening, possibly expensive. But that's no excuse. The main reason nothing changes is complacency. Oxford is not a self-critical place. The assumption is: this is Oxford. We've muddled along this way for nearly a millenium. If you don't like it, go somewhere else.

My friend Mark once got into an argument with an elderly don at Oriel. Mark was trying to convince the don that the Finals system was unfair and should be scrapped. The don didn't disagree with any of Mark's specific assertions, but merely replied that the Finals system had been around for a century. "That's not a reason to keep it," Mark insisted.

The don shrugged. "My boy, tradition is self-justifying."

This sense of complacency is satirized by C. S. Lewis, writing in the first half of the century: "The real Oxford is a closed corporation of jolly, untidy, lazy, good for nothing, humorous old men, who have been electing their own successors since the world began and who intend to go on with it. They'll squeeze under the Revolution or leap over it when the time comes, don't you worry."

Suggesting that all is not well to members of this closed corporation is huffily dismissed as hubristic—the more so when the suggestions come from students or foreigners. (One day I fumed to a sympathetic don about the need for student evaluation of teaching and course content. "You've convinced *me*," he said, "that student course evaluation would benefit both students and dons. And I'll bring that up at the next faculty meeting. But I doubt things will change. You know what they'll say. They'll say, 'This is not America.'")

This attitude stands in sharp contrast to the American attitude about change. Americans, as Hollywood has told all the world, love change. Enough is not enough; we want more. We want new consumer goods, bigger houses, new improved toilet-bowl cleaners. We want self-improvement. We adore self-help and pop-psychology books.

The downside of this attitude is obvious. It can degenerate into mere selfishness and greed: *me me me, more more more*. But just because this attitude, at its worst, can be obnoxious, it does not follow that a blind resignation and complacency is any better. For the positive side of this "American" attitude shouldn't be underestimated. At its best, it involves an optimism, a continual striving for the good: the good toothpaste and the more convenient fast food, but also the good life and the more just society. Ideally, this assertiveness about wanting more is coupled with a willingess to be introspective and searchingly self-critical.

This is why few American universities have been as stagnant as Oxford has been. Harvard, for instance, has drastically altered its undergraduate curriculum several times during this century, and the book has not closed yet on curriculum changes. The curriculum, the resources, and the admissions process are all being continually reevaluated to reflect student needs and to keep pace with the changing demands of society. Students, community members, faculty members, and alumni are all asked for their ideas. Efforts are made to ensure a more racially and socio-economically diverse student body, a more diverse faculty, and a curriculum that reflects the diversity of American thought. These efforts have not been uncontroversial. They have inspired bitter opposition as well as passionate advancement. But it is the continual spirited controversy that prevents the university from stagnating.

Most crucially, élite American universities self-consciously strive to be communities. Yale College's Dean of Freshmen, Richard Brodhead, put it like this in a welcome address to freshmen:

> You come here to a place full of diversity. I ask each of you, in the way you organize your engagement with this multiform human world, to take seriously the notion that you could be helping to create a model of an exemplary community . . . It is for you to work out the positive content of a proper community. Obvious suggestions would be that you not coerce one another, that you not intimidate one another, that you practice tolerance and respect for one another (not just when it's easy)—but these are paltry, minimal requests. The more exciting hope would be that you would be not just respectful in the face of each other's difference, but actively, mutually inquisitive: willing to open yourself to what seems foreign and so to overcome the insularity of each homebound life.

American students take the community-building project extremely seriously, sometimes, perhaps, too seriously: a low-level of hysteria sometimes prevails, and minor issues erupt easily into campus-wide dramas, filling bulletin boards, conversations, and student newspapers for months at a time. But that notion of a jointly created community is one that is dear to me, and that is what seemed most lacking at Oxford. Oxford micromanages student lives when it comes to rules about gowns, examinations, mealtimes, and so on. But when it comes to the big issues—how shall we live together? How shall we create an atmosphere in which people can learn and thrive?—Oxford is strangely silent. The dons seem to regard these as irrelevant concerns, and students follow their lead.

I don't mean to idealize places like Harvard and Yale. Certainly Harvard has a lot further to go before the decision-making process is truly open. Compared to some other American universities, *Harvard* is smug and archaic. But compared to Oxford, it's on the cutting edge.

British people and American people have different assumptions about the value of efficiency and change. This is particularly true at Oxford, where change is often resisted simply for tradition's sake. An American friend of mine, Sam, told me a story that illustrates this. Sam was reading for a D.Phil. in politics at Merton College. Like many students, he was annoyed to discover, upon arrival at Oxford, that he had to purchase a gown. This rather flimsy piece of polyester sold for about £15 at the High Street stores. Sam, an entrepreneurial minded young man, decided that this was ridiculous. He contacted a clothing wholesaler, and discovered that the actual cost of producing the gowns was closer to three pounds each. Sam decided to launch a venture that would earn him some extra spending money while benefiting all Oxford students. He would buy up a thousand gowns, and sell them to students for £7 each.

It made sense to him and to all his American friends, and the English undergraduates to whom he spoke agreed that they would be happy to get cheaper gowns. So Sam wrote letters to each Oxford college, explaining his scheme. He asked them to make undergraduates aware that High Street stores made a huge profit on each gown, and that he could supply identical products at lower prices. He further asked that colleges permit students to charge the purchase of gowns to their monthly college bill, or "battels" account.

Sam expected colleges to be pleased with his idea. After all, they presumably wanted to save their students money. At worst, he figured that allowing students to charge gowns to their college account might prove administratively too difficult, but that colleges would be willing to make students aware of his scheme.

A few colleges responded with enthusiasm, and congratulated Sam on coming up with a scheme to save students money. But most colleges either didn't respond at all or responded with firm negatives: "We are not interested in your proposal." One college sent on Sam's letter to several High Street gown suppliers, who sent Sam hostile letters threatening to sue him for libelously claiming that they made a profit on their gowns (which they did). It turned out later that this college owned the buildings rented by the stores.

When Sam called the colleges that had refused to consider publicizing his plan, to ask why they weren't interested, he was shocked at the responses he received.

"We're just not interested, can't you understand that?" said one college bursar, and hung up on him.

"Who are you?" said another. "Why should we speak to you?"

Another shouted at him: "You North Americans think that you can simply come in here and change everything. Well, we don't want your changes! We didn't ask you how to run our University!"

Sam was baffled. In America, no one would have said, "Who are you?" They would have said, "You can save us money? Wonderful! What a bright young man!" Naturally: it's the Horatio Alger myth all over again. Young man emerges from nowhere with a good idea. Old tycoon, bored with subservience, puts his arm around the newcomer's shoulder: "Young man, I like your spirit. I'll see to it that you go far."

There is another story, possibly apocryphal, about the American at Christ Church who got rusticated (suspended) for charging tourists to have tea in his rooms. In America, the joke goes, the college would probably have just asked for a cut of the profits.

In many ways, Oxford is not part of the twentieth-century capitalist world. It preserves many inefficient and ridiculous practices that could not survive anywhere else. It operates according to its own logic, as Sam discovered. I do not mean to imply that efficiency should be the highest value of an educational institution—there are other, more important, social goals. There may well be many times when the less efficient road is the better one, so far as education is concerned. But when inefficiency actually interferes with the educational goals of a university, then something ought to change.

To some extent, Oxford is simply an extreme example of a very British attitude. Efficiency is not the highest goal; even Britain's Tories have always softened neo-classical free-market policies with a bit of inefficient paternalism. For Americans, this means that life in England is filled with frustrations. The inefficiency of British institutions is a perenially favorite topic. If only supermarket checkout counters were enlarged, and bags provided in advance, the lines would be so much shorter! If only all stores opened on Sundays, shopping on Saturdays wouldn't be such a nightmare! If only more people opened up late-night convenience stores, they would make a fortune! If only Oxford had a decent orientation program, so much less student time and angst would be wasted! If only the colleges pooled their library holdings, there could be one huge, well-staffed library open all night!

But complacency prevents change. This drives many Americans wild with exasperation. Even left-wing Americans like myself, no fans of free-market economics, begin to long for a little competition to liven up the Oxford scene. Almost against our will, we devise ways to make Oxford more rational, profitable, efficient. An American friend of mine jokes that Oxford's inefficiency "gets you in touch with your inner management consultant."

I think he is right. Management consultancy is the hot career these days, and major American firms like McKinsey aggressively recruit Rhodes and Marshall Scholars, promising them salaries equivalent to those offered to MBA holders. That means $100,000 a year, right out of Oxford. It's little wonder that they succeed in luring many American Oxonians to their firms. But, as my friend suggested, there may be more to it than that: "I sometimes think," he told me, "that Oxford represents a conspiracy to turn American graduates into management consultants. This place is so maddeningly inefficient that it actually drives us into the arms of McKinsey and BCG. By the end of two or three years at Oxford, we Americans, no matter how politically radical, are literally dying for a good, rational dose of the entrepreneurial, free-enterprise mentality."

By this point in the year, as I sat in the sun, I thought that I had Oxford figured out. But I wasn't sure where that left me. I had one or two more years of Marshall money to spend at Oxford, and so far, my academic work had been a waste of time. I no longer expected Oxford to change. If things were going to change, I was going to have to make them change. I was going to have to lower my expectations and alter my approach. Was there any way, I wondered, to make my remaining time at Oxford worthwhile?

If I wanted to try to switch to the M.Litt., the master's by thesis only, I needed to act quickly. But I didn't have a thesis supervisor, and I didn't really have much of a thesis proposal yet. And I suspected that as I had told David, Hugh Ford would be reluctant to lose any students.

I thought about taking the easy, lazy option, and just sticking with the M.Phil. But that was unpalatable; I felt an almost physical revulsion when I thought of the seminars, the essays, the exams—another year of dreary, dull coursework in a subject I found unchallenging and unengaging.

And the M.Litt.: assuming that they would let me switch, would I really want to write a 50,000 word thesis in less than a year, starting from scratch? And was I really all that interested in the subject? Yes, I was interested in questions of European cultural identity, but I wasn't sure I was *that* interested. After all, it wasn't a topic that I had picked out of nowhere, a topic that interested me more than any other in the world. Instead it was a topic chosen in an effort to make the best of a bad bargain. Yes, I could probably be reasonably happy if I wrote on that topic. But not wildly happy. I didn't think I would benefit much intellectually from the exercise. And frankly, Europe was not my main interest. I hadn't come to Oxford intending to study European Politics or culture; Hugh Ford had roped me into it through a neat combination of bribery and threats, making me think that I should feel fortunate to have a place in any M.Phil. program. And I had been too scared to really protest.

I remembered Ford's words. Unfortunately, he'd said, I don't know who would be able to supervise you in politics, but I have a new program of my own, the M.Phil. in European Politics, and I'd be willing to take you on . . .

I had been so relieved at having a program and so grateful that I had stifled the voice inside me that was saying, even then, "Hey! But you're not *interested* in European Politics!" Now, in May, I wished I had listened to that voice. I wished I had thought harder about what I did want to study, and I wished that I had made a fuss in order to ensure that I'd be *able* to study what I wanted to study. I wished I hadn't let my awe at being at Oxford keep me from complaining when things didn't go well. And now I had wasted the better part of a year.

Miranda, with her strong interest in Eastern Europe, was willing to stick with European Politics despite the program's flaws. For her, the chance to write a thesis and take optional seminars on Eastern Europe outweighed the dreariness of the required first year work. But I didn't have a burning interest in European Politics, and the more I thought about it, the more I was certain that European Politics just wasn't for me. Even doing the M.Litt., with a decent supervisor, I wouldn't be very happy.

Now it was May, the last term of the year. If I didn't want to finish the M.Phil., and I didn't really feel excited about the M.Litt., what could I do? Was there anything else? Could I switch to a different field, one in which I had more inherent interest?

I picked up my blanket and waded back to St. Aldate's, elbowing several shrill pre-adolescent Italians out of my way. Back in my room, I took down my copy of the Examination Decrees, the fat book describing each degree. I looked in the table of contents. BAs, M.Phils, M.Litts, D.Phils . . . and yes, there they were. The M.Sc. and the M.St. One-year master's degree programs. I scanned the list of courses. Comparative Social Research. Jurisprudence. Social Anthropology.

I stopped at Anthropology. I turned to the right page. Yes, a one-year degree in anthropology.

I had once come very close to studying anthropology as an undergraduate. When I was in my second year of college, I wasn't happy with History and Literature, my concentration. It was pleasant, it was interesting, it was very easy for me. But it didn't thrill me, didn't fascinate me. I wanted a subject which would fascinate me. I was eighteen and I wanted to look at the big questions. I wanted to know how people conceived of the universe, why they thought of it as they did, how societies incorporated change, why some ideas and people changed everything and others didn't. What people believed in and how they made sense of their lives.

I had thought about it for a long time and then decided that I wanted to switch from history and literature to anthropology. Anthropology fascinated me. Even anthropologists seemed fascinating to me, carrying with them the aura of strange cultures and odd rites.

I talked it over with my history and literature tutor, Charles, a long, thin man with a beard and a painfully slow southern drawl. He always wore V-necked sweaters over shirts with unfashionably wide collars. He was widely acknowledged by students to be the most boring man in the world.

"I can understand that you'd like something exciting," said Charles, slowly. I thought I might die of old age before he finished his sentence. "But you're good in this program. You'll do well."

"But that's just the trouble," I broke in. "It's not a challenge."

Charles sighed. "There are more things in life than challenges. There's prestige, for one. Anthropology is interesting, I'm sure, but you know as well as I do that it's not considered a *serious* degree here. Whereas history and literature is an honors-only concentration, highly respected intellectually. Which would you rather have when you graduate? A degree in what's widely considered a fluff subject, like anthropology? Or a degree from one of the most élite programs here, history and literature? Think about it."

I thought about it, and, I am ashamed to say, I agreed with Charles in the end. I was a good little girl, and I was on the fast track. I didn't want to jump off for the sake of an academic program that I might not like anyway. Oh, I justified it to myself fairly easily: I had never taken an anthropology course. I might hate it after all. I was becoming increasingly immersed in student politics and public service; I didn't have much time left over for academic work. Why not stick with hist. and lit.? It wasn't so bad, really, and if it wasn't challenging maybe that was a virtue. I needed all the energy I had for other things.

But when you came right down to it I stayed in history and literature because I wasn't confident enough to risk stepping off the fast track. I was scared. And we all know what happened: I threw myself into extracurricular activities. Did extremely well in hist. and lit. without ever paying much attention to my work. Wasn't miserable, but didn't feel like I was learning very much. Applied for fellowships, with an ill-considered plan of study that made sense and looked great on paper and sounded good to fellowships selection committees. Like hist. and lit., PPE was easy, it was safe, it was undeniably serious, mainstream, and fast-track. Only problem: it really didn't interest me. Then when I decided not to do that, the only option presented to me was European politics. Equally safe, mainstream, fast-track. I snatched the opportunity.

And now here I was, bored silly. As an undergraduate I had at least been busy, with all my public service work to occupy my intellectual and emotional energies. This kept me from fretting too much about how bored I was academically. But at Oxford I wasn't doing much. Yes, I was rowing, coxing, playing rugby, going to parties. But ultimately those things are no substitute for thinking. I had lots of time to contemplate just how intellectually starved I was. Safe, mainstream, fast-track, and bored.

So I decided to switch to the M.St. in social anthropology. I had decided against switching to anthropology once before, for all the wrong reasons. Faced with the choice one more time, I didn't want to make the wrong decision again. My next year at Oxford would probably be the last time in my life that anyone would be giving me money with which to do whatever I wanted. So I should forget the fast track, and *do* what I wanted. That meant getting out of European politics altogether, minus a degree. But who would ever care? I wanted to be a writer, to go into public health or politics. No one was ever going to give a damn whether or not I had an M.Phil. in European politics.

It took all my tact and courage to explain this to Hugh Ford. I liked Ford, despite my unhappiness with the European politics program and with his teaching style, and I hated to hurt his feelings by saying I wanted to switch. Sure enough, he looked dismayed.

"But why not just stick it out?" he said. "You passed the qualifying exam with very respectable marks."

I told him that I had realized during the course of the year that I wasn't well-suited to the study of political science. I agreed that it was important, and said I was glad to have learned all I had during the year—but now I wanted to learn about something else, something that I had always been interested in.

"But—anthropology!" wailed Ford. 'It's not—it's just not a serious subject. And the M.St.—Christ Church wouldn't have admitted you if they'd known you would want to read for the M.St. It's not a serious degree. The M.Phil. is so much more highly respected! I can't understand why you want to do this to yourself!"

No one who matters to me or to my future will ever give a damn, I thought to myself. How many people in the US, at least, have any idea how an M.Phil. differs from an M.St., or from an M.Litt., or an M.Sc.? A master's degree is a master's degree, as far as most people are concerned. But obviously I couldn't say this, so I just looked contrite. And stubborn.

Finally Ford gave up. "Well," he said glumly, "you should do what makes you happy. I'm sorry that the European politics M.Phil. didn't turn out to be what you wanted. Let me know if you need my assistance in sorting this out: I'll try to help if I can."

I thanked him and left.

There was a lot of sorting-out to be done.

First I had to convince the Marshall Commission to let me switch courses. This meant convincing Ruth Davis. I still quivered nervously when I recalled my first telephone conversation with her, over a year ago. And I knew that there had been a rash of course-changing in my

Marshall group, so I was prepared for Ruth to greet my petition with a very cold welcome. Sure enough, when I blurted out my desire to switch to anthropology, there was an ominous silence on the other end of the line.

Finally, Ruth spoke. "You haven't by any chance been speaking to Celia, have you?"

Celia was a Marshall I had barely seen all year. The last I had heard, she was doing Middle Eastern Studies.

"Uh, no, why?"

"She called me up fifteen minutes ago and said she wanted to switch to anthropology."

I assured Ruth that I had not conspired with Celia in any way. This wasn't enough, though.

"You've already switched once this year," she reminded me. "The Commission wasn't terribly happy about that."

"I know," I said. "But I really have thought about this a lot, and I genuinely think I'll be happier in anthropology. And I promise that I won't ask again."

Ruth sighed. "All right. We don't want you to feel as though you're wasting your time here. And I can see that you're very enthusiastic about anthropology. Put it all into writing and I'll try to persuade the Commission to give you one more chance."

I knew that if Ruth Davis was pulling for me, the Commission would be sure to let me switch. But I still had two more hurdles to overcome. For one, I needed to convince the anthropology faculty to admit me as a student, several months past the usual application deadline.

This wasn't too difficult, in the end. As at Harvard, anthropology at Oxford was not treated with the respect it deserved by other, older disciplines. This made the faculty very eager for students, preferably students with good academic credentials. And since most anthropologists like their field, it wasn't hard to convince them that I liked it too. In fact, they seemed to think it was entirely understandable that students should want to disrupt their M. Phil. courses in other subjects in order to do a lesser degree in anthropology.

"I don't think there will be any problem about admitting you," the admissions secretary told me cheerfully. "We quite understand that you're eager to switch. Last year two Rhodes and a Marshall switched in around this time. Now there's you and your friend Celia. Don't worry, we'll rush your application through."

A week later I got a letter advising me that I had been admitted to read for the Master of Studies in Social Anthropology.

The one remaining hurdle was to convince Christ Church to allow me to switch. I resignedly donned my gown, set my alarm for 8 a.m., and went to see the Senior Censor.

The man who had been Senior Censor at the beginning of the year had gone into forced retirement "for health reasons." Wild rumors spread through College about the "real" reasons for his resignation. But I was pleased with the change, because I hadn't found the old Censor particularly easy to deal with. I hoped that the new Censor would be more easy going.

He was. He greeted me with a smile and a wink. "As you know, we do not permit students to switch courses, and as you know, we have already allowed you to switch once, at the beginning of the year. As you also know, we do not normally admit students to read anthropology, or to read for the degree of Master of Studies."

I nodded contritely.

"However, I don't want you to be unhappy here. So I'm going to let you switch. Just in case anyone ever asks you what I said to you, assume great scowls of disapproval, assume gnashing teeth and fearful lectures. And good luck to you!"

I laughed. "Thanks. I hope I won't ever have to bother you again."

He rolled his eyes. "Don't dare!" he said, and dismissed me.

And that was that.

The month remaining of the term passed quickly. The weather remained lovely, and everyone was outside much of the time. Given the vagaries of the English weather, there was a sense that each day might be the very last; the "summer," still technically to come, might well be uniformly gray and cold. So no one did much work.

I certainly did no work. I was in academic limbo, and therefore had no work—anthropology wouldn't start until the following October. I called the Institute of Social Anthropology and asked for a reading list; as I had no background in anthropology, I was eager not to start at a disadvantage. The admissions secretary greeted my request with surprise; apparently there was no list of suggested readings for entering students. She finally suggested that I contact the admissions director. I wrote a letter to him with the same request, but got no answer, so I gave up. (A list of books about the anthropology of the Middle East, the admissions director's special area, finally arrived in late July.)

I returned all of my overdue books to the library at the Social Studies Faculty Centre, and was greeted with envious stares from my former European politics classmates, now slogging away at their first optional subjects.

"God, I envy you," said David.

"Switch!" I told him.

"I can't. You know why? I shot myself in the foot by

flubbing the qualifying exam. You were right—Hugh Ford didn't make a fuss, he's letting me stay in the program. But the trouble is, it's on sufferance. I couldn't switch, because no other program would take me, since I failed the qualifying exam. So I either stay in European Politics, or I leave Oxford."

"Leave, then. Make your film, David."

"Yeah, maybe I will." He sighed. "We'll see. But good luck! Go sit in the sun—you have no work to do!"

I didn't go sit in the sun. Instead, I went down to the river. It was Eights Week, the highlight of the rowing year. I had chosen to row only in a non-competitive graduate boat that term, so I wasn't racing in Eights myself, but I went to see the show and cheer on the Christ Church boats. The river was crowded with several thousand spectators, most getting drunk on Pimm's and feasting on strawberries.

Christ Church didn't excel, but most crews performed respectably enough. The Gatorade kit, long forgotten, had finally come in. We all proudly displayed the orange and green Gatorade emblem on our clothing. That night, the end of the rowing season was celebrated at a boat-club bop in the College bar. I celebrated by having a few beers with the other people in my graduate boat; we had not done well in the one small regatta we had entered the previous week, but we had had a good time. The men's first VIII, macho and gallant to the last man, celebrated by forcibly cutting off the hair of their long-haired male cox, who struggled and wept as the scissors cut though his pony tail.

Ah, Oxford! At other universities, it might be called physical assault and harassment; but down in the Christ Church bar it was just the youthful high spirits of the future governing élite.

PART FIVE

EPILOGUE

SOME SORT OF
LEARNING PROCESS

MY FIRST YEAR at Oxford ended with a whimper. I had
no academic work to do, so the year just petered out
gently. I read a lot, and explored the countryside around
Oxford. I visited Wales and Scotland with Jerome. I began
to make plans for applying to American graduate schools.
I worked on this book.

The second year was better than the first. I started
my anthropology course, and enjoyed it. This was not
because it was immune from the problems plaguing other
Oxford programs. It wasn't. The same problems were
there, by now like familiar old friends: lecture question-
periods monopolized by dons, poor resources, a curriculum that hadn't been substantially revised since around
1965. There were no required department-wide seminars,
so I had little contact with my fellow graduate students.
The department blundered on with the same mixture of
muddle and benign neglect that characterizes so many
programs at Oxford.

But this time my expectations were more realistic.
And as I had expected, I enjoyed the material much more
than I had enjoyed European Politics. And I got lucky: I
had a good supervisor. He was a little odd—he conducted
tutorials from a semi-fetal position while chain-smoking
a pipe—but I liked him enormously. He occasionally
referred to me as "dear girl," and he offered benevolent
pats on the shoulder as he sent me off to read several
thousand pages of ethnographies. He was willing to let

me investigate topics of my own choosing. He was critical when necessary and offered praise where praise was due. Tutorials with Hugh Ford had involved me sitting there glumly while Ford rambled on vaguely about lack of structure. With my anthropology tutor, real conversations took place, and I found myself looking forward to my weekly tutorials, some I hadn't done since undergraduate days.

The anthropology faculty was friendlier than the politics faculty had been. Perhaps this was because the anthropology faculty was a bit of a black sheep within Oxford. Its reputation suffered from the suspicion of the rest of the university that anthropologists were not "serious" academics. And it's true that an air of elegant amateurism hung about the Institute for Social and Cultural Anthropology. An old Victorian building on Banbury Road, the Institute was homey and cluttered with photos of aged or deceased British anthropologists: Evans-Pritchard, Malinowski, Fortes, Edmund Leach, Audrey Richards. The upper rooms contained still uncataloged remnants of forgotten fieldwork expeditions, like Mauritanian bows and fire-making sticks from East Timor.

Most of my friends from the previous year seemed happier, too. My Marshall group returned to Oxford, minus two people who had decided not to return, but everyone else seemed, if not ecstatically happy, at least resigned. We had lower expectations. We were prepared to go out and get what we wanted; we didn't expect Oxford to help us get much of anything. Miranda announced that she planned to stay and do a D.Phil.; she and Tom announced their engagement. She said that the European Politics optional seminars were much better than the core seminars had been. David spent the summer working on a film-making project in Germany, and returned with a thesis idea. Justin announced that he was going to run for Congress as soon as he turned twenty-five. "I've learned to value the American political system," he told me crisply. "It's a damned sigh better than the inegalitarian system they've got here." He no longer wore cravats. My flatmate, Peter, the Australian, spent every weekend climbing mountains all over Europe. Rob grew a beard and began to skip seminars with great frequency. Ellen went to France to study medieval literature, and Antoinette got engaged to Winston, her noble savage. Peggy, the ambitious American, went touring in India for a year, and became head of a small aid organization. Mark decided to continue on as Oriel Dean for one more year, and then to go to graduate school in America. Jerome decided to spend a year in the US, getting an American law degree. This merely postponed the difficulties we would eventually have to face, but still it made me very happy.

At Christ Church, there were eight Americans among the new graduates, double the amount in my class. Talking to them made me realize how far I had come since the previous Michaelmas.

Early in Noughth Week, I had tea with Jake and Kenny, two of the new graduates. They were both worried.

"I don't know who my supervisor is," fretted Jake.

"I haven't heard anything from my department," agreed Kenny.

"But," said Jake hopefully, "I guess if there was anything I needed to know right now, they'd tell me, right? I mean I'll get a mailing or something, explaining what lectures to go to, and when orientation is, and all that?"

"Not likely," I said.

They looked at me, taken aback.

"But, they have to tell us what we need to do," said

Kenny. "We're new here. When's College matriculation? When's University matriculation? When do lectures start? Where are lectures? When are things due? What's due? Who's in charge? How do we find out? We don't even know who to ask about things, or where their offices are. I mean, they can't just keep us guessing.'

"Yes they can," I said. "This is Oxford."

"But that's stupid. Freshman week at Stanford there was a calendar of events," said Jake plaintively. "There were orientation and information sessions in each dorm."

"Not here," I replied. "This place seems to function on the principle that you just ought to *know* things. No one will *tell* you. Nothing will be clear. You're supposed to be psychic. 'If you have to ask, you obviously don't know.'"

"What?" said Kenny.

"Nothing." I sighed. "I know it's incredibly confusing at first. Not just at first. It will probably be confusing all year." So I took out a piece of paper and wrote down all the essential information I wished I had known the previous year. I explained who the Censor was, and where he could be found. I suggested strategies for identifying and contacting supervisors. I told them which office had copies of lecture lists, and which bulletin boards often contained essential information that would be posted nowhere else. I explained that if they wanted to go to language classes or get computer accounts they had to go now, because by the time notices went up, registration would be over. I told them what to do if they wanted to change courses.

"Most of all," I said, "figure out what you want to do, and do it. No one will ever *ask* you what you want to do, and they'll just put you to work on something trivial. But on the other hand, if you're firm, you can do pretty much whatever you want here."

"I'm doing a taught course," Kenny objected. "There's got to be some sort of curriculum."

I shrugged. "To some extent, the notion that there are any 'taught courses' for graduates is misleading. Don't expect a curriculum in the American sense, with a clear philosophy of whatever discipline you're in. On the graduate level, Oxford really doesn't 'teach' anything. But that doesn't mean you can't learn anything. If you know what you want to learn, Oxford can be great—you'll have loads of free time, and you can do whatever you like."

"What's the point of being here then, if you're not taught anything?" Jake laughed uneasily. "We could take the year off and go sit in a library anywhere in the world, if that was all we wanted. Oxford isn't a think-tank; it's supposed to be a teaching institution."

"Good point." I searched for some way to justify going to Oxford. "But there are a lot of interesting people around here. True, they're interesting despite Oxford, not because of it, and many of them are disappointed by Oxford. But the name draws them from all over the world—so take advantage of meeting the other graduate students."

Jake didn't look convinced.

"You'll decide for yourself," I told him.

Kenny and Jake looked a bit disbelieving. I could see the cogs turning in their minds: *But this is Oxford, the most famous university in the world! Only an ingrate could be anything but wildly happy and intellectually satisfied here! If we're confused, it must be our own fault. It couldn't be Oxford's fault.*

I shrugged. I felt like the Ancient Mariner. They would have to see for themselves.

About a month later, I was on my way to Jerome's room when Kenny stopped me tentatively. He looked troubled.

'Kenny, what's up?"

"Uh, not much."

"How's it going?"

"Oh, well, OK." He paused.

"How's your course?" I probably shouldn't have asked.

Kenny was reading international relations. He was miserable. He was confused. He was studying things that seemed pointless. He didn't understand them. Lectures were a waste. There was no real discussion in seminars.

"And," he said, "I feel like my brain is rotting. Really: I've never felt so uninspired. I wrote more sophisticated essays four years ago, when I was a freshman. I feel so frustrated."

Kenny wasn't the only unhappy first year. André, an anthropology student from France, came up to me one day in the library. He was having trouble finding the books for his tutorial essay, but he was worried about more than that. "What do you think we're supposed to be learning?" he asked. "What are you doing in your tutorials? I cannot grasp the structure of the course."

I shook my head. "I don't know, exactly. There isn't really a set curriculum. Maybe we could take a look at some old exams—that might be a way to figure out just what it is that they think we're learning."

He sighed. "I am used to having things be more clear."

It is a measure of how much I had adapted to British styles, and how much my expectations had changed, that I was surprised to hear another first year, from Canada, complain about her supervisor. She had the same supervisor I had. I liked him very much, and I was surprised that Susan didn't.

"I feel that I don't get any feedback from him," she told me. "He just sits there with his eyes shut, smoking his pipe, while I read my essays. He seems so distant and uninterested. And he just assigns me reading that I'm not interested in. It's all pre-1950!"

"I think he'll give you constructive feedback, if you ask for it," I responded. "He probably just doesn't realize that you want something more. And just try telling him you'd rather read something different. I'm sure he'll agree—he's letting me choose some of my own topics."

Susan shook her head. "What's the point? I don't think he has any intellectual passion. I'm going to switch supervisors."

"But the things you criticize him for aren't really personal quirks—he's simply behaving like a typical Oxford supervisor. It's the culture. Don't assume that because he doesn't jump for joy at your essays and speak in superlatives, he lacks intellectual passion. Passion's just not an emotion that's in vogue around here."

Susan shrugged. "You may be right. Perhaps I'm being unfair. I realize that it's Oxford itself that I'm objecting to. But I want to try to make a fresh start with a new supervisor."

QUOTH THE
ANCIENT MARINER

IN NOVEMBER, DEMOCRAT Bill Clinton was elected President of the United States. Most of us Americans at Oxford rejoiced; a new world seemed to have opened up. Oxford became a hot topic in the American media. The English rejoiced, too, or at any rate they made the best of it: suddenly Clinton was Oxford's favorite graduate. Everyone over forty claimed to have known him well, and a self-congratulatory mood prevailed. "Dons glory in their boy as leader of Western world," gloated a headline in the London *Independent*. "Oxford Man Leads World," agreed *Cherwell,* the student newspaper. Hey, guys, I thought, let's try not to take all the credit here. The Oxford Union (the debating society) was more tongue in cheek: "We're so pleased that an Oxford man has been elected president that we're naming this term after his wife," said the Union's calendar of events for Hilary Term 1993.

The *Independent* felt that Oxford had been good for Clinton: "His Oxonian credentials provided him with a reassuring patina of tradition and academic prestige." They quoted Clinton as saying that his time at Oxford was very rewarding intellectually: he was "very impressed" by Oxford. He found it "exhilarating . . . simply incredible."

Well, maybe Clinton was just being polite when he said that. Because frankly, I suspect that if his two years at Oxford were intellectually productive, it was because of the friends he made and the books he read, not because of any help his tutors gave him. Like many Americans before and after him, he didn't even bother to finish his degree, instead leaving for Yale Law School with his course unfinished.

If Clinton was telling the truth, and he really did find his Oxford academic experiences exhilarating, I envy him.

My own attitude towards Oxford, by now, was one of tolerant cynicism. As the Christ Church Dean had advised at the previous year's Newcomers' Dinner, I had succeeded in making it my own.

I was no longer blinded by gratitude at being given the opportunity to study at the world's most famous university. I had earned my place, and I deserved to get the best from Oxford. Oxford was my university: mine to cherish when it deserved cherishing, mine to criticize, mine to change.

In the end, I *had* gotten something out of Oxford intellectually. I learned a fair amount about European politics, and a good deal about anthropology. More importantly, my time at Oxford forced me to define myself, by showing me what I was not. I had been forced to articulate and assess my own cultural assumptions. And when I examined my assumptions, I discovered that although Oxford *could* be my own, I didn't really *want* it to be my own.

I had made many good friends at Oxford, particularly among the graduates, and I would miss them when I was gone. But I was glad to be going back home to America, with all its faults. After some time away from America, I could see its many faults more clearly, but I think that America remains a far more open and hopeful society than England. At any rate, its upper layer is more easily penetrable by those below.

I remembered the intimidating image of Oxford stu-

265

dents I had had before I arrived: sophisticated, witty, brilliant, and superbly confident. Now I knew better. Most of the undergraduates I got to know, at Christ Church and elsewhere, were intimidated themselves. For the most part, they approached their academic work with a mixture of fear, boredom, and resentment. Treated like children by their tutors, they acted like children in the classroom and towards one another. Thus the frequency of cruel juvenile pranks like the cutting of the cox's pony tail, and the absence of any visible sense of social or political responsibility. The English undergraduates were as intimidated as I was, if not more so, by the weight of history and the shadow cast by books like *Brideshead Revisited*. They made contorted attempts to appear as effortlessly glib, relaxed, and upper class as they imagined *Brideshead*'s Sebastian Flyte to have been.

And why, after all, shouldn't they be immature and resentful? Young, upper-middle-class Britons are stuck in the stagnating center of a declining culture. The signs are all around them: McDonald's is on Cornmarket, the main shopping street, and *Wayne's World* is at the Magdalen Street cinema. The "brain-drain" continues unabated as the best and the brightest in academics and business are lured away by the higher salaries on the other side of the Atlantic. On the High Street, the recession is closing down famous old shops. The book reviews are filled with glum articles about the decline of the British novel; foreigners keep winning the Booker Prize. The top twenty British box office hits of 1992 were all from Hollywood. A BBC survey found that more than half of Britons would emigrate if they had the choice. The tablolids are filled with salacious stories about the crumbling monarchy. In the business section, the sterling crisis is charted.

This is nothing new. The British upper-class world

has been shrinking fast since the Second World War. In John le Carré's 1964 novel *Tinker, Tailor, Soldier, Spy,* spy-master George Smiley laments this:

> He saw with painful clarity an ambitious man born to the big canvas, brought up to rule, divide, and conquer, whose visions and vanities were all fixed . . . upon the world's fame; for whom reality was a poor island with scarcely a voice that would carry across the water.

But today's privileged young English men and women, and even most younger dons, have not even the consolation of having been born to the big canvas. Smiley's pain is the pain that comes from losing what he, and others of his generation, once had. Today's generation lacks even the glamor of pain and betrayal. They never had the big canvas. They were born to a poor island, still rigidly conscious of the glorious past, and told to adjust to the unglorious present and the gray future represented by Prime Minister John Major.

No wonder they sulk! No wonder work hardly seems worth the effort. If you know the future is gray, that the fantasy of Empire is only a fantasy, it's easiest not to try, to pretend not to care. Denied even the right to feel Smiley's pain, it's no wonder they try to recreate the certainties of the past, with dining societies, rugby, the academic traditions of the Victorians. No wonder they seek comfort in tradition and hierarchy, and glory vicariously, condescendingly, in Bill Clinton's success.

And that is what may ruin Oxford in the end. You can only get by for so long on tradition and a pile of nice old buildings. Sooner or later more is required: compassion, imagination, energy. There's a whole big world out there which has no interest in drinking societies or outdated academic structures. A university cannot be an ivory tower; sooner or later it has to acknowledge the world in which it finds itself. And if Oxford can't provide an atmosphere that fosters compassion, imagination, and energy, sooner or later students—and money—will start going somewhere that does.

Some people will be tempted to dismiss this as an Anglophobic tirade from an American who didn't happen to get what she wanted from Oxford. But I don't mean to be Anglophobic; Oxophobic might be a better term. There's nothing wrong with Britain or the British, except that British society still sets up places like Oxford as the best that Britain can offer. And Oxford is emphatically *not* the best that Britain can offer.

For most Britons, life has been improving since the War, and has presented opportunities undreamt of by previous generations. The old upper-class playgrounds like Oxford are growing dingy and unkempt; increasingly, the best and most interesting people either visit them and hurry away with a sigh of relief, or never bother to go at all. If they go to university at all (and most students in Britain never get the opportunity), they go to one of Britain's newer, less grand, more innovative, and exciting universities. And you won't catch many working-class people shedding a tear over the decline of Oxford. On the contrary—to many Britons, the sooner Oxford fades into obscurity, the better.

Oxford doesn't have to fade into obscurity. Oxford could, instead, take stock of its position in a rapidly changing society, and resolve to play an active role in bringing about positive change, in educating future leaders from non-traditional backgrounds (i.e., more women, more minorities, more state-school applicants) in bold and innovative ways. But today Oxford remains, by and large, a university for the privileged, and its atmosphere and programs are increasingly irrelevant. It muddles on passively.

I am not the only one, on either side of the Atlantic, to feel saddened and disillusioned by contemporary Oxford. Anyone desirous of reading about Oxford from the point of view of British undergraduates should find a copy of *The Oxford Myth*, edited by Rachel Johnson. In a series of essays written by undergraduates in the mid-eighties, an image of Oxford similar to the one I have laid out here emerges, an Oxford characterized by pretension, alienation, and self-disgust. And most of all by a sense of sadness and betrayal: to the many undergraduates who arrive, hopeful and conscientious, Oxford is a disappointment. Take, for instance, these sample comments from essays in *The Oxford Myth*:

> Looking back on what I have written, Oxford emerges as a rather unpleasant place to have spent three years . . . among other things it seemed to lack any imagination . . . No new vision lit up the future and animated political discussion . . . It was an era of imitation . . . No one was free enough to invent or to dream or to hope.

> Life in college can encourage breathtaking insularity.

> The worst undergraduate epidemic, the dogged pursuit of a pleasureless pleasure by each generation's supposedly most exceptional intellects, is utterly inexplicable except as a desperate attempt to turn expectations into reality.

> The majority of undergraduates . . . neither dedicate themselves to work nor reject it for something else. They commit themselves to nothing. They put in spasmodic bursts of endeavour, usually the day before the tutorial, the fruits of which are small

and quickly forgotten. They treat each subject only superficially; they read little and cease to go to lectures . . . They take nothing seriously. All in all it is a half-hearted and profoundly debilitating state of affairs.

Oxford is a place where people are fantastically depressed.

And so on. These comments, although made eight years ago, still ring true. In 1992–93, the Oxford University Student Union did a survey of undergraduate students. Seventy-five percent reported having had problems with the teaching at Oxford. Forty-five percent had had problems with their tutor. Forty percent had considered leaving Oxford altogether at one time or another. At Christ Church, a few highly motivated students started a magazine, *House Bound,* about College life. They complained about widespread student apathy and intolerance. Not surprisingly, the magazine was published anonymously.

The following is from a recent feature article in the London *Sunday Times*, entitled "The Establishment: It's Back:"

British society is deeply conservative. The enduring importance of class and hierarchy, epitomized by the Establishment, the old school tie and Oxbridge, is [a product of] the ability of the class system to mutate, evolve, and metamorphose from decade to decade, from century to century. It has the adaptive powers of nature's longest-surviving creatures. Britain, as a result, is like an ancient geological formation . . . The idea of a sense of national regeneration becomes a chimera. Power may be diffused, but the Establishment somehow remains, a wet blanket draped across the top of society, a fitting emblem for a society historically stifled by hierarchy and a deep lack of ambition.

CLOSE ENCOUNTERS:
THE QUEEN

IN DECEMBER OF my second year, the Queen came to visit Christ Church.

The Queen is the nominal head of Christ Church, a royal foundation. She only comes to check up on her college every fifteen years or so. This time around, she informed Christ Church that she wanted to meet some students—perhaps after her *annus horribilis*, with her children's front-page shenanigans, she thought some unrelated young people might make a nice break.

She said that she wanted to meet students informally, in their natural haunts. Christ Church agreed, and promptly repainted and refurnished the JCR, which had been languishing for years in a haze of grease and cigarette smoke. Among the graduate students, this prompted cynical reflections on Stalin's rides through the Russian countryside. Peasants were forced in advance to repaint their cottages, and they were given decent clothes and commanded to smile for the occasion.

There was a ballot to determine which graduate students would get to meet the Queen at an event in the JCR. I guess I got lucky: a week before the Queen's arrival, I received an embossed card from the JCR Committee. It was decorated with a number of little crests, ribbons, and other decorative doodads. I was invited to "Sherry in the Presence of the Visitor, Her Majesty Queen Elizabeth." (The Visitor. It sounded like something out of *Close Encounters* or the *Twilight Zone*.)

According to the invitation, dress was to be "lounge suits." Now this may mean something to the English. To a free-associating American, it brings to mind only two things: lounge lizards and leisure suits. I know that Queen Elizabeth has never been famed for her style, but I assumed that even she wouldn't stoop to the level of a polyester leisure suit. I decided to ignore the instructions as irrelevant. I wore a skirt and jacket.

On the day of the Visit, huge crowds of royalty-watchers thronged Christ Church to watch the Queen go from a Cathedral service to the JCR. They were held back by wire fences. (As the uppity *Oxford Mail* put it, "Wall of Iron Surrounds Queen".) Security was high; I had to present identification to the police in order to get into College.

Apparently no one is supposed to enter a room after the Queen. I didn't know that. And so, needless to say, I managed to be the only person to arrive at the sherry party *late*. It was an accident—I was confused about the time. The plainclothes police scowled at me as they examined my invitation outside the JCR. Finally they allowed me to slip in.

"Hi!" I chirped to friends standing stiffly around the room.

I was greeted by an agonized chorus of "Shhh!" I spotted Jake. He frantically gestured me to his side.

"Stand over here," he hissed. "You're late!"

"No, I'm not," I said. "The Queen doesn't come until twelve-thirty."

"She's over there, dummy!" He pointed to the drinks table. Sure enough, there was a familiar-looking hat.

"Oooh. Whoops. Do you think this means I shouldn't go over there to get a drink?"

Jake rolled his eyes. "Yes, I think so."

"Darn."

"Listen, she'll come over here in a few minutes and speak to everyone in the group. If she offers you her hand, you're supposed to curtsy."

"No way."

"What do you mean, no way?"

"I'm a 'little-r' *republican,* Jake."

Jake was looking more and more aggrieved.

"Look," I said crossly. "I don't know *how* to curtsy. I've never done it. I'm not going to start now. Anyway—" I thought I should say something soothing—"I don't think she'll be giving anyone her hand. Her hands seem to be pretty full."

The Queen had a bouquet of flowers in one hand and a glass of sherry in the other. She had her famous purse hanging from the crook of her right arm, and a Cathedral program balanced in the crook of her left. I wondered what she would do if her nose started to itch.

"How come she has no *crown?*" I asked peevishly.

"Ssh!" said Jake.

She was wearing her overcoat, too. I thought that she must be pretty hot. I was sweating myself, and the fumes from the JCR's newly applied paint were making me feel slightly dizzy. I wanted a glass of orange juice, but the Queen seemed to have inconsiderately offered the last one to a large frumpy lady-in-waiting. (This was a sad shock; I have always envisaged ladies-in-waiting as light, graceful nymphs. On the contrary—they were all over fifty, and they all wore sensible shoes.) The Queen and the lady-in-waiting were chatting with a group of undergraduates. Looking around, I noted that while we graduates seemed to be a genuine random cross-section of the GCR population, the undergraduates were disproportionately of the public school sporting set. Something fishy must have been going on with their ballot.

Finally the Queen got to our group. She went from

person to person, asking polite questions. She was very short, I noticed: she had thick three-inch heels and she still only came up to my chin.

Then, after Jake, it was my turn.

"And where are you from?" she asked.

"Nowhere very interesting, I'm afraid," I responded. Jake kicked me. "New York."

"New York," gasped the Queen, apparently thrilled. I thought she might be about to ask me how one acquired a green card.

"Yes!" I agreed. "New York!"

"Really!"

"Yes!"

We gazed raptly into each other's eyes. She was one heck of a conversationalist.

Finally she said, "There seem to be a lot of Americans at Oxford."

"Oh, yes, a lot," I agreed.

"You must find it . . . *different* here than in New York!"

"Oh, yes." That was true.

She was clutching her sherry glass tightly. "And what are you studying?"

"Anthropology."

"Oh!"

"Yes!"

"Oh. Anthropology. And what will you do with that?"

"Nothing?" I suggested hopefully.

"Nothing? Oh!"

I felt sorry for her. She had to have dozens of conversations like this every day. "Well, I think I'd like to be a writer."

"Oh! Really!"

"Yes!"

We nodded at each other, smiling inanely, for several

seconds. Finally she turned to the woman next to me. "And where are *you* from?" she asked.

"The Gambia, in Africa," replied the woman, a new graduate called Miriam.

I guess the Queen didn't like The Gambia, because she turned rapidly away from Miriam with an agonized smile. "And where are *you* from?" she asked the next person in line.

Later that afternoon, after the Queen was gone, I went over to the Tutor for Student Welfare's office. I needed to get a form stamped in order to defer my US student loans for another year. I was nervous: I knew that I would have to encounter Mrs. Edgerton, the assistant to the Tutor for Welfare. The previous year, she had been none too friendly about stamping my loan form.

The office was empty, but I heard voices coming from an inner room. I loitered for a while, coughing politely to indicate my presence. No one emerged. Finally I nervously poked my head around the corner. Mrs Edgerton and another woman were sitting and chatting, coffee cups in their hands. They looked up.

"Oh, I'm so sorry to interrupt you!" I said, in an effort to forestall an angry rebuke. "Could I just leave something for you to do when you get a chance, Mrs. Edgerton?"

But today she liked me. She beamed at me. "Oh, you're not interrupting us at all. Not at all. We're just having some coffee to make up for having had some *wine* earlier." She laughed girlishly. "In honor of the Queen's visit, you know."

"Oh, yes," I agreed cautiously. "The Queen."

"Quite. Let me come and help you. What's the trouble?"

This was too good to be true. She walked into the main office with me as I explained what I needed.

"Oh," she said severely, when I showed her the form. "The Tutor for Welfare likes to do those himself."

"But—last year *you* just stamped it for me."

"Quite," she agreed. She swayed slightly, looked me over, and, perhaps because I was admitting that I had needed to borrow to finance my undergraduate education, she seemed to decide that I was a class ally.

"The way it works," she said savagely, biting each word, "is that there is a new Tutor for Welfare this year, Dr. Morgan. He's a history don. The old Tutor thought I should handle those forms. The new one is different. He thinks that if you don't have a university degree, there's nothing—" she tapped her ears—"between here and here."

"Oh," I said uneasily. "I guess there are always a lot of people like that in universities."

"Absolutely." She looked at me with increasing fondness. "They're all over! They think that because of your education or your accent, you're not a human being! So they pay you nothing, and they treat you like dirt."

"You need a union," I said brightly. "When I was at Harvard, the support staff unionized. It made a big difference—the university had to start taking them seriously from then on. The union's slogan was 'We can't eat prestige.'"

She laughed bitterly. "Oh, they'd never allow it. They think you should feel lucky to be here." She glared towards the Tutor for Welfare's empty office. "Let me tell you. I have worked at this college for twenty-five years. *Twenty-five* years. *Dr. Morgan's* been here for five, and the Dean for one! I hold this place together. I'm assistant for Special Events. *I* organized the Queen's visit for the Dean and the Censor and Dr. Morgan. I wrote all the letters. I made all the telephone calls. *Everything*. I did all the work. So you'd think, wouldn't you, that perhaps I'd be invited to the dinner, or the sherry party, or the cathedral service."

She was angrily twisting my loan deferral form in her hands. I winced. "But no," she continued, voice tight. "No. Then Dr Morgan came in today with another don, both in their gowns, after the sherry party, laughing like anything, and do you know what that man said to me when he happened to look my way? He said, 'Oh, if you want to take *fifteen minutes* off to stand outside and watch as the Royal procession *leaves,* you may.' That's for twenty-five years."

I shook my head sympathetically. "That's awful." I hoped Dr. Morgan wasn't coming up the stairs.

But her emotion had made her throw caution to the winds. "I suggested that as they were letting students and tutors meet the Queen, they should have a ballot for three or four of the staff to go, too. And they looked at me as thought I was insane." She sniffed.

It was clear that Mrs. Edgerton had had enough of being a good, deferential employee. This was a lifetime of resentment surfacing. Her voice was rapid and her face was flushed angrily.

"This is a stultifying country," she informed me. I nodded. "When I was young, and I first got a job here, I wrote to my grandfather and said, 'I'm working at Oxford University.' He wrote back, and do you know what he said?"

I didn't.

"Not, 'Congratulations.' Oh no. He was a foul-tempered, tyrannical old man. He wrote, 'Never forget that your great-grandmother was a skivvy at Oxford University. Do not forget your place.'" She paused, quivering with indignation. "A *skivvy!* A maid. Well, I don't have a place! I don't know my place! My great-grandmother had a place. My *mother* had a place. But I'm not my mother. I'm a human being!"

I wasn't sure what to say. I was saddened, and moved. Somehow "Right *on,* sister!" didn't seem like it would strike quite the right note.

"You're right," I finally said simply. "It's pretty terrible. That's why, no offence, I'm glad I'm not English. I couldn't stand to be stuck in this society. It's too rigid, too prejudiced."

Mrs. Edgerton seemed to be calming down. She smiled at me. "You're right. I'm sorry. I guess it's the wine." She pulled a tissue out of one tweed pocket.

"That's OK," I said. "You have every right to be angry. I'd be angry too." It was clear to me now why she was so often bad tempered. A bright, ambitious woman, whose only misstep was to have been born in the wrong class and to have gone to work at Oxford, where class stratifications live and thrive.

In a burst of conspiratorial good will, she straightened out my loan deferral form and rummaged around for a stamp. "Who cares?" she said. "I'm perfectly capable of doing this myself. I've done these forms for two decades, after all. Dr. Morgan will be annoyed, but I think it's about time to make him annoyed about a thing or two."

"Past time," I agreed. "Good luck."

"To you, too," she said, handing me the completed form. She smiled. "Have a good Christmas."

DEATH THROES?

WILL OXFORD LAST as it is?

Maybe not. The last few years have seen an unprecedented questioning of élite British institutions. Charles and Diana have separated. The Queen is paying taxes. The Tory government has stumbled from humiliation to humiliation. At Oxford, women dons have succeeded in getting the University to make a commitment to creating more senior faculty positions for women. In the Christ Church GCR, a women's group has been started. And perhaps most importantly, the Mrs. Edgertons of Oxford are getting fed up. Little by little, a desire for change seems to be spreading.

I thought of Edmund Wilson, visiting Oxford decades ago and cheerfully asserting that he wanted to "plumb the depths of old, decayed, conservative English academic life in its death throes." For the sake of all the people I got to know in England, I hope that the death throes don't go on much longer. Sooner or later, even paper flowers wilt and die.